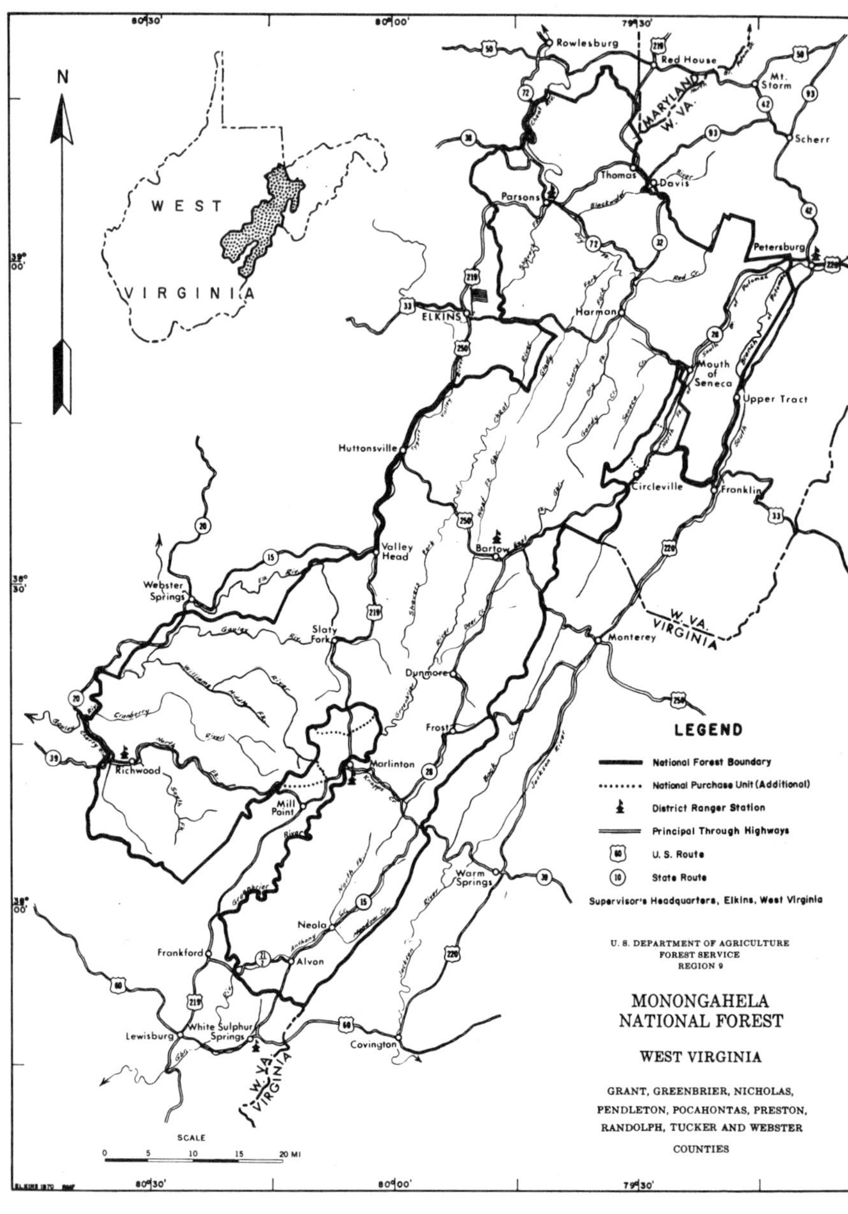

LEGEND
National Forest Boundary
National Purchase Unit (Additional)
District Ranger Station
Principal Through Highways
U. S. Route
State Route
Supervisor's Headquarters, Elkins, West Virginia
U. S. DEPARTMENT OF AGRICULTURE
FOREST SERVICE
REGION 9
MONONGAHELA
NATIONAL FOREST
WEST VIRGINIA
GRANT, GREENBRIER, NICHOLAS,
PENDLETON, POCAHONTAS, PRESTON,
RANDOLPH, TUCKER AND WEBSTER
COUNTIES
SCALE
0 5 10 15 20 MI
WEST
VIRGINIA
N
Rowlesburg
Red House
Mt. Storm
Scherr
Thomas
Davis
Parsons
Petersburg
ELKINS
Harman
Mouth of Seneca
Upper Tract
Huttonsville
Circleville
Franklin
Valley Head
Bartow
Webster Springs
Slaty Fork
Monterey
Dunmore
Frost
Richwood
Marlinton
Mill Point
Warm Springs
Neola
Frankford
Alvon
Lewisburg
White Sulphur Springs
Covington
MARYLAND
W. VA.
VIRGINIA
80°30'
80°00'
79°30'
39° 00'
38° 30'
38° 00'

Forest Wildlife Plants of the Monongahela National Forest

by

Roy B. Clarkson

Wm. Homer Duppstadt

and

Roland L. Guthrie

Department of Biology
West Virginia University

THE BOXWOOD PRESS

Distributed
by
The Boxwood Press
183 Ocean View Blvd.
Pacific Grove, California, 93950
408/375-9110

Library of Congress Cataloging in Publication Data

Clarkson, Roy B. 1926-
Forest Plants.

Includes index.

1. Forest flora—West Virginia—Monongahela National Forest—Identification.
2. Monongahela National Forest.

I. Duppstadt, William Homer, joint author.
II. Guthrie, Roland Lee, 1928-
III. Title.

QK193.C48 581.9754'5 80-21670

ISBN: 0-910286-82-5 (pbk.)

Printed in U.S.A.

PREFACE

THE MONONGAHELA NATIONAL FOREST contains a varied assemblage of forest types and associated plants. The purpose of this book is to provide **nontechnical** keys, descriptions and illustrations of the most common plants found in forested areas within the Monongahela. **It contains both summer and winter plant illustrations and identification keys.** Plants occurring primarily along the roadsides and in open fields are not included. Plants that are not commonly found or are of little value to wildlife are also omitted. **Whenever possible, technical terminology has been replaced with common terms.**

The book is designed primarily for the use of forest personnel, although it may be useful to hikers, backpackers, sportsmen, and others entering the forests of the region. It is designed to be carried in the field in pack or pocket.

The authors acknowledge the assistance of many persons in the preparation of this handbook. Among these are: Dr. Earl L. Core and the late Dr. P.D. Strausbaugh for use of descriptions and illustrations from *Flora of West Virginia;* Dr. Core, Dr. Nelle P. Ammons, and Dr. Ralph Buchsbaum for similar material from *Woody Plants in Winter,* published by the Boxwood Press; Dr. Melvin Brown and Dr. Russell Brown for special drawings and for the extensive use of illustrations from *Woody Plants of Maryland;* C.P. Peters for the use of one illustration from *The Book of Shrubs* by Wm. C. Grimm, published by The Stackpole Company; Charles Dischinger and Linda Rader for assistance in preparing the keys; Arnold Schulz, United States Forest Service, for his suggestions and assistance; Anita Hicks, Donna Parker, and Barb Power for help in organizing the material; and Irene Duppstadt and Jean Bland for typing the manuscript.

This project was supported by funds provided by the USDA, Forest Service, Region 9.

Roy B. Clarkson

Morgantown, West Virginia
October, 1980

CONTENTS

THE MONONGAHELA NATIONAL FOREST

INTRODUCTION

THE MONONGAHELA NATIONAL FOREST is located along the Allegheny Mountain Range of the Appalachian System entirely within the State of West Virginia. It extends from near Eglon, Preston County, in a southwesterly direction for a distance of about 100 miles to within six miles of White Sulphur Springs, Greenbrier County. From east to west it extends from near Petersburg, Grant County, to the junction of Cherry River with Gauley River in Nicholas County, a distance of about 80 miles. It contains many of the most interesting botanical and scenic areas of the State. This area is little more than one-tenth the total area of West Virginia, yet, because of a considerable diversity of altitude, temperatures, geologic strata, rainfall and other factors, it contains more than three-fourths of the total number of species of vascular plants collected in the State.

The area is readily accessible by car, over U.S. Routes 33, 219, 220, and 250 and W.Va. Routes 28, 32, and 92.

TOPOGRAPHY

The Monongahela is naturally divided into two geologic provinces: The Ridge and Valley Province and the Allegheny Plateau Province.

Ridge and Valley Province

The eastern part of the area is included in the Ridge and Valley Province. The western boundary of this province is the crest of Allegheny Front Mountain which runs in a NE/SW direction. In the north, the Allegheny Front forms a steep slope that is easily followed from Bear Rocks, Grant County, southward to near Onego, Pendleton County. From here it follows Timber Ridge southward to the vicinity of Circleville, Pendleton County. The province then "jogs" westward for ten miles and follows Back Allegheny Mountain southward.

The Allegheny Front slopes sharply from an elevation of 4,000 feet south of Bear Rocks to an elevation of 2,500 feet on Laurel Run, Grant County, less than one mile to the east. Farther south, in Pocahontas County, a difference in elevation between Bald Knob (4,842 feet) and the county road 1.75 miles east (2,934 feet) is even more striking.

The topography of this section, as the name suggests, is a lowland interspersed with mostly longitudinal ridges. The pattern of drainage throughout the Ridge and Valley Province is of the trellis type with the main streams flowing in a N/S direction and with numerous, short tributaries. The northern portion of this Province is drained by branches of the Potomac River, the southern portion by the Greenbrier River.

An interesting region located on the western boundary of the Ridge and Valley Province in northern Pocahontas County is known as the "Birthplace of Rivers." Here are found the headwaters of the Greenbrier, Gauley, and Elk rivers, which flow south and west to the Kanawha; the Jackson, which flows east to the James; the South Branch, which flows north to the Potomac; and the Cheat and Tygart, which flow north to the Monongahela.

Allegheny Plateau Province

The part of the Monogahela National Forest lying west of the Allegheny Front is included with the Allegheny Plateau Province. This portion is characterized by greatly dissected high altitude plateaus interspersed with scores of rugged peaks that rise to elevations of over 4,000 feet. Spruce Knob, elevation 4,860 feet, the highest point in West Virginia, and Bald Knob, elevation 4,842 feet, the second highest point in the state, are included here.

The plateaus are best seen in eastern Randolph and Tucker counties where the Allegheny Front slopes gently westward forming extensive, almost level areas at elevations of over 4,000 feet. The exposed rock in this region is largely of the highly resistant Pottsville Conglomerate series. This broad expanse of relatively level land provides little protection to the vegetation from strong westerly winds which almost constantly sweep the region. These winds, along with past fires and possibly other factors, have resulted in the development of large areas of "huckleberry plains." Poor drainage in some areas results in extensive shallow bogs.

Farther west and south the plateau is highly dissected and forms a panorama of steep, rugged mountains separated by narrow valleys. The drainage pattern is typically dendritic, consisting of numerous winding streams fed by many convoluted branches.

The main stream in the northern part of this section is Shaver's Fork of Cheat River, which heads at Thorny Flat west of Cass, Pocahontas County, and flows almost due north through Randolph and Tucker counties to Parsons, where it joins with Black Fork to form Cheat River. Cheat River then meanders north through a wide valley to the National Forest Boundary north of St. George, Tucker County. Black Fork is formed at Hendricks, Tucker County, by the junction of Dry Fork and Blackwater rivers, the two other principal streams of the northern portion.

The southwestern portion of the area is drained by the Elk, Williams, Cranberry, and Cherry rivers. These streams rise near the tops of the ridges of the Allegheny Front and flow westward to the Kanawha River.

CLIMATE

The wide range in elevation and the considerable span of latitude of the Monongahela National Forest result in a great deal of variation in the climate of different sections.

Temperatures

According to Weather Bureau records, the average annual temperature of the Allegheny Plateau is between 6°F and 7°F lower than that of the Ridge and Valley. The lowest recorded temperatures are -37°F at Lewisburg, Greenbrier County, and -30°F at Bayard, Grant County. Temperatures below freezing have been reported during every month of the year at upland stations. The highest temperature on record in the area, 104° F, was reported from the Ridge and Valley.

Frost data are very incomplete, but available records show an average growing season of 147 to 150 days in the Ridge and Valley and 119 to 145 days in the Allegheny Plateau, where killing frosts have been reported as late as June 17 and as early as September 10.

Precipitation

Rainfall, in all parts of the area, is normally ample for the growing of crops and for the growth of mesic species. There is a marked difference, however, in the amount of precipitation between the Allegheny Plateau and the Ridge and Valley. On the plateau the average annual rainfall ranges from 41 to 51 inches; the Ridge and Valley receives an average annual rainfall of 27 to 42 inches. During the driest season on record, 1930, the precipitation was less than twenty inches at some locations on the plateau and even less in the other sections.

At least traces of snow are known from some locality within the Monongahela National Forest during every month of the year except August. The greatest amount of snowfall occurs during the month of February. The average annual snowfall varies from over 91 inches in Canaan Valley, Tucker County, to less than 25 inches in the eastern section at Franklin, Pendleton County.

Wind

The prevailing winds throughout the area come from a westerly direction. These winds normally contain considerable moisture, much of which condenses and falls as rain or snow as the winds are cooled in their passage over the high Allegheny Plateau. As the winds reach the Ridge and Valley east of the plateau, they become warmer and less precipitation is noted. This largely accounts for the much higher precipitation in the Plateau region, especially on the western slopes of the mountains. This difference has a significant differentiating effect on the flora of these two regions.

Another, more direct effect of wind is seen in the vegetation of the large wind-swept "plains" of Tucker, Randolph, Pendleton, and Grant counties. Here the westerly wind blows almost constantly, resulting in the growth of "banner trees" in which limbs fail to develop on the western side of the tree, producing a lopsided growth form.

Ice Formation

There are no records available concerning the formation of ice on the vegetation of the higher elevations. This phenomenon is of common occurrence, however, and has an effect on the plant life of these areas. Ice formation is very common above 3,200 feet during all of the winter months. This is most often a thick glaze formed by freezing rain or snow, which results in damage to deciduous trees of many species.

GEOLOGY

The oldest geologic strata exposed in the area are of the Ordovician Period. Most of the exposed strata, however, are of the Silurian, Devonian, and Mississippian periods.

It is well known that the vegetation of a particular area is greatly affected by the nature of the underlying soil. The soil, in turn, is determined by the nature of the rock from which it was derived. These effects are various and in many instances difficult to determine. In other cases, however, the effect of the underlying strata on vegetation is easily seen.

In general, throughout the area, the mountain tops and the high plateau regions are underlain with sandstones and conglomerates. In such areas the soils are mostly acid. There are a great many plants that are common in these areas and entirely lacking in alkaline soils. Prominent among these are the members of the heath family (Ericaceae). This group is widespread in the acid soils of the mountains, especially in the plateau region of Randolph, Tucker and Grant Counties. The numerous bogs and high altitude swamps have a low pH and contain a typical vegetation. The extensive forests of Red Spruce occur at higher altitudes where the soils are acid. Many of the ferns, the lycopods and a great variety of herbaceous plants require acid soil and are associated with the above formations.

Alkaline soils support a different flora, the most common component of which is Kentucky Bluegrass *(Poa pratensis),* which achieves its best growth on calcareous soils. Among the ferns, Goldie's Shield Fern *(Dryopteris goldiana)* and Bladder Fern *(Cystopteris bulbifera)* require such soil.

SUMMER KEY TO THE GENERA

SELECT the one of the two numbered pairs of contrasting characters that seems most suitable and proceed to the number indicated. When the character selected leads to a genus, turn to the page given after the name of the genus.

1. Plants without seeds or flowers (fernlike, mosslike, or rushlike). .... **Non-seed plants.** 2
1. Plants with seeds borne singly or in cones or with true flowers. .... **Seed plants.** 16

2. Leaves small, scalelike, crowded, or overlapping, sporangia in axils of modified leaves forming a conelike structure (in most species). .... *Lycopodium* (**Club Moss, Groundpine**), p. 32
2. Leaves fernlike with sporangia clustered on the leaves in various ways. 3

3. Fertile leaves or fertile portions of the leaves conspicuously unlike the sterile. 4
3. Fertile leaves or segments green and leaflike. Reproduce by spores borne in sporangia arranged in clusters or lines on the lower sides or margins of the leaves. Sporangial clusters sometimes covered by a membrane. 5

4. Leaves twice divided with sporangia on the margins of the division of the fertile frond. .... *Osmunda,* p. 34
4. Sterile leaves once-divided with the fertile frond forming hard, rounded, berrylike divisions within which the spores are found. .... *Onoclea,* p. 36

5. Sporangial clusters round, mostly back from the margins of the leaves. 6
5. Sporangial clusters mostly longer than broad, or marginal on the leaves. 12

6. No covering on the clusters of the sporangia. 7
6. Covering present on the sporangial clusters, at least when young. 9

7. Rootstalk on the surface of the soil; blade narrow lobed. .... *Polypodium,* (**Polypody**), p. 52
7. Rootstalk buried; blade triangular. 8

8. Leaf divisions jointed at the main axis; upper leaf surface hairless. .... *Gymnocarpium,* (**Oak Fern**), p. 38
8. Leaf divisions not jointed; upper leaf surfaces covered with fine hairs. .... *Phegopteris* (**Beech Fern**), p. 40

9. Rootstalk slender; leaf blade thin, deciduous. 10
9. Rootstalk stout, leaf blade thick, evergreen. 11

10. Covering on sporangia, hoodlike when young, attached at the side, soon withering. Bulblets sometimes present on lower leaf surface. .... *Cystopteris,* (**Bladder Fern**), p. 37
10. Covering on sporangia, kidney shaped. .... *Thelypteris* (**New York Fern**), p. 39

11. Covering of sporangial clusters circular, umbrellalike. .... *Polystichum* (**Christmas Fern**), p. 46
11. Covering of sporangial clusters shield-shaped. .... *Dryopteris* (**Shield Fern, Wood Fern**), p. 42

12. Sporangial clusters longer than broad, not near the midrib, blade pinnately divided. .... *Asplenium* (**Spleenwort**), p. 48
12. Sporangial clusters forming marginal bands on the leaves, or, if separate, covered by tissue. 13

13. Sporangial clusters separate. 14
13. Sporangial clusters forming marginal bands. 15

14. Sporangial clusters borne on marginal teeth. .... *Dennstaedtia* (**Hay-scented Fern**), p. 47
14. Sporangial clusters covered by discontinuous flaps of marginal tissue. .... *Adiantum* (**Maidenhair Fern**), p. 50

15. Plants large, terrestrial; sporangial clusters borne on a heavy marginal vein extending around the leaf. .... *Pteridium* (**Bracken Fern**), p. 51
15. Plants of medium or small size, usually on rocks; sporangial clusters borne near the tips of separate veins, leaves firm, stalks dark, leaf-blade hairy. .... *Cheilanthes* (**Lip Fern**), p. 49

16. Seeds not enclosed within a fruit; trees and shrubs. ....**GYMNOSPERMS**, 17
16. Seeds enclosed within a fruit when mature. .... **FLOWERING PLANTS**, 22

17. Seed solitary (not borne on a cone scale), partially enveloped in a fleshy covering. .... *Taxus,* (**Yew**), p. 53
17. Seeds borne on cone scales. 18

18. Mature leaves scalelike and opposite, immature leaves slender and in threes, cones berrylike. .... *Juniperus* (**Juniper**), p. 61
18. Leaves in clusters of 2 or more, or solitary and spirally arranged. 19

19. Leaves solitary. 20
19. Leaves in clusters, evergreen, 2-5 in a sheathed cluster. .... *Pinus* (**Pine**), p. 57

20. Leaves flat, 2-ranked, with two white stomatal bands beneath. 21
20. Leaves somewhat 4-sided. .... *Picea* (**Spruce**), p. 56

21. Leaves sessile. ....*Abies* (**Fir**), p. 54
21. Leaves short-stalked. .... *Tsuga* (**Hemlock**), p. 55

22. Mostly herbaceous plants with vascular bundles scattered through the pith. Leaves with closed venation; mostly parallel-veined, net-veined in a few genera. Parts of flowers usually in 3s or 6s, never in 5s. Herbaceous except in the genus *Smilax* (**Greenbriers**). **MONOCOTYLEDONS**,23
22. Herbaceous and woody plants with the vascular bundles usually arranged in a ring about the pith. Leaves net-veined, with open venation. Flower parts in 4s or 5s. .... **DICOTYLEDONS**, 40

23. Calyx and/or corolla none, or of scalelike or chaffy divisions. 24
23. Calyx and/or corolla leaflike or colored. 31

24. Plants with jointed stems, sheathing leaves, and flowers enclosed by scales. 25
24. Flowers not enclosed by scales. 29

25. Stems round; leaf sheath split. ....(**Grasses**), 26
25. Stems triangular; leaf sheath not split. (**Sedges and Bulrushes**), 27

26. Each spikelet 1-flowered. .... *Danthonia* (**Poverty Grass, Mt. Oat Grass**), p. 65
26. Spikelets 2 to many flowered. ... *Panicum* (**Panic Grass**), p. 66

27. Flowers perfect. 28
27. Flowers either staminate or pistillate. ...... *Carex* (**Sedge**), p. 69

28. Flowers 2-ranked giving a flat appearance to branches of the inflorescence. .... *Cyperus* (**Sedge**), p. 67
28. Flower scales overlapping all the way around the branches of the inflorescence. .... *Scirpus* (**Bulrush**), p. 68

29. Flowers on a stalk, covered by a hood. 30
29. Flowers not covered by a hood. .... *Typha* (**Cattail**), p. 62

30. Flower stalk elongated. . *Arisaema,* (**Jack-in-the-Pulpit**), p. 70
30. Flower stalk short, compact. .... *Symplocarpus* (**Skunk Cabbage**), p. 71

31. Plants rushlike, calyx small, greenish or brownish. .... *Juncus* (**Rush**), p. 72
31. Plants not rushlike, calyx and corolla larger, sepals colored like the petals. Stamens mostly 6, one before each sepal and petal. Fruit a many-seeded pod or berry. 32

32. Stems woody; flowers many, radiating from a single point on a stalk arising in the leaf axils, with male and female flowers on separate plants; fruit a berry; leaves net-veined. .... *Smilax* (**Greenbrier**), p. 82
32. Stems herbaceous, leafy (bearing one or more well-developed leaves); fruit a berry, or capsule. 33
32. Leaves all or mostly basal, or apparently so, in some species absent at flowering time; fruit a capsule. 38

33. Leaves usually 3 in one whorl, net-veined; flower solitary. .... *Trillium,* p. 80
33. Leaves alternate. 34

34. Flowers axillary or terminal, solitary or few, or with flowerstalks radiating from a single point. 35
34. Flowers in a terminal branched inflorescence. 37

35. Flowers terminal, yellowish; stem forked or branching above. 36
35. Flowers axillary, rose-purple. *Streptopus* (**Twisted Stalk**), p. 79

36. Style 1, stigma 3-cleft or entire. *Disporum* (**Hairy Disporum**), p. 78
36. Style 3-parted to about the middle. *Uvularia* (**Bellwort**) (not included in text).

37. Leaves 2 or 3, heart-shaped at base; sepals 4, white; stamens 4. .... *Maianthemum* (**Canada Mayflower**), p. 77
37. Leaves several, broadly oval, oblong or oval, lance-shaped; sepals 3 and petals 3, stamens 6; flowers white; style single. .... *Smilacina* (**Plumelily**), p. 76

38. Flowers solitary, nodding; leaves 2 (or 1), mottled; plants from deep-seated compact underground stems. .... *Erythronium* (**Trout lily, Fawn lily**), p. 74
38. Flowers several, radiating from a single point. 39

39. Plants with the odor and taste of onion; fruit a capsule; leaves may not be present at flowering time. .... *Allium* (**Ramp, Wild Onion**), p. 73
39. Plants not onionlike; fruit a berry. *Clintonia* (**Bead Lily**), p. 75

40. Flowers without petals or without both sepals and petals. 41
40. Flowers with both sepals and petals; petals not united. 74
40. Flowers with both sepals and petals. Petals more or less united. 128

41. Flowers naked, imperfect, one or both kinds in catkins (aments). 42
41. Flowers not in catkins. 58

42. Only 1 kind of flower in catkins (pistillate or staminate). 43
42. Both kinds of flowers (pistillate and staminate) in catkins. 49

43. Pistillate flowers in short catkins. Herbs. 44
43. Staminate flowers in slender catkins or heads. Trees or shrubs. 45

44. Leaves opposite. .... *Urtica* (**Nettle**), p. 133
44. Leaves alternate. .... *Laportea* (**Wood Nettle**), p. 132

45. Leaves pinnate. 46
45. Leaves simple. 47

46. Husk indehiscent; nut rough; pith chambered. .... *Juglans* (**Walnut**), p. 93
46. Husk splitting into segments; nut ribbed but smooth; pith continuous. .... *Carya* (**Hickory**), p. 96

47. Staminate flowers in heads; fruit a triangular nut, occurring usually two within a bur with unbranched spines. .... *Fagus* (**Beech**), p. 115
47. Staminate flowers in slender catkins. 48

48. Involucre forming a prickly bur with branched spines enclosing 2 to 4 nuts. .... *Castanea* (**Chestnut**), p. 116
48. Involucre forming a cup, partially covering a single nut (acorn). .... *Quercus* (**Oak**), p. 117

49. Fruit many-seeded. 50
49. Fruit 1-seeded. 51

50. Bracts of catkin entire or slightly toothed; stamens few, stigmas short; buds with one scale; leaves several times longer than broad, short petioled. .... *Salix* (**Willow**), p. 86
50. Bracts of catkin irregularly cleft; stamens numerous; stigmas elongated; buds with several scales; leaves about as long as broad, long petioled. .... *Populus* (**Poplar**), p. 89

51. Calyx regular, sap milky, fruit a multiple of drupes, berrylike. .... *Morus* (**Mulberry**), p. 131
51. Calyx, none, or rudimentary. 52

52. Style and stigma 1; fruits in balls. *Platanus* (**Sycamore**), p. 162
52. Style and stigma 2. 53

53. Shrub with fragrant fernlike leaves. *Comptonia* (**Sweet-fern**), p. 92
53. Trees or shrubs; leaves not fernlike. 54

54. Staminate flowers in catkins, without a calyx; pistillate flowers in a small spike or head; nuts unwinged. 55
54. Both staminate and pistillate flowers in catkins, the staminate with a 2- to 4-parted calyx, the pistillate without a calyx; nuts winged. 57

55. Nut surrounded by leathery, leaflike bracts. .... *Corylus* (**Hazelnut**), p. 103
55. Nut not surrounded by bracts. 56

56. Nut enclosed in bladderlike sacs. .... *Ostrya* (**Iron wood, Hop Hornbeam**), p. 107
56. Nut with a 2- to 3-lobed bract at the base. .... *Carpinus* (**American Hornbeam, Muscletree**), p. 106

57. Stamens 2; fruiting bracts papery, 3-lobed or entire, deciduous. .... *Betula* (**Birch**), p. 108
57. Stamens 4; fruiting bracts woody and wavy-edged or 5-toothed, persistent. .... *Alnus* (**Alder**), p. 112

58. Seeds few (1-2) in each cell of the ovary, rarely 3 or 4. Pistil 1, simple or compound. 59
58. Seeds many in each cell of the ovary; calyx present, ovary inferior. .... *Aristolochia* (**Dutchman's Pipe**), p. 136

59. Ovary superior. 60
59. Ovary inferior. Shrubs and trees. 73

60. Stems with swollen nodes; stipules sheathing the stem at the node. 61
60. Stems not of this character. 63

61. Herbs. 62
61. Trees. .... *Platanus* (**Sycamore**), p. 162

62. Sepals 6, the 3 inner ones turned inward, usually developing wings and surrounding the fruit. .... *Rumex* (**Dock**), p. 137
62. Sepals 4 or 5, equal and erect in fruit; achenes usually enclosed by the fruiting calyx; styles 2 or 3, deciduous. .... *Polygonum* (**Bindweed**), p. 138

63. Herbs. 64
63. Shrubs or trees. 66

64. Styles 10; ovary 10-celled. .... *Phytolacca* (**Pokeweed**), p. 139
64. Style, if present, 1; flowers unisexual. 65

65. Leaves opposite. .... *Urtica* (**Nettle**), p. 133
65. Leaves alternate. .... *Laportea* (**Wood Nettle**), p. 132

66. Leaves alternate. 68
66. Leaves opposite, fruit winged. 67

67. Fruit with two wings. .... *Acer* (**Maple**), p. 206
67. Fruit with one wing. .... *Fraxinus* (**Ash**), p. 258

68. Ovary 3-celled. .... *Ceanothus* (**New Jersey Tea**), p. 213
68. Ovary 1- to 2-celled. 69

69. Stigmas and styles 2. 70
69. Stigma and style 1. 71

70. Leaves doubly toothed. Fruit winged. .... *Ulmus* (**Elm**), p. 127
70. Leaves singly toothed. Fruit a drupe. *Celtis* (**Hackberry**), p. 130

71. Anthers opening lengthwise. .... *Dirca* (**Leatherwood**), p. 224
71. Anthers opening by uplifted lids. 72

72. Small trees with some leaves lobed. .... *Sassafras,* p. 150
72. Shrubs with no lobed leaves. .... *Lindera* (**Spice Bush**), p. 151

73. Style 1. .... *Pyrularia* (**Buffalo Nut**), p. 135
73. Styles 2. .... *Hamamelis* (**Witch Hazel**), p. 161

74. Stamens numerous, usually more than 10. 75
74. Stamens definite and not more than twice as many as the petals. 91

75. Calyx free from the ovary. 76
75. Calyx more or less joined to the ovary. 124

76. Pistils several or many, distinct, or united at base; leaves alternate. 77
76. Pistils strictly 1, simple or compound. 86

77. Stamens inserted on the calyx. 78
77. Stamens inserted on the receptacle. 83

78. Pistils distinct, ripening into pods or drupes. 79
78. Pistils united, enclosed by the calyx tube and fastened to it. ... 81

79. Pistils 5 to 8 ripening into pods that split along 1 side; shrubs; leaves toothed or entire. .... *Spiraea,* p. 163
79. Pistils few or many, ripening to dry, one-seeded fruits or one-seeded fleshy fruits. 80

80. Pistils not enclosed in a fleshy calyx tube; fruit very fleshy; one-seeded. . *Rubus* (**Blackberry, Raspberry, Dewberry**), p. 174
80. Pistils enclosed in a fleshy calyx tube. .... *Rosa* (**Rose**), p. 182

81. Ripe pistils papery or leathery (so-called seeds) enclosed in a very fleshy, usually edible calyx tube. 82
81. Ripe pistils very hard and bony. . *Crataegus* (**Hawthorn**), p. 173

82. Styles 2 to 5, cavities of the ovary as many as the styles. .... *Pyrus* (**Mountain-ash, Crab Apple, Chokeberries**), p. 164
82. Cavities of the ovary twice as many as the styles. ....*Amelanchier* (**Sarvis, Service Berry**), p. 169

83. Herbs; petals yellow; ovary with one ovule. .... *Ranunculus* (**Buttercup**), p. 141
83. Trees or shrubs. 84

84. Stipules none. .... *Asimina* (**Pawpaw**), p. 149
84. Stipules encircling the twigs. 85

85. Leaves entire, unlobed or with basal lobes. ...... *Magnolia,* p. 144
85. Leaves entire, lobed or shallowly notched at the apex. .... *Liriodendron* (**Tulip-tree**), p. 148

86. Leaves marked with translucent or black dots. .... *Hypericum* (**St. John's Wort**), p. 219
86. Leaves not dotted. 87

87. Herbs. 88
87. Shrubs or trees. 89

88. Leaves compound or dissected. .... *Actaea* (**Baneberry**), p. 142
88. Leaves 2 in number (1 leaf on sterile plants), umbrellalike and lobed. .... *Podophyllum* (**May Apple**), p. 143

89. Leaves opposite. .... *Acer* (**Maple**), p. 206
89. Leaves alternate. 90

90. Inflorescence attached to a leaflike bract. *Tilia* (**Basswood**), p. 216
90. Inflorescence without such bracts. .... *Prunus* (**Cherry**), p. 183

91. Stamens of the same number as the petals and opposite them. 92
91. Stamens alternate with the petals or of a different number. 95

92. Woody climbers. 93
92. Herbs or shrubs. 94

93. Leaves simple. .... *Vitis* (**Grape**), p. 215
93. Leaves palmately compound. .... *Parthenocissus* (**Virginia Creeper**), p. 214

94. Sepals 2, distinct, herbs. ...... *Claytonia* (**Spring Beauty**), p. 140
94. Calyx with sepals united, 4 to 5-toothed, shrubs. .... *Ceanothus* (**New Jersey Tea**), p. 213

95. Ovary superior. 96
95. Ovary wholly or partly inferior. 120

96. Ovaries 2 or more, separate, or somewhat united at the base. Stamens separate, borne on the receptacle. 97
96. Ovary 1. 100

97. Herbs; leaves fleshy. .... *Sedum* (**Stone Crop**), p. 154
97. Herbs; leaves not fleshy. 98

98. Ovaries with separate styles or sessile stigmas. .... *Ranunculus* (**Buttercup**), p. 141
98. Ovaries, or lobes of the ovary, 2 to 5, with a common style. .. 99

99. Plants fleshy; stamens just twice as many as the pistils. .... *Sedum* (**Stone Crop**), p. 154
99. Plants not fleshy; stamens not twice as many as the pistils; flowers larger, mostly showy. .... *Geranium,* p. 193

100. Pistil simple, placenta borne on the carpel wall. 101
100. Pistil compound, as shown by its cells, placentas, styles or stigmas. 105

101. Leaves umbrellalike, lobed. *Podophyllum* (**May Apple**), p. 143
101. Leaves not umbrellalike. 102

102. Flowers imperfectly or not at all butterflylike. 103
102. Flowers butterflylike. 104

103. Thorny trees. .... *Gleditsia* (**Honey Locust**), p. 187
103. Unarmed shrubs; leaves simple. .... *Cercis* (**Redbud**), p. 189

104. Fruit beanlike; trees or shrubs; leaves pinnate; foliage not glandular dotted. .... *Robinia* (**Black Locust**), p. 190
104. Fruit jointed of 3 or more joints; herbs; leaves 3-foliolate. .... *Desmodium* (**Stick Tights**), p. 191

105. Ovary 1-celled. 106
105. Ovary 2- to several-celled. 109

106. Corolla irregular. 107
106. Corolla regular. 108

107. Petals 4; stamens 6. .... *Dicentra,* (**Dutchman's Breeches, Squirrel Corn, Bleeding Heart**). .... p. 152
107. Petals 5; stamens 5. .... *Viola* (**Violet**), p. 220

108. Ovule solitary. .... *Rhus* (**Sumac**), p. 194
108. Ovules more than 1. Leaves dotted. ....*Hypericum* (**St. John's Wort**), p. 219

109. Flowers irregular; trees or shrubs. 110
109. Flowers regular. 111

110. Leaves simple, alternate, not toothed. .... *Rhododendron,* p. 236
110. Leaves palmately compound, opposite, leaflets toothed. ....*Aesculus* (**Buckeye**), p. 212

111. Stamens neither just as many nor twice as many as the petals. 112
111. Stamens just as many or twice as many as the petals. 114

112. Trees or shrubs. 113
112. Herbs; leaves opposite; petals 5. .... *Hypericum* (**St. John's Wort**), p. 219

113. Stamens fewer than the petals. .... *Fraxinus* (**Ash**), p. 258
113. Stamens more numerous than the petals. *Acer* (**Maple**), p. 206

114. Ovules and seeds only 1 or 2 in each cell. 115
114. Ovules and seeds several or many in each cell; leaves compound. 119

115. Herbs; flowers perfect; cells of the ovary 5; flowers more or less showy. .... *Geranium,* p. 193
115. Trees or shrubs. 116

116. Leaves palmately compound 5- to 7-foliate. ....*Aesculus* (**Buckeye**), p. 212
116. Leaves simple. 117

117. Leaves palmately veined. .... *Acer* (**Maple**), p. 206
117. Leaves pinnately veined; alternate; erect shrubs or trees. ... 118

118. Petals or corolla-lobes oval; stamens fastened to the base of the corolla. .... *Ilex* (**Holly**), p. 199
118. Petals elongate, free from each other and from the stamens. .... *Nemopanthus* (**Mountain-holly**), p. 204

119. Shrubs. .... *Staphylea* (**Bladdernut**), p. 205
119. Herbs. .... *Oxalis,* p. 192

120. Ovules and seeds more than 1 in each cell. 121
120. Ovules and seeds only 1 in each cell. 123

121. Ovary 1-celled. .... *Tiarella* (**Foam Flower**), p. 155
121. Ovary 2- to many-celled; styles 2-3; stamens 5 or 10. 122

122. Leaves opposite. .... *Hydrangea,* p. 156
122. Leaves alternate. .... *Ribes* (**Gooseberry**), p. 157

123. Stamens 5 or 10. 124
123. Stamens 2, 4, or 8. 127

124. Shrubs or small trees. 125
124. Herbs; styles 2-5; fruit fleshy. 126

125. Leaves simple. .... *Crataegus* (**Hawthorn**), p. 173

125. Leaves compound. .... *Aralia,* p.226

126. Leaves whorled; fruit red. ..... *Panax* (**Ginseng, Sang**), p. 230
126. Leaves alternate; fruit black. .... *Aralia,* p. 226

127. Shrubs or trees; flowers perfect. .. *Cornus* (**Dogwood**), p. 231
127. Trees; pistillate and staminate flowers on separate trees. ....*Nyssa* (**Black Gum**), p. 225

128. Stamens more numerous than the lobes of the corolla. 129
128. Stamens not more numerous than the lobes of the corolla; stamens alternate with the corolla lobes or fewer in number. 142

129. Ovary 1-celled; sepals 2. .... *Dicentra* (**Dutchman's Breeches, Squirrel Corn; Bleeding Heart**), ... p. 152
129. Ovary 2 or more celled. 130

130. Stamens attached to the corolla; styles 4; filaments separate; shrubs or trees. .... *Diospyros* (**Persimmon**), p. 257
130. Stamens free from the corolla, or borne at its base; style 1. 131

131. Sepals and petals attached below the ovary........................ 132
131. Sepals and petals attached on top of the ovary. Erect shrubs, or if trailing, berry not white. 138

132. Margin of the leaves without teeth. 133
132. Margin of the leaves with very tiny teeth (sometimes without teeth in *Gaultheria*). 138

133. Leaves evergreen. 134
133. Leaves deciduous. 136

134. Prostrate, nearly herbaceous. *Epigaea* (**Trailing Arbutus**), p. 245
134. Erect shrubs. 135

135. Corolla somewhat irregular. .... *Rhododendron,* p. 236
135. Corolla regular with 10 narrow pouches into which the anthers are tucked. .... *Kalmia* (**Mt. Laurel**), p. 244

136. Corolla somewhat irregular. .. *Rhododendron* (**Azalea**), p. 236
136. Corolla regular. 137

137. Corolla 4-lobed. ......*Menziesia* (**Allegheny Menziesia**), p. 246
137. Corolla 5-toothed. .... *Lyonia* (**Maleberry**), p. 247

138. Leaves evergreen. 139
138. Leaves deciduous. 140

139. Plants low, 5-15 cm high. .... *Gaultheria* (**Teaberry**), p. 248
139. Plants taller, 5-15 dm high. .... *Pieris* (**Mt. Fetterbush**), p. 249

140. Shrubs with depressed-spherical capsules; corolla nearly spherical. ....*Lyonia* (**Maleberry**), p. 247
140. Trees with oval-pyramidial, upright capsules and sour twigs. .... *Oxydendrum* (**Sourwood**), p. 250

141. Berry 10-seeded. .... *Gaylussacia* (**Huckleberry**), p. 251
141. Berry many-seeded. .... *Vaccinium* (**Blueberry**), p. 252

142. Ovary superior. 143
142. Ovary inferior. 145

143. Corolla regular; stamens as many as the corolla lobes, free from the corolla or nearly so; ovary 1, not deeply lobed, 2- to 10-celled. 144
143. Corolla irregular; stamens with anthers 5, free from the corolla. .... *Rhododendron* (**Azaleas**), p. 236

144. Petals or corolla-lobes oval; stamens attached to the base of the corolla. .... *Ilex* (**Holly**), p. 199
144. Petals elongate, free from each other; stamens not attached to the base of the corolla. *Nemopanthus* (**Mountain-holly**), p. 204

145. Flowers in heads with bracts; stamens united by their anthers to form a ring or tube surrounding the pistil. 150
145. Flowers not in heads; leaves opposite or whorled. 146

146. Herbs; creeping, evergreen. *Mitchella* (**Partridge Berry**), p. 259
146. Shrubs. 147

147. Stamens 4; leaves opposite or whorled and with stipules. .... *Cephalanthus* (**Buttonbush**), p. 260
147. Stamens 5; leaves opposite and without stipules. 148

148. Corolla tubular, irregular. ..... *Lonicera* (**Honeysuckle**), p.261
148. Corolla round or urn-shaped, regular. 149

149. Leaves simple. .... *Viburnum,* p.262
149. Leaves pinnate. .... *Sambucus* (**Elderberry**), p. 269

150. Stems wandlike; leaves sessile or nearly sessile. Style branches of the disc-flowers with elongate hairy appendages. .... *Solidago* (**Goldenrod**), p. 273
150. Stems upright; basal leaves usually present; heads of both ray and disc flowers; style branches of the disc flowers not appendaged. .... *Senecio* (**Groundsel, Ragwort**), p. 272

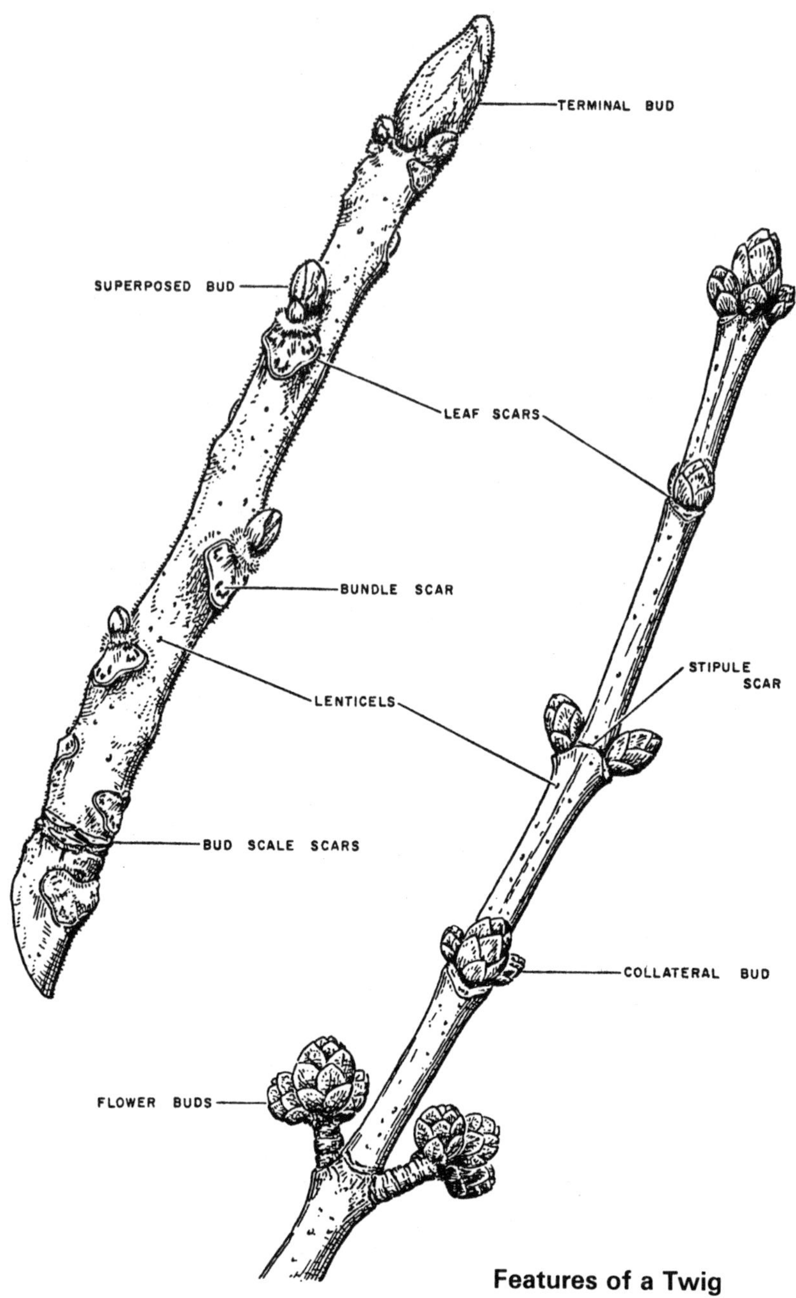

Features of a Twig

WINTER KEY TO THE GENERA OF WOODY PLANTS

1. Leaves evergreen. 2
1. Leaves deciduous. 15

2. Leaves 8 mm or less in width, needlelike or scalelike. 3
2. Leaves 12 mm or more in width. 8

3. Leaves in clusters. .... *Pinus* (**Pine**), p. 57
3. Leaves not in clusters. 4

4. Leaves alternate, elongate. 5
4. Leaves whorled or opposite, of two types, awl-shaped in whorls of 3 on young growth, scalelike, opposite on older branches; foliage sprays not flattened. .... *Juniperus* (**Juniper**), p. 61

5. Leaves square in cross-section. .... *Picea* (**Spruce**), p. 56
5. Leaves flattened. 6

6. Low trailing shrubs to 1 m high; leaves smooth, alternate. .... *Taxus,* (**Yew**), p. 53
6. Trees. 7

7. Leaves sessile. .... *Abies* (**Fir**), p. 54
7. Leaves with short petioles. .... *Tsuga* (**Hemlock**), p. 55

8. Leaves opposite. .... *Lonicera* (**Honeysuckle**), p. 261
8. Leaves alternate. 9

9. Plants climbing by tendrils. .... *Smilax* (**Greenbrier**), p. 82
9. Plants not climbing. 10

10. Stems erect, more than 20 cm high. 11
10. Stems low; under 20 cm high. 14

11. Leaves rough, margin smooth, slightly toothed. 12
11. Leaves not smooth on the margin, armed with spiny teeth. .... *Ilex* (**Holly**), p. 199

12. Fruits persistent, in several-flowered inflorescences. .... *Pieris* (**Mt. Fetterbush**), p. 249
12. Not as above; leaves more than 3 cm long. 13

13. Buds moderate or large, scales several. .. *Rhododendron,* p. 236
13. Buds tiny, scales 2 or none. .... *Kalmia* (**Mt. Laurel**), p. 244

14. Stems red-bristly; fruit dry. *Epigaea* (**Trailing Arbutus**), p. 245
14. Stems smooth; fruit fleshy, red. .. *Gaultheria* (**Teaberry**), p. 248

15. Leaf scars opposite or whorled. 16
15. Leaf scars alternate. 50

16. Leaf scars whorled. 17
16. Leaf scars opposite. 18

17. Buds small, often sunk in bark. *Cephalanthus* (**Buttonbush**), ... p. 260

17. Buds oblong, spreading; twigs smooth; soft-wooded shrubs. .... *Hydrangea,* p. 156

18. Climbing or scrambling, without tendrils or aerial roots. .... *Lonicera* (**Honeysuckle**), p. 261
18. Not climbing. 19

19. Bundle traces distinct, 3 or more in a line. 20
19. Bundle traces 1 or many; if many, scattered or in a ring or nearly confluent in a line. 47

20. Leaf scars large and broad. 21
20. Leaf scars small or narrow. 23

21. Trees, twigs without milky juice. ... *Aesculus* (**Buckeye**), p. 212
21. Soft-wooded shrubs. 22

22. Lenticels very conspicuous. ...... *Sambucus* (**Elderberry**), p. 269
22. Lenticels not conspicuous. .... *Hydrangea,* p. 156

23. Leaf scars elongate, straight or curved. 24
23. Leaf scars not as above. 35

24. Bud scale 1; leaf scars straight or curved, but not horseshoe-shaped. 25
24. Bud scales 2 or more or none. 26

25. Buds gummy within. .... *Viburnum,* p. 262
25. Buds not gummy within. .... *Salix* (**Willow**), p. 86

26. Bud scales none (the young foliage rusty brown). .... *Viburnum,* .... p. 262

26. Buds with 2 or more scales. 27

27. Bud scales 2, not overlapping. 28
27. Bud scales more than 2. 32

28. Youngest growth gray, or grayish-brown, not hairy. 29
28. Young growth often highly colored (red, green, purple, etc.). 31

29. Leaf buds long, slender, tapering, lead-colored. *Viburnum,* p. 262
29. Leaf buds not long and slender. 30

30. Buds dark red or rusty brown, scurfy. .... *Viburnum,* p. 262
30. Buds gray or brown, not scurfy. ... *Cornus,* (**Dogwood**), p. 231

31. The opposite leaf scars not raised and meeting or nearly so in a "V." .... *Acer* (**Maple**), p. 206
31. The opposite leaf scars somewhat raised and connected to each other by a narrow line on each side. *Cornus* (**Dogwood**), p. 231

32. Buds sessile. 33
32. Buds stalked. 34

33. Branches short, numerous, rigidly spreading. *Viburnum,* p. 262
33. Not as above. .... *Acer* (**Maple**), p. 206

34. Leaf scars meeting in a point. .... *Acer* (**Maple**), p. 206
34. Leaf scars often meeting in a straight line. ..... *Viburnum,* p. 262

35. Leaf scars very small and inconspicuous; pith often more or less excavated. .... *Lonicera* (**Honeysuckle**), p. 261
35. Leaf scars larger, pith continuous. 36

36. Buds covered by the base of the petiole. . *Cornus* (**Dogwood**), ... p. 231
36. Buds not covered. 37

37. Leaf scars long-hairy at the top. 38
37. Leaf scars not long-hairy. 39

38. Buds sessile. .... *Acer* (**Maple**), p. 206
38. Buds stalked. .... *Virburnum,* p. 262

39. Bud scales none; twigs without raised lines. ... *Viburnum,* p. 262
39. Buds with scales; twigs without raised lines. 40

40. Exposed scales 2 to 4. 41
40. Exposed scales more than 4. 44

41. Buds stalked. .... *Acer,* (**Maple**), p. 206
41. Buds not stalked. 42

42. Leaf scars connected by lines. *Lonicera* (**Honeysuckle**), p. 261
42. Leaf scars not connected by lines. 43

43. Stipule scars present, almost connecting the leaf scars. ....
.... *Staphylea* (**Bladdernut**), p. 205
43. Stipule scars none. .... *Acer* (**Maple**), p. 206

44. Buds superposed; leaf scars raised. ... *Lonicera* (**Honeysuckle**),
.... p. 261
44. Buds not superposed. 45

45. Soft-wooded shrubs. .... *Hydrangea,* p. 156
45. Trees or shrubs, not soft-wooded. 46

46. Leaf scars meeting in a point. .... *Acer* (**Maple**), p. 206
46. Leaf scars not meeting. .... *Viburnum,* p. 262

47. Bundle traces many; sap not milky; pith continuous. ....
.... *Fraxinus* (**Ash**), p. 258
47. Bundle trace 1. 48

48. Soft-wooded shrubs with flaking bark; pith continuous. ....
.... *Hypericum* (**St. John's Wort**), p. 219
48. Not as above with leaf scars 2 mm or more broad. 49

49. Leaf scars connected by lines; buds superposed. ....
.... *Cephalanthus* (**Buttonbush**), p. 260
49. Leaf scars not connected by lines; trees with moderate lenticels.
.... *Fraxinus* (**Ash**), p. 258

50. Climbing or scrambling. 51
50. Not climbing. 56

51. Climbing by tendrils or aerial roots. 52
51. Twining or scrambling, without aerial roots or tendrils. 55

52. With aerial roots; (Caution! Poison ivy). .. *Rhus* (**Poison Ivy**),
.... p. 194
52. With tendrils. 53

53. Tendrils borne on persistent leaf-base; stems green. ....
.... *Smilax* (**Greenbrier**), p. 82
53. Tendrils opposite the leaf scar. 54

54. Tendrils ending in flat disks. ....
.... *Parthenocissus* (**Virginia Creeper**), p. 214
54. Tendrils not ending in disks; pith continuous. .. *Vitus* (**Grape**),
.... p. 215

55. Buds superposed; stems not prickly; leaf scars U-shaped. .... *Aristolochia* (**Dutchman's Pipe**), p. 136
55. Buds solitary; stems prickly; leaf scars elongate. *Rosa* (**Rose**), ... p. 182

56. Bearing spines or prickles. 57
56. Without spines or prickles. 66

57. Bearing spines (stiff outgrowths of the twig). 58
57. Bearing prickles (superficial outgrowths). 62

58. Spines in 2s and unbranched, representing stipules. .... *Robinia* (**Black Locust**), p. 190
58. Spines scattered and branched or not, representing modified twigs. 59

59. Leaf scars on torn membranes; spines branched. .... *Gleditsia* (**Honey Locust**), p. 187
59. Not as above. 60

60. Spines very sharp pointed and without buds or leaf scars. .... *Crataegus* (**Hawthorn**), p. 173
60. Spines are thornlike twigs having buds and/or leaf scars. 61

61. Stipule scars none. .... *Pyrus* (**Crabapple, Chokeberry, Mountain-ash**), p. 164
61. Stipule scars present. .... *Prunus* (**Cherry**), p. 183

62. Leaf bases persistent, torn at the top. *Rubus* (**Blackberry**), p. 174
62. Leaf bases not persistent. 63

63. Leaf scars irregulary cracked. .. *Robinia* (**Black Locust**), p. 190
63. Leaf scars not as above. 65

64. Leaf scars nearly encircling the thick stem. .... *Aralia,* p. 226
64. Leaf scars not as above. 65

65. Buds elongated, stalked; pith porous. *Ribes* (**Gooseberry**), p. 157
65. Buds ovoid; pith continuous. .... *Rosa* (**Rose**), p. 182

66. Without leaf scars but with persistent leaf-bases; pith central in branches. .... *Rubus* (**Blackberry**), p. 174
66. With leaf scars. 67

67. Bundle traces distinct, 3 or more in a line. 68
67. Bundle trace 1, or many traces scattered or nearly confluent in a line. 123

68. Leaf scars very narrow. 69
68. Leaf scars broader. 89

69. Leaf scars straight or U-shaped. 70
69. Leaf scars horseshoe-shaped, or ringlike, nearly or completely encircling the bud. 85

70. Stipule scars encircling the twig. .... *Magnolia,* p. 144
70. Stipule scars smaller or none. 71

71. Leaf scars half-encircling the twig; tall shrub; buds gummy. .... *Pyrus* (**Mountain-ash**), p. 164
71. Leaf scars shorter. 72

72. Bud scale 1 .... *Salix* (**Willow**), p. 86
72. Bud scales 2 or more. 73

73. Pith porous in old twigs. .... *Ribes* (**Gooseberry**), p. 157
73. Pith continuous 74

74. Sap milky. .... *Rhus* (**Sumac**), p. 194
74. Sap not milky. 75

75. Aromatic. 76
75. Not aromatic. 78

76. Bark not peeling horizontally around the stem. .... *Lindera* (**Spice Bush**), p. 151
76. Bark peeling horizontally around the stem. 77

77. Bark pleasantly aromatic, with odor of wintergreen. .... *Betula* (**Birch**), p. 108
77. Bark unpleasantly aromatic. .... *Prunus* (**Cherry**), p. 183

78. Leaf scars low, straight. .... *Rosa* (**Rose**), p. 182
78. Leaf scars raised, or curved. 79

79. Lateral buds short-ovoid. 80
79. Lateral buds elongate-ovoid. 81

80. Stipule scars present. .... *Betula* (**Birch**), p. 108
80. Stipule scars absent. .... *Pyrus* (**Mountain-ash**), p. 164

81. Buds curved, the scales twisted; pith small, angled. ....*Amelanchier* (**Service Berry**), p. 169
81. Not as above. 82

82. Buds symmetrical; pith small, flattened or 3-angled. ....*Betula* (**Birch**), p. 108
82. Without this combination of characters. 83

83. Buds wooly or gummy. ....
.... *Pyrus* (**Crabapple, Chokeberry, Mountain-ash**), p. 164
83. Buds not as above. 84

84. Buds oblong or elongated-oval. ....
.... *Pyrus* (**Crabapple, Chokeberry, Mountain-ash**), p. 164
84. Buds short-oval. .... *Prunus* (**Cherry**), p. 183

85. Stipule scars encircling the twig. . *Platanus* (**Sycamore**), p. 162
85. Stipule scars shorter or none. 86

86. Leaf scars torn; not aromatic. . *Robinia* (**Black Locust**), p. 190
86. Leaf scars nearly encircling the bud. 87

87. Sap milky. .... *Rhus* (**Sumac**), p. 194
87. Sap not milky; nodes swollen. .... *Dirca* (**Leatherwood**), p. 224

88. Pith chambered throughout or at the nodes only. 89
88. Pith continuous. 90

89. Twigs rather thick, pith chambered throughout; leaf scars large.
....*Juglans* (**Walnut**), p. 93
89. Twigs slender, pith chambered at the nodes; leaf scars small. .....
.... *Celtis* (**Hackberry**), p. 130

90. Pith with firmer diaphragms at intervals. Often missing in *Asimina* (**Paw Paw**), ... 91
90. Pith without firmer diaphragms. 92

91. Buds densely covered with reddish-brown hairs. ....
.... *Asimina* (**Paw Paw**), p. 149
91. Not as above. .... *Nyssa* (**Black Gum**), p. 225

92. Sap milky. 93
92. Sap not milky. 94

93. Bud scales 2 or 3. .... *Rhus* (**Sumac**), p. 194
93. Bud scales several. .... *Morus* (**Mulberry**), p. 131

94. Lowest scale of lateral buds centrally located over the leaf scar; pith angled. .... *Populus* (**Poplar**), p. 89
94. Not as above. 95

95. Low shrub with leaves persistent until late winter, fernlike. ....
.... *Comptonia* (**Sweet-fern**), p. 92
95. Not as above. 96

•

96. Stipule scars elongated; resin in blisters in sheltered places. .... *Betula* (**Birch**), p. 108
96. Not as above. 97

97. Buds stalked. 98
97. Buds not stalked. 102

98. Buds long and spinelike. .... *Fagus* (**Beech**), p. 115
98. Not as above. 99

99. Leaf scars 2-ranked. 100
99. Leaf scars in more than 2 ranks. 101

100. Buds yellowish. .... *Hamamelis* (**Witch Hazel**), p. 161
100. Buds black or brown, only the flower buds stalked. .... *Cercis* (**Red Bud**), p. 189

101. Aromatic; buds greenish yellow. . *Lindera* (**Spicebush**), p. 151
101. Not aromatic; buds reddish. .... *Alnus* (**Alder**), p. 112

102. Pith flattened or 3-angled. 103
102. Pith round. 105

103. Bud scales not overlapping. .... *Alnus* (**Alder**), p. 112
103. Bud scales overlapping each other. 104

104. Bud scales 4-6 .... *Corylus* (**Hazel Nut**), p. 103
104. Bud scales usually 2 or 3. .... *Betula* (**Birch**), p. 108

105. Twigs with 3 small vertical ridges below the leaf scars. 106
105. Not as above. 107

106. Leaf scars 2-ranked. .... *Cercis* (**Redbud**), p. 189
106. Leaf scars in more than 2 ranks. .... *Prunus* (**Cherry**), p. 183

107. Buds long and spinelike; stipule scars long. ... *Fagus* (**Beech**), ... p. 115
107. Not as above. 108

108. Buds small and appressed. 109
108. Not as above. 111

109. Leaf scars on raised leaf cushions; bark peeling horizontally, inner bark with a disagreeable odor. *Prunus* (**Cherry**), p. 183
109 Leaf scars low. 110

110. Lateral buds triangular. .... *Celtis* (**Hackberry**), p. 130
110. Lateral buds minute, not triangular. *Cornus* (**Dogwood**), p. 231

111. Leaf scars 2-ranked. 112
111. Leaf scars in more than 2 ranks. 116

112. Bud scales 2, not overlapping. .... *Alnus* (**Alder**), p. 112
112. Bud scales 2, overlapping or more than 2. 113

113. Bud scales with vertical stripes. *Ostrya* (**Hop Hornbeam**), p. 107
113. Bud scales not striped. 114

114. Bud scales 2. .... *Tilia* (**Basswood**), p. 216
114. Bud scales several. 115

115. Buds nearly round, with 4-6 scales. *Corylus* (**Hazelnut**), p. 103
115. Buds oblong, somewhat 4-sided, with about 12 scales. .... *Carpinus* (**American Hornbeam**), p. 106

116. Exposed bud scales 2. .... *Cornus* (**Dogwood**), p. 231
116. Exposed bud scales more than 2, or the buds naked. 117
117. Without stipules or stipule scars. 118
117. With stipules or stipule scars. 120

118. Aromatic; twigs green. .... *Sassafras,* p. 150
118. Not aromatic. 119

119. Buds wooly or gummy. .... *Pyrus* (**Crabapple, Chokeberry, Mountain-ash**), p. 164
119. Buds not wooly or gummy. ... *Pyrularia* (**Buffalo Nut**), p. 135

120. Stipule scars elongated. .... *Betula* (**Birch**), p. 108
120. Stipule bases present, or stipule scars short. 121

121. Stipule scars on bases of leaf cushion; inner bark with disagreeable odor; lenticels elongated. .... *Prunus* (**Cherry**), p. 183
121. Stipule scars not on a leaf cushion. 122

122. Lenticels horizontally elongated. .... *Prunus* (**Cherry**), p. 183
122. Lenticels not horizontally elongated. .... *Crataegus* (**Hawthorn**), p. 173

123. Stipule scars nearly or quite encircling the twig. 124
123. Not as above. 127

124. Buds long and pointed. 125
124. Buds not as above. 126

125. Leaf scars small. .... *Fagus* (**Beech**), p. 115
125. Leaf scars large. .... *Magnolia,* p. 144

126. Buds large, flattened. .... *Liriodendron* (**Tuliptree**), p. 148
126. Buds short, ovoid. .... *Ulmus* (**Elm**), p. 127

127. Bundle traces many, mostly in 3 groups; leaf scars lobed. .. 128
127. Not as above. 129

128. Pith chambered. .... *Juglans* (**Walnut**), p. 93
128. Pith continuous. .... *Carya* (**Hickory**), p. 96

129. Bundle traces not in 3 groups. 130
129. Bundle trace 1. 136

130. Sap milky. 131
130. Sap not milky. 132

131. Without stipule scars. .... *Rhus* (**Sumac**), p. 194
131. With stipule scars; buds ovoid. .... *Morus* (**Mulberry**), p. 131

132. Pith angular, more or less star-shaped. 133
132. Pith round or nearly so. 134

133. Bud scales numerous. .... *Quercus* (**Oak**), p. 117
133. Bud scales 2 or 3. .... *Castanea* (**Chestnut**), p. 116

134. Buds asymmetrical. .... *Tilia* (**Basswood**), p. 216
134. Buds nearly symmetrical. 135

135. Scars of 2 kinds: leaf scars with 3 bundle traces, and branch scars with numerous bundles in an elipse. .... *Pyrularia* (**Buffalo Nut**), p. 135
135. Not as above. .... *Corylus* (**Hazel Nut**), p. 103

136. Pith chambered or porous. 137
136. Pith continuous. 138

137. Bud scales 2, overlapping. .... *Diospyros* (**Persimmon**), p. 257
137. Bud scales several, buds triangular. . *Celtis* (***Hackberry***), p. 130

138. Bundle trace broken into 3. 139
138. Bundle trace unbroken. 140

139. Twigs aromatic, green. .... *Sassafras,* p. 150
139. Not as above; buds superposed. .... *Ilex* (**Holly**), p. 199

140. Leaf scars on large leaf cushions; buds round to spindle-shaped; twigs angled near the nodes. .... *Spirea,* p. 163
140. Leaf scars not on leaf cushions. 141

141. Bud scales 2, bundle trace semicircular. .... *Diospyros* (**Persimmon**), p. 257
141. Not as above. 142

142. Leaf scars about as high as wide. 143
142. Leaf scars wider than high. 147

143. Twigs aromatic, green. .... *Sassafras,* p. 150
143. Not as above. 144

144. Terminal bud not larger than lateral buds, or absent. ....
.... 145
144. Terminal bud larger than the lateral buds; outer bud scales shorter than the bud. 146

145. Twigs brown or red. .... *Oxydendrum* (**Sourwood**), p. 250
145. Twigs gray. .... *Lyonia* (**Maleberry**), p. 247

146. Bark shredding; capsules bristly. ....
.... *Menziesia* (**Allegheny Menziesia**), p. 246
146. Not as above. .... *Rhododendron,* p. 236

147. Soft-wooded, or aromatic. 148
147. Neither soft-wooded nor aromatic. 149

148. Soft-wooded; not aromatic. ... *Ceanothus* (**New Jersey Tea**),
.... p. 213
148. Aromatic; not soft-wooded. .... *Sassafras,* p. 150

149. With stipules or stipule scars. 150
149. Without stipules or stipule scars. 151

150. Buds sometimes superposed. .... *Ilex* (**Holly**), p. 199
150. Buds not superposed. .... *Spirea,* p. 163

151. Bud scales 2, twigs glabrous. ....
.... *Nemopanthus* (**Mountain-holly**), p. 204
151. Not as above. 152

152. Buds ovoid or oblong. 153
152. Buds round or nearly so. 155

153. Fruit present in winter, consisting of small round capsules. ......
.... *Lyonia* (**Maleberry**), p. 247
153. Fruit absent in winter. 154

154. Twigs green or red or warty. ..... *Vaccinium* (**Blueberry**), p. 252
154. Twigs not green or warty. .. *Gaylussacia* (**Huckleberry**), p. 251

155. Fruit absent in winter; shrubs; twigs green or red or warty. ......
.... *Vaccinium* (**Blueberry**), p. 252
155. Fruit present in winter; trees; fruits oblong capsules. ....
.... *Oxydendrum* (**Sourwood**), p. 250

LYCOPODIUM L. **Clubmoss**

Low perennials with erect or trailing, often much-branched stems, and small evergreen, 1-nerved leaves arranged in many rows. Sporangia solitary in the axils of certain leaves or on the upper surface. Spores sulfur-yellow.

a. Spikes sessile or nearly so. Main stem subterranean; aerial branches treelike. .... 1. ***L. obscurum***
a. Spikes on elongated stalks. Main stem on or near the surface. ... . 2. ***L. flabelliforme***

1. ***L. obscurum*** L. (obscure), ***Groundpine, Tree Clubmoss***

Underground stems with distinct upper and lower sides, subterranean, bearing erect, treelike stems 1-3 dm high, divided at the summit into several bushy branches; leaves narrow, extending along the stem, those on the upper and lower surfaces shorter and flatter against the stem than the lateral ones, yielding flattish branchlets; cones 1-3, erect, sessile or nearly so. Moist rich woods and rocky barrens. **The plants resemble miniature pine trees.**

LYCOPODIUM obscurum

L. flabelliforme Blanchard (fan-shaped), **Groundpine**

Horizontal stems on or near the surface, merely covered by duff; upright stems erect, irregularly branched, the branches very flat, 2-4 mm wide, the divisions erect or spreading, clothed with small overlapping, flattened leaves in 4 rows, the lateral ones bearing toothlike tips; cones 1-3, erect on stalks, 2.5-6 cm long. Dry woods and open hillsides.

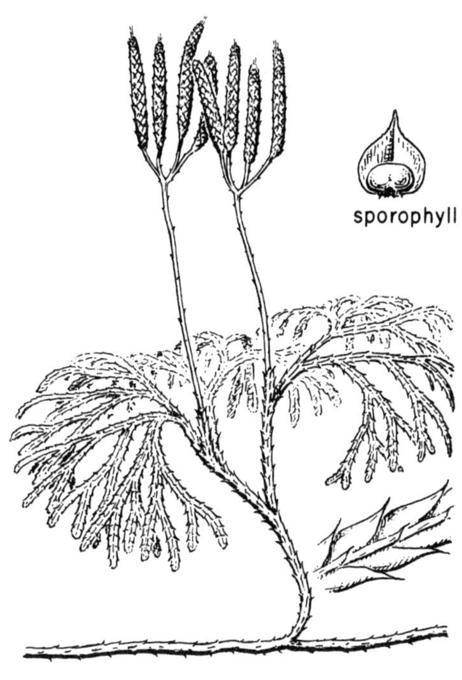

LYCOPODIUM flabelliforme

OSMUNDA L. **Cinnamon Fern, Interrupted Fern**

Fertile leaves or fertile portions of the leaf lacking chlorophyll, much contracted and bearing sporangia on the margins of the divisions.

a. Leaves twice divided, usually with separate sterile and fertile forms, divisions of the sterile leaf with a tuft of wool at the base. . . . . 1. ***O. cinnamomea***

a. Leaves twice divided with fertile parts in middle, no wool at the base of the divisions of sterile leaves. . . . . 2. ***O. claytoniana***

1. ***O. cinnamomea*** L. (Cinnamon-colored), **Cinnamon Fern**

Sterile leaves 6-18 dm tall, brown-wooly when young; the fertile leaves arising within the circle of sterile leaves, brown, soon withering. **Fertile leaves become cinnamon-colored. Divisions of sterile leaves with tufts of "wool" at their bases.** Common in a wide range of habitats.

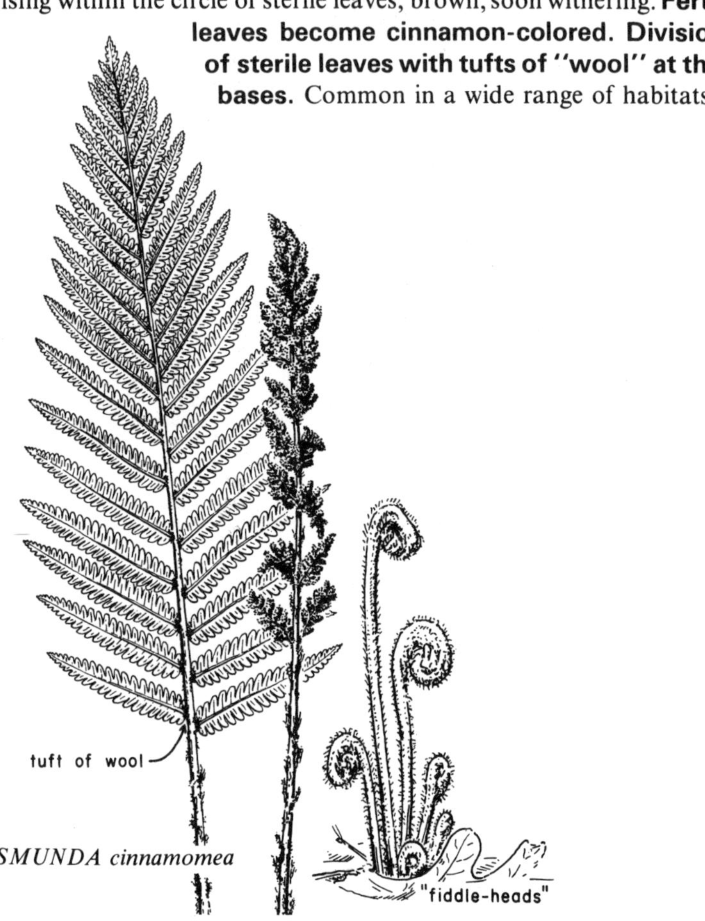

OSMUNDA cinnamomea

O. claytoniana L. (for John Clayton), **Interrupted Fern**

Leaves 5-13 cm tall, loosely wooly when young, becoming hairless with age; the fertile divisions of the leaf, 2-5 pairs, green at first, becoming brown with age, withering early. **Fertile divisions of the leaf occur in the middle of the leaf, thus "interrupting" the sterile divisions.** Common in many habitats, especially in old fields and on road banks.

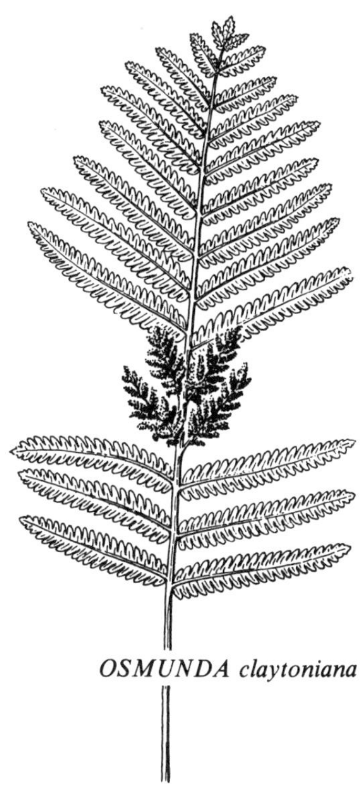

OSMUNDA claytoniana

ONOCLEA L. **Sensitive Fern**

Coarse ferns having two distinctly different leaves, the sterile leaflike, suberect, withering with frosts; the fertile strictly erect, with divisions modified to form hard, rounded divisions in which the sporangial clusters are concealed, ultimately splitting open; persisting throughout the winter.

O. sensibilis L. (sensitive to frost), **Sensitive Fern**

Fertile leaves 3-7.5 dm tall, the fertile portion twice divided; sterile leaves 3-13 dm tall, broadly triangular, deeply divided, the central shaft winged; the divisions with entire or wavy margins. **Fertile leaves become brown and hard with age and persist through the winter.** Moist meadows and damp woods.

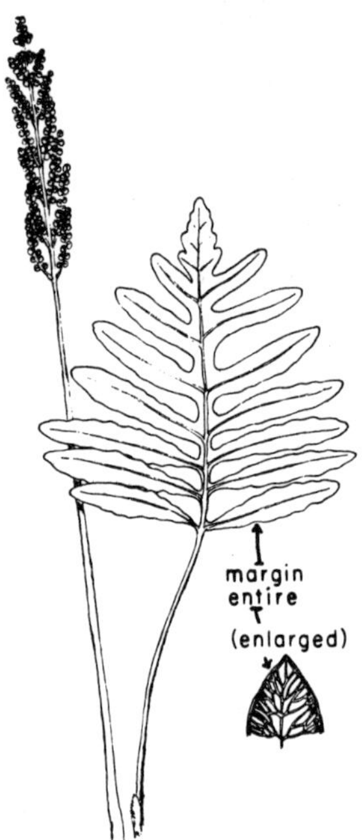

ONOCLEA sensibilis

CYSTOPTERIS Bernh. **Bladder Fern**

Delicate ferns with 2-4 divided leaves, the ultimate divisions coarsely toothed. Sporangia occur in roundish spots, each borne on the back of a vein. Covering on cluster of sporangia membranous, hoodlike, attached by a broad base on its inner side.

C. bulbifera (L) Bernh. (bearing bulbs) **Bladder Fern**

Leaves of delicate texture, attaining a length of 3-7.5 cm, with a long, tapering tip. Bulbets are formed on the lower surface of the leaves; these become detached and in time, may grow into new plants. **Our only fern with bulblets on the lower surface of the leaf.** Common in moist open woods, on stones and cliffs.

CYSTOPTERIS bulbifera

GYMNOCARPIUM Newman. **Oak Fern**

Leaves erect, spreading or drooping; blades divided 1-3 times, triangular, the divisions toothed, or deeply divided. Sporangial clusters circular, or nearly so, borne on the back of the blades, without a covering.

G. dryopteris (L.) Newman (oak fern) **Oak Fern**
(Dryopteris disjuncta (Ledeb.) C.V. Mort)

Leaves hairless, 10-30 cm wide, broadly triangular, thrice-divided, the divisions widely spreading. Moist spruce woods and cold mountain swamps. **Recognized by the broadly triangular 3-parted leaves with round sporangial clusters.**

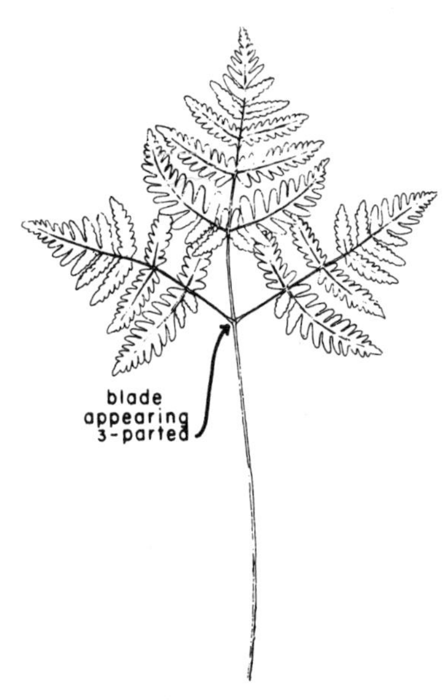

GYMNOCARPIUM dryopteris

THELYPTERIS Schmidel **New York Fern**

Underground stem cordlike, with a row of aerial deciduous leaves. Blade broadest at or near the middle, with round-lobed divisions. Sporangial cluster small, round with a kidney-shaped covering.

T. noveboracensis Nieuwl (of New York), **New York Fern**
(Dryopteris noveboracensis (L.) Gray***).***

Leaves 3-6 dm high, twice divided, lance-shaped in outline, tapering both ways from the middle; divisions deeply subdivided, lance-shaped, the lobes oblong; veins mostly simple; sporangial clusters near the margin. Woods and thickets, commoner in damp locations and in acid soil. **An easy fern to identify because the leaf tapers both ways.**

THELYPTERIS noveboracencis

PHEGOPTERIS Fee. **Beech Fern**

Underground stem cordlike, scaly, aerial leaves borne in a row. Blade triangular, with pinnate segments. Sporangial clusters round, lacking a covering.

a. Leaves narrower than long; wings of central axis not extending down to lowest division. .... ***P. connectilis***

a. Leaves nearly or quite as broad as long; united upper and lower basal segments of opposite divisions forming a fiddle-shaped wing along the central axis. .... ***P. hexagonoptera***

P. connectilis Watt. (joined together), **Long Beech Fern** ***(Dryopteris phegopteris*** (L.) Christens***)***

Leaves 8-26 cm long, longer than broad, hairy on the veins beneath; central axis chaffy; divisions deeply cut, the lowest pair bent downward. Moist and rocky ravines generally at high elevations in the mountains. **Lowermost leaf divisions are bent downward and do not form a wing at their base.**

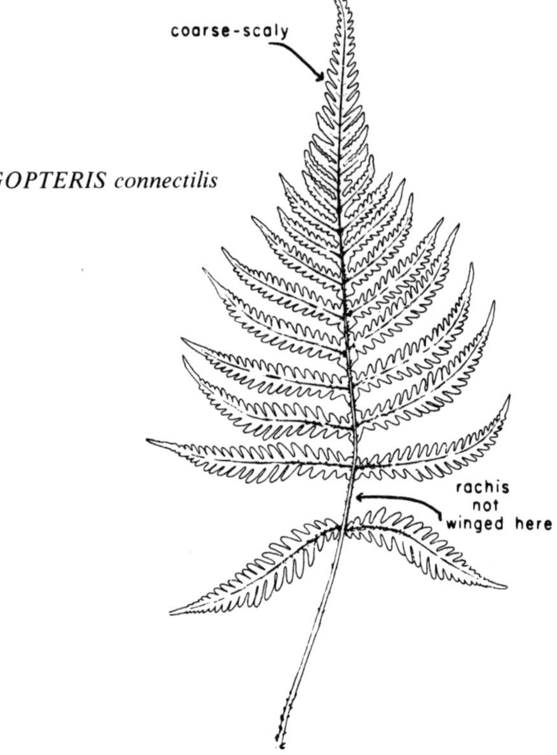

PHEGOPTERIS connectilis

P. hexagonoptera Fee. (six-cornered fern), **Broad Beech Fern**
(Dryopteris hexagonoptera (Michx.) Christens***)***

Leaves 14-30 cm broad, triangular, broader than long, slightly hairy on the lower surface; central axis scarcely chaffy; segments of the lowest leaflets often pinnately lobed. Moist woods and thickets. **Lowermost leaf divisions form a wing along the central axis.**

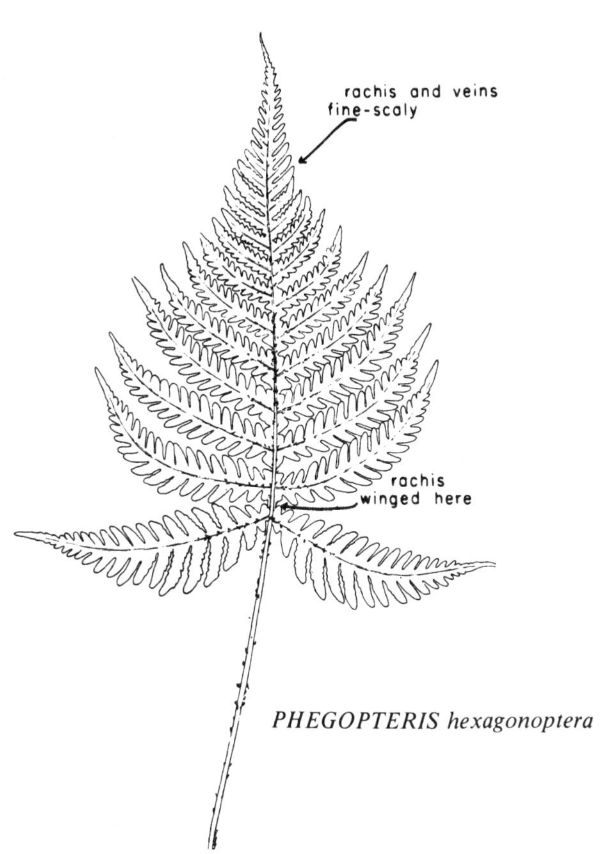

PHEGOPTERIS hexagonoptera

DRYOPTERIS Adans. **Shield Fern, Wood Fern**

Leaves erect, spreading, or drooping, clustered, evergreen in some species; blades 1-3 divided, the divisions usually toothed, lobed, or subdivided. Sporangial clusters round, or nearly so, borne on the back of the unmodified leaf. Covering of sporangial clusters round to kidney-shaped, attached at or near the center. Many hybrids occur and identification is sometimes difficult.

a. Blade narrowly oblong, lowest divisions triangular; sporangial covering smooth. .... ***D. cristata***
a. Blades relatively broad. .... b

b. Blade once divided. c
b. Blade twice divided. .... d

c. Sporangial cluster marginal, leaves firm and evergreen. .... ***D. marginalis***
c. Sporangial clusters close to midribs; blade abruptly sharp-pointed. .... ***D. goldiana***

d. Leaves remain well into winter, main axis smooth or nearly so, innermost bottom division little-broadened. . ***D. spinulosa***
d. Leaves evergreen, finely granular on the upper main axis. .... ***D. intermedia***

D. cristata (L.) Gray (crested), **Crested Shield Fern**

Leaves stiff and erect, 3-6 dm long, elongate oblong or lance-shaped in outline, not evergreen: divisions triangular-oblong, the lowest deeply divided, the divisions oblong, obtuse, finely toothed; sporangial clusters halfway between midrib and margins, their cover kidney-shaped. Sphagnum bogs and wet woods. **Has narrow leaves when compared to other ferns of this group.**

DRYOPTERIS cristata *DRYOPTERIS marginalis*

D. marginalis (L.) Gray (marginal) **Marginal Shield Fern**

Leaves oval in outline 3-7 dm long, evergreen, hairless; divisions lance-shaped; subdivisions oblong, obtuse, not toothed; sporangial clusters on or near the margins. Rich woods and rocky banks. **Thick, firm evergreen leaves with sporangial cluster on margins of divisions** (clusters may be missing in winter.).

D. goldiana (Hook.) Gray (for its discoverer) **Goldie's Shield Fern**

Leaves 6-10 dm long, broadly oval in outline; divisions oblong lance-shaped, the subdivisions oblong-slender, toothed; sporangial clusters borne near the midribs, their covering large, circular. Rich woods and rocky ravines. **Sporangial clusters close to midvein of divisions, blade abruptly sharp-pointed.**

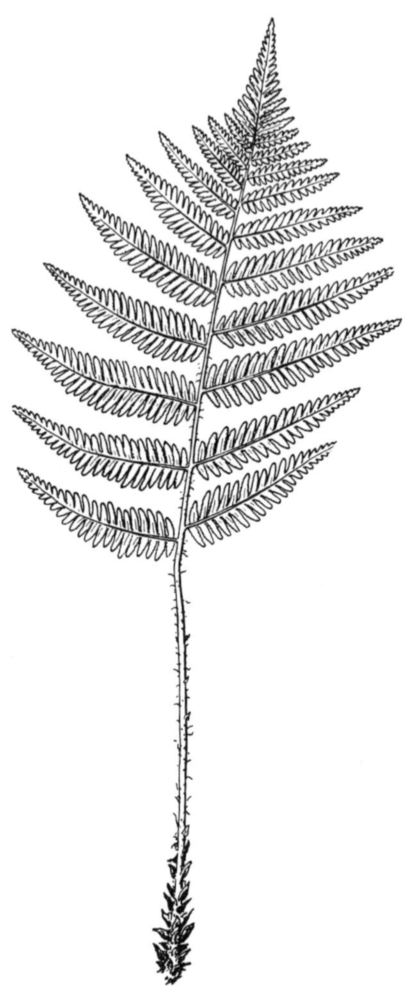

DRYOPTERIS goldiana

D. spinulosa (O.F. Muell.) Watt. (with minute spines)
Spinulose Shield Fern

Leaves ovate-lanceolate in outline, three-times divided, 3-8 dm long; divisions elongated-triangular, ascending; **lower subdivisions markedly unequal in length, those on the lower sides much longer,** inner subdivisions of basal row much longer than the next outer ones, toothed lobes have tiny spines; covering of sporangial clusters smooth. Common in rich woods.

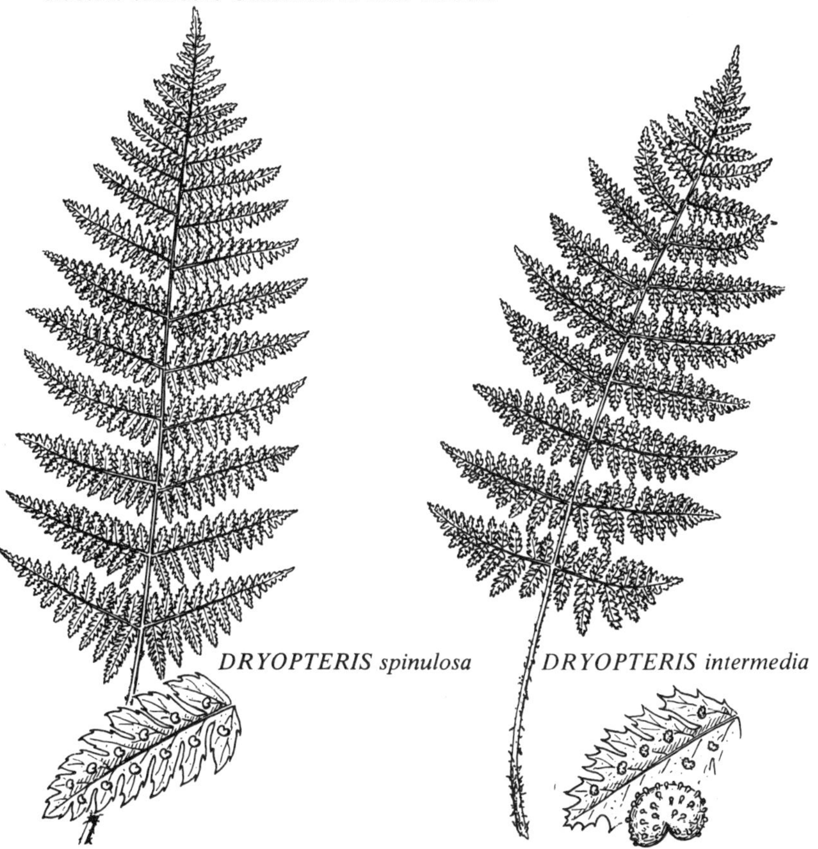

D. intermedia Gray (intermediate), **Intermediate Wood Fern**

Leaves evergreen, 25-50 cm long; **leaflets at right angles to the main axis, the inner leaflets of the basal row usually shorter than the next ones;** covering of sporangial clusters with stalked glands. Rich woods and rocky ravines throughout the region.

POLYSTICHUM Roth **Christmas Fern**

Leaves firm, evergreen, erect, axis chaffy; divisions of the blade with an upward projecting basal lobe. Sporangial clusters round.

P. acrostichoides (Michx.) Schott. (resembling *Acrostichum*)
Christmas Fern

Leaves 2-5 dm high, oblong or lance-shaped, divided, the upper spore-bearing divisions much smaller than the lower, sterile ones; divisions long, lance-shaped, with a lobe projecting on the upper side near the base. Woods and rocky hillsides. **Sporangia are thickly clustered on small divisions on terminal one-third of leaf. Leaf divisions have an upward projecting basal lobe. Evergreen.**

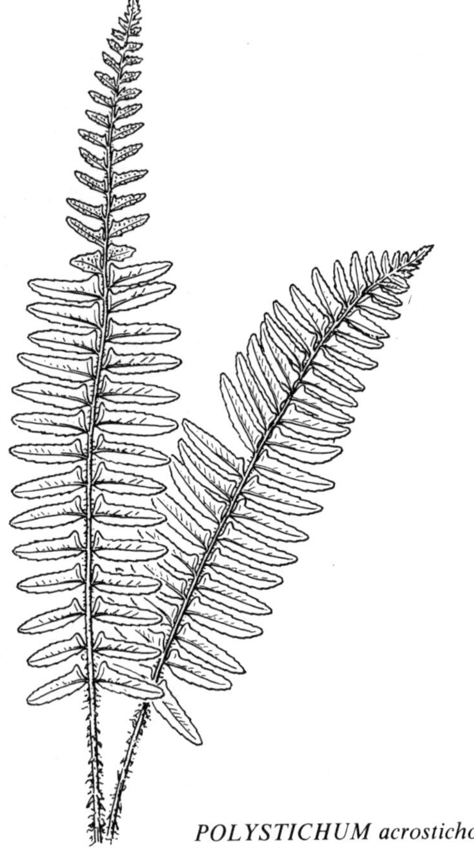

POLYSTICHUM acrostichoides

DENNSTAEDTIA Bernh. **Hay-Scented Fern**

Ferns with slender, creeping, hairy underground stems. Leaves erect, 2-3 divided, 3-12 dm long. Sporangial clusters marginal, the sporangia grouped on a tiny receptacle borne within a cup-shaped covering formed partly of the somewhat modified reflexed lobe of the leaf margin.

D. punctilobula (Michx.) Moore, (with dotted lobes)
Hay-Scented Fern

Leaves 3-9 dm long, 12.5-27.5 cm wide, oval, lance-shaped to triangular, lance-shaped, sharp-pointed,usually 3 times divided, thin and delicate, the under surface glandular and hairy; leaf stalks dark brown at the base. **Has the odor of newly mown hay. Often takes over mountain pastures where it is detested by farmers. Sporangial clusters are on margin within a cup-shaped covering. A good indicator of past fire.** Widely distributed throughout, particularly in higher elevations after fire.

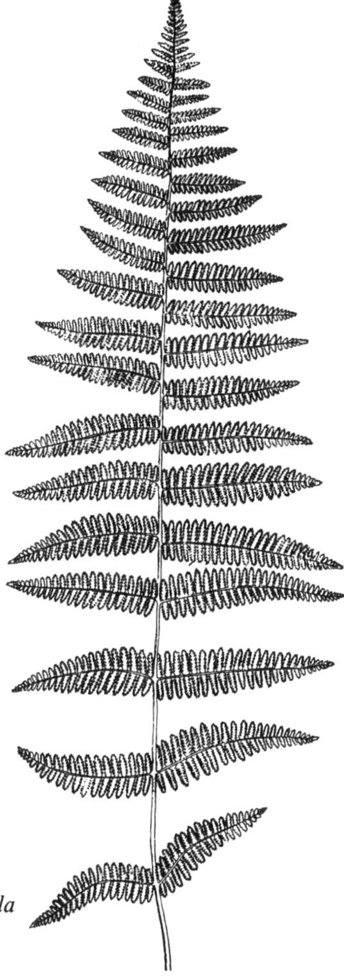

DENNSTAEDTIA punctilobula

ASPLENIUM L. **Spleenwort**

Ferns with simple, lobed or 1-3 divided, usually uniform leaves. Sporangial clusters straight or somewhat curved, oblong to thin. Covering of sporangial cluster attached along one edge to the upper (inner) side of the fertile vein.

a. Main axis of leaf green; leaf stalk dark, at least at the base; frond 1-2 divided, not prolonged to a tail-like tip. ***A. montanum***

a. Main axis of leaf dark throughout; leaves erect; divisions lanceolate, alternate, lobed on the upper side of the base. .... ***A. platyneuron***

A. montanum Willd. (of mountains), **Mountain Spleenwort**

Leaves evergreen, triangular lance-shaped, sharp-pointed, 5-13 cm long; main axis of leaf green, winged near the tip, 1-2 divided; divisions triangular, the lowest cut into oblong or oval toothed lobes, the upper becoming gradually simpler; not prolonged into a tail-like tip, **leaf stalk tufted, dark brown at base and green above.** Occurs where soil acidity is high; on sandstone or shale cliffs.

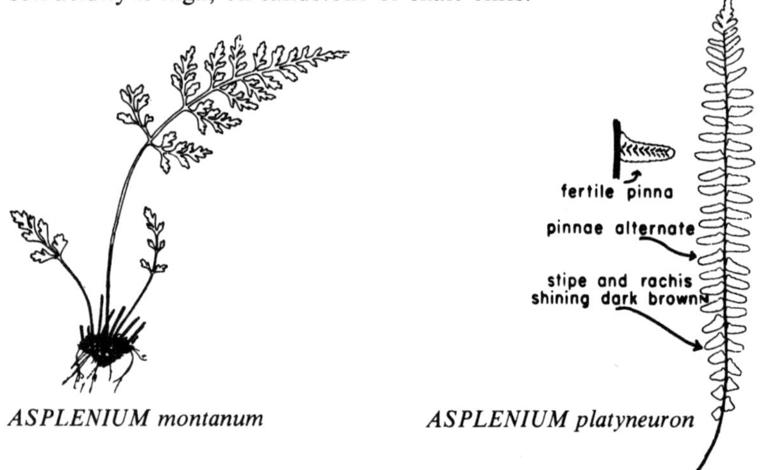

ASPLENIUM montanum *ASPLENIUM platyneuron*

A. platyneuron (L.) Oakes (broad-nerved), **Ebony Spleenwort**

Leaves 2-4 dm long, 2.5-6 cm wide above the middle, once divided; divisions 20-40 pairs, mostly alternate, sessile, margin wavy, toothed, or incised, lobes on the base of the upper side of the divisions. Fertile leaves usually longer than the spreading, sterile ones. **Main axis of leaf dark throughout.** On rocks or rocky banks, common on both acid and limestone soils, especially under black walnut trees.

CHEILANTHES Sw. **Lip Fern**

Small ferns on rock habitats, with mostly hairy, wooly or scaly, 1-3 divided leaves. Sporangial clusters rounded, marginal; separate or somewhat confluent. Margins of segments modified and reflexed to form the covering over the sporangia.

C. lanosa (Michx.) D. C. Eat. (Wooly), **Hairy Lip Fern**

Leaves 1-3.5 dm high, **twice divided, the divisions deeply subdivided; leaf-stalk tufted, brown, covered with long, rusty, jointed hairs.** This is a common species of the Devonian shales of eastern West Virginia, rarely found elsewhere in this region.

CHEILANTHES lanosa

ADIANTUM L. **Maidenhair Fern**

Leaves with black glossy leaf stalks; sporangial clusters borne on the margin of a lobe of the leaf. Leaf reflexed forming a covering over the sporangia.

A. pedatum L. (palmately forking), **Maidenhair Fern**

Leaves 2-5 dm high, the leaf stalk forking at the summit, several divisions branching from the outer side of each fork; subdivisions numerous, thin, fan-shaped, with irregularly lobed, upper margins. This is one of our better known ferns and none of our species possesses a more delicate, graceful beauty. It thrives in moist, shaded places, and is found in ravines and rich woods. **Easily recognized by the fan-shaped leaf.**

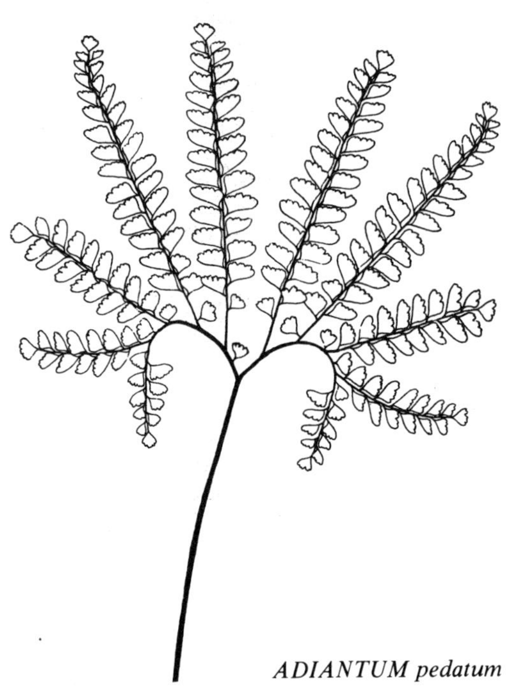

ADIANTUM pedatum

PTERIDIUM Gleditsch. **Bracken Fern**

Sporangia in a continuous line around the entire margin of the fertile leaf, covered by the reflexed margin that forms the covering over the sporangia.

P. aquilinum (L.) Kunn (of an eagle), **Bracken**

Leaf 5-20 dm high, leaf blade usually triangular, the 3-divided branches twice subdivided; terminal segments about 5-8 mm wide, the margins of the ultimate segments hairy; longest entire segment or entire part of a segment 4 times as long as broad. **Sporangia in a continuous line around the leaf margins.** Common in a wide variety of habitats, particularly in acid soil following fire, where it may become a troublesome weed. Covers large areas at higher elevations. **Poisonous to livestock when included in hay. A good indicator of past fire.**

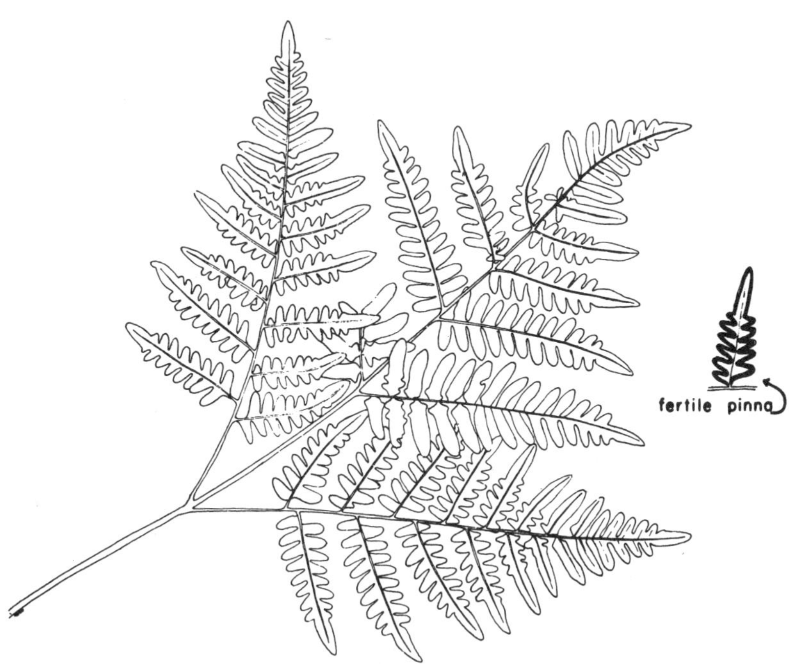

PTERIDIUM aquilinum

POLYPODIUM L. **Polypody**

Sporangial clusters round, without a covering, borne on the under side of the leaves, on the ends of the free veinlets.

P. virginianum L. (Virginian), **Common Polypody**

An evergreen fern with firm, green, smooth, once-divided leaves 1-3.5 dm long and 2.5-7.5 cm wide. Sporangial clusters brown, borne about midway between the midrib and the margins of the lobes. **An easily recognized fern because of its large uncovered sporangial clusters. One of the most common ferns growing on moist, shaded rocks.** This fern occurs in rocky places, or occasionally on the trunks of trees or on logs.

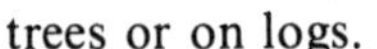

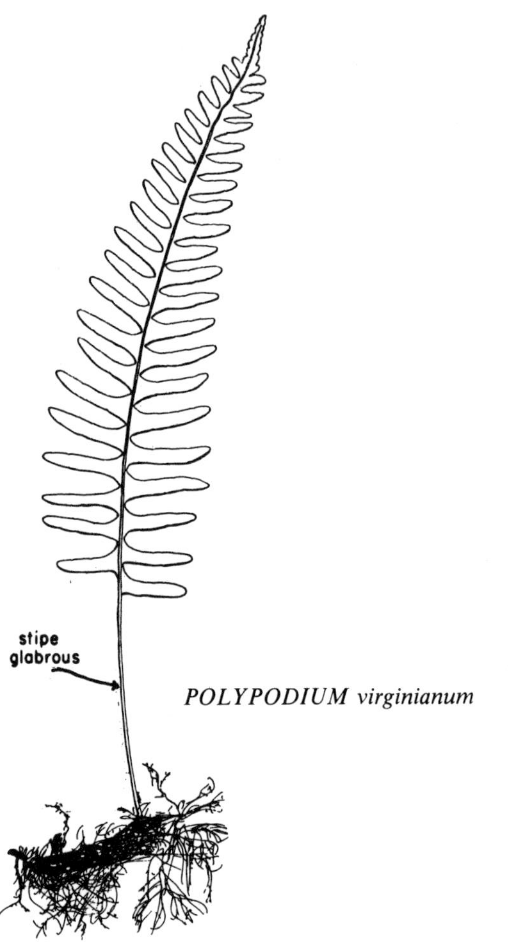

POLYPODIUM virginianum

TAXUS L. **Yew**

Low evergreen shrubs with sharp-pointed elongate leaves appearing alternate in two opposite rows on the branches; the seed is nearly enclosed by the fleshy, bright red covering.

T. canadensis Marsh. (of Canada)
American Yew, Canada Yew, Ground-hemlock

A low, trailing evergreen shrub, 1 m or less in height; **leaves arranged in 2 ranks, dark green above, with yellowish green bands beneath, 12-30 mm long, about 2 mm wide, remain attached to twigs upon drying;** mature seed nearly covered by a red fleshy covering, seed up to 6 mm long, may persist into winter. Rich swampy to moist woods and thickets at high elevations.

WINTER

The above characteristics can be observed in winter.

TAXUS canadensis

ABIES Mill. **Fir**

Evergreen trees with elongate, flat, sessile leaves spirally arranged but appearing nearly 2-ranked. Leaves shorter and crowded on the upper side of the twig on cone-bearing branches. Cones upright, cylindric or barrel-shaped, maturing in one year, the cone scales fall from the persistent axis at the time of seed fall.

A. balsamea (L.) Mill. **Balsam Fir, "Blister Pine"**

A beautiful evergreen tree up to 25 m tall, the trunk rarely reaches 0.5 m in diameter in our area; leaves narrowly elongate, not sharp-pointed, 1-3 cm long; marked with 2 white stomatal bands beneath; large circular leaf scars remain when the leaves ultimately fall; cones upright, cylindrical or barrel-shaped, forming on the topmost branches, 6-10 cm long; bracts oval, toothed, tipped with a slender point, shorter than, or equal to the scales. Bracts longer than the cone scales in var. ***phanerolepis,* Bracted Balsam Fir.** Bark warty with resin blisters (hence the common name "Blister Pine." Occurs in West Virginia only in sphagnum bogs and swamps.

Distinguished from our other evergreens by the flattened leaves without petioles, with 2 conspicuous white stomatal bands beneath, arranged in two somewhat diverging rows. Leaves not sharp-pointed. Cones large, upright—disintegrate on the tree.

WINTER

The above characters may be observed in winter except the cones will be represented only by the stiff upright central axis still attached to the tree.

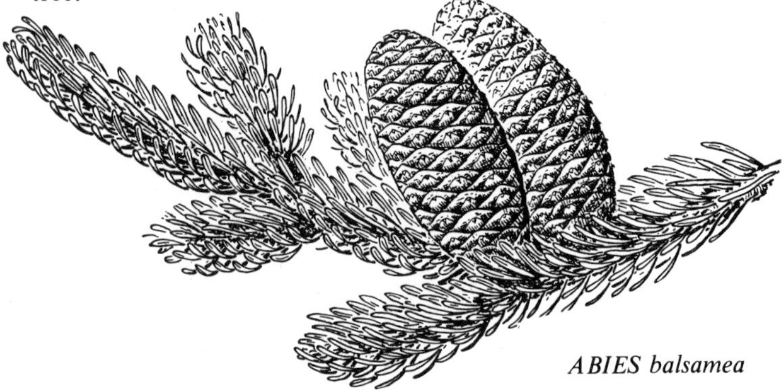

ABIES balsamea

TSUGA Carr. **Hemlock**

Handsome evergreen trees with flat, elongate, alternate leaves on short petioles, appearing to grow in 2 opposite rows on the branches, fall quickly upon drying. Leaves have two conspicuous white stomatal bands beneath. Cones small, oval, drooping.

T. canadensis (L.) Carr. (of Canada) **Eastern Hemlock**

An evergreen tree up to 35 m high and 12 dm in diameter, with spreading branches; leaves soft, short-petioled, elongate, not sharp-pointed, 8-12 mm long; reddish bark deeply furrowed, with prominent ridges; cones oval, 1-2.5 cm long, maturing in one year. In damp woods and ravines. **May be easily identified by the flat, petioled leaves with 2 prominent white stomatal bands beneath, arranged in opposite rows that give the branch a flat appearance. Leaves not sharp-pointed. Cones are small.**

WINTER

All of the above characters may be used for winter identification.

TSUGA canadensis

PICEA Dietr. **Spruce**

Evergreen trees, with sessile, short, elongate,4-angled, needle-shaped leaves, attached at the base to short, peglike woody stalks; leaves fall quickly upon drying. Cones oval, drooping, the many cone scales thin, persistent.

P. rubens Sarg. (reddish) **Red Spruce**

An evergreen tree up to 35 m high and 9 dm in diameter; very young branchlets hairy; **leaves needlelike,** 12-15 mm long, **sharp-pointed, 4-sided, diverging all around the branch like the bristles on a bottle-brush;** conspicuous peglike structures remain on the branches where the leaves have fallen; inner bark reddish, outer bark roughened by thin brownish-grey scales; cones mature in one year and fall off in autumn or early winter, oval, 3-4 cm long, brown, the scales oval, smooth, or slightly toothed at the tip. Well-drained uplands, mountain tops or borders of swamps. Formerly very abundant at higher elevations, often forming pure stands at elevations above 3,500 feet.

WINTER

The above characters may be used for winter identification.

PICEA rubens

PINUS L. **Pine**

Evergreen trees with the leaves narrowly elongate (needlelike), arranged in bundles of 2-5, persistent for several years. **Pines are the only conifers having leaves with a sheath at the base binding 2 or more leaves together.** The sheath is deciduous in soft pines and persistent in hard pines. Cones require 2 years for maturing (3 years in a few species), but often hang on the tree for several years; cones armed (having a spine near the tip of the scale) or unarmed.

a. Leaves 5 in a bundle, bundle sheath deciduous; cone scales unarmed (soft pine). .... ***P. strobus***
a. Leaves 2-3 in a bundle, bundle sheath persistent (hard pines). ....b

b. Cone scales armed with a sharp spine (spines small and may not be present in ***P. echinata***). c
b. Cone scales unarmed, leaves in 2s. .... ***P. resinosa***

c. Spine of cone scales small, 1-3 mm long. .... d
c. Spine of cone scales large, 5-6 mm long, leaves in 2s. . ***A. pungens***

d. Leaves in 3s, rigid, 1.8-3 mm broad. .... ***P. rigida***
d. Leaves in 2s, 0.5-1.5 mm broad, 4-8 cm long. .... ***P. virginiana***
d. Leaves in 2s and 3s, 0.5-1.5 mm broad, 7-13 cm long. ***P. echinata***

WINTER KEY

The above key may be used for identification in winter.

P. strobus L. (ancient name for some tree), **Eastern White Pine**

A large evergreen tree up to 50 m high and 12 dm in diameter; leaves 5 in a cluster, 7-13 cm long, marked with white stomatal bands, the bundle sheath quickly falls; bark on old trunks in flat-topped ridges but not scaly as in our other native pines; mature cones 1-1.6 dm long, curved with the scales resin-dotted, without a terminal prickle. Rich woods especially in the lower slopes and bottomlands. **Our only pine with 5 leaves in a cluster and the only soft pine in eastern North America.**

PINUS strobus *PINUS virginiana*

P. virginiana Mill. (Virginian)
Scrub Pine, Virginia Pine, Jersey Pine

A scrubby tree to 20 m high and a diameter of 6 dm; **leaves in 2s, twisted 4-8 cm long, gray-green or yellow-green;** bark with shallow furrows forming dark brown scales; often with many old, open cones persistent on the tree, oval, 3-7 cm long; scales with a slender prickle and a dark purplish-brown band on the inner lip of the scale. **Leaves resemble those of the planted Scotch Pine in number and length, however, Scotch Pine has a smaller cone that is very minutely armed.** Barren, rocky soil.

P. rigida Mill. (rigid) **Pitch Pine**

A tree to 25 m high, and a diameter of 5 dm; leaves in clusters of 3, 5-12 cm long, stiff, dark green; rough dark-brown bark and hard, resinous wood; mature cones oval, 3-9 cm long, often clustered with many old open cones persistent on the tree, scales bearing a thick, curved prickle. Rocky or barren soil. **Our only native pine with leaves in 3s, and cone scales with a thick, curved prickle.**

PINUS rigida *PINUS echinata*

P. echinata Mill. (spiny), **Shortleaf Pine, Yellow Pine**

A straight tree to 45 m high, 10 dm in diameter; leaves mostly in clusters of 2, but usually with clusters of 3 on the same tree, 7-13 cm long, slender, flexible; bark consisting of large rectangular plates; mature cones small, oval, 4-5 cm long; scales with a small, deciduous prickle. Dry or rocky soil. **Leaves in 2s and 3s. Cone scales armed with a tiny prickle.**

P. pungens Lamb. (sharp-pointed) **Table Mountain Pine**

A tree up to 20 m high and 10 dm in diameter; leaves in clusters of 2 or occasionally 3, rigid, 3-6 cm long, dark green; bark formed into irregular reddish-brown plates; cones strongly clustered, oval, 5-10 cm long, persistent for several years, sometimes remaining closed until opened by the heat of fire; heavy woody scales with a stout, sharp, hooked spine 5 mm long. Uplands. **Leaves in 2s (sometimes 3s). Cones very tight to branches, cone scales very stout and sharp, our most stoutly armed pine cone.**

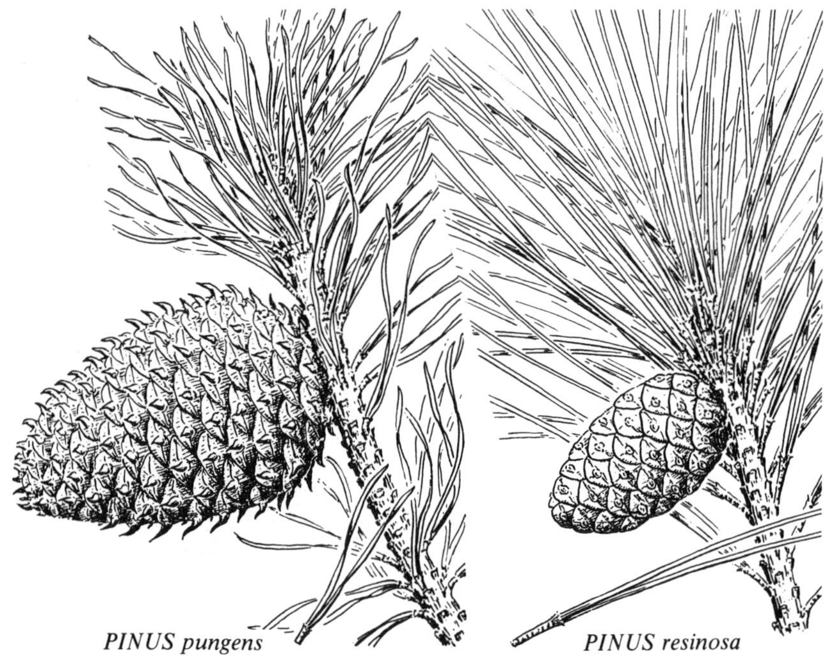

PINUS pungens *PINUS resinosa*

P. resinosa Alt. (resinous) **Red Pine, Norway Pine**

A tall tree growing to 50 m tall and 15 dm in diameter; leaves dark green, 2 in a bundle, up to 16 cm long; bark smooth, reddish; cones oval, 5 cm long; **the only hard pine in North America with unarmed scales.** Native to only two locations in W.Va., but used extensively in reforestation. **Leaves in 2s; cone scales unarmed. Our only native pine having 2 medium-length needles that break cleanly in two when bent double.** (Resembles the planted Austrian Pine in needle number and needle length; however, Austrian Pine needles are not brittle and the cone is minutely armed.)

JUNIPERUS L. **Juniper**

Small trees or shrubs with sessile leaves arranged opposite or whorled. Cones globe-shaped, berrylike because of the fusion of the fleshy scales, light blue with a whitened waxy coating.

J. virginiana L. (Virginian) **Red-cedar**

A tree usually less than 25 m high, pyramidal in form; **leaves on young twigs awl-shaped, spiny-tipped in whorls of 3,** 4-8 mm long, **those of the older branches opposite, scalelike, closely pressed to the twigs and overlapping,** arranged in 4 rows, giving a square shape to the twig; the thin reddish-brown bark peels off in long narrow strips; **cones berrylike, light blue, waxy, about 6 mm in diameter,** an important food for the cedar waxwing. Dry hillsides especially east of the higher Alleghenies on limey soils.

WINTER

The above characteristics may be used for winter identification.

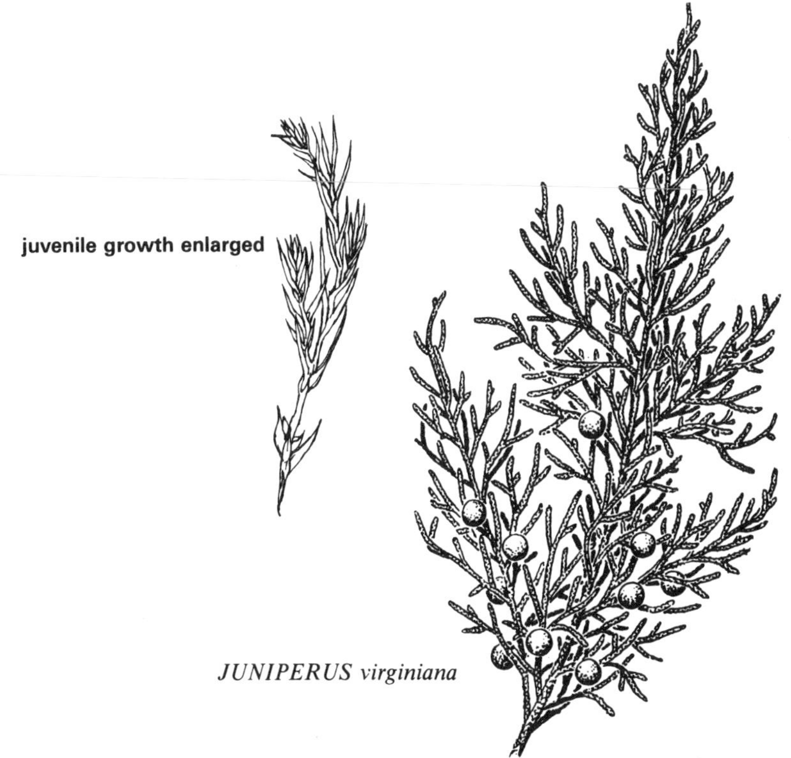

JUNIPERUS virginiana

TYPHA L. **Cattail**

Staminate and pistillate flowers separate but borne on the same stalk, the staminate flowers uppermost. Leaves 6-23 mm broad.

T. latifolia L. (broad-leaved), **Broad-Leaved Cattail**

Stems stout, 1-2 m high; staminate and pistillate portions of the spike each 8-15 cm or longer. Flowers in August-September. Abundant locally in marshes, roadside ditches and other poorly drained areas. The dried fruiting spikes and bleached leaves are conspicuous during the winter.

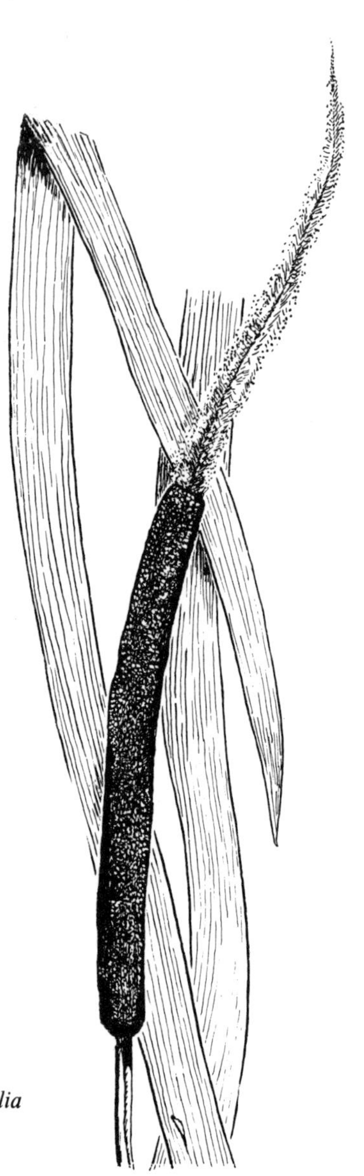

TYPHA latifolia

Note: The identification of grasses requires special terminology. The terms used here are illustrated on page 64. Because grasses and sedges are easily confused, a comparison of the two groups is given below.

Comparison of Grasses and Sedges

	Sedges	**Grasses**
Stems	Not jointed at the nodes. Usually solid. Often triangular in cross-section.	Jointed at the nodes. Usually hollow in internodes. Circular in cross-section.
Leaves	3-ranked, alternate. Sheaths usually closed around stem.	2-ranked, alternate. Sheaths usually open around stem.
Fruit	An achene (a small, one-seeded dry fruit with the outer covering not fastened to the enclosed seed).	A grain (a small, one-seeded dry fruit with the outer covering attached to the enclosed seed).

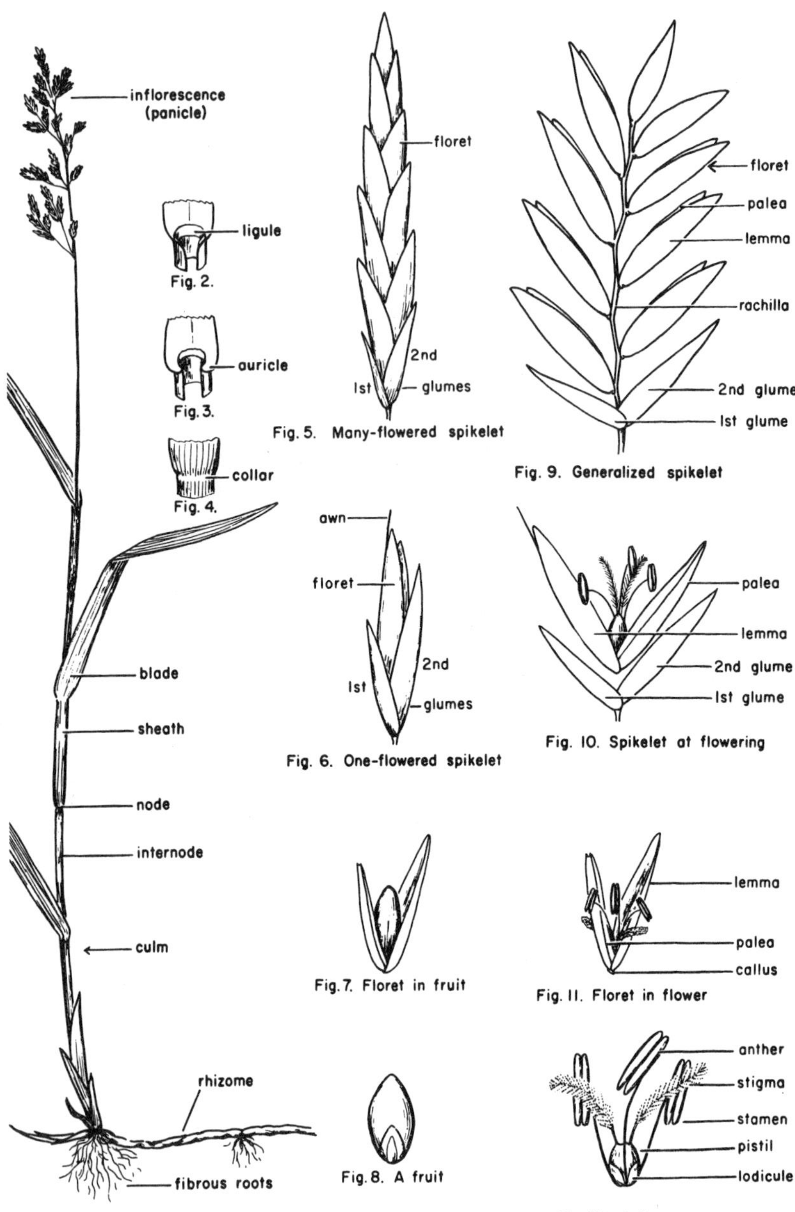

Figure 1. Complete plant

Fig. 5. Many-flowered spikelet

Fig. 6. One-flowered spikelet

Fig. 7. Floret in fruit

Fig. 8. A fruit

Fig. 9. Generalized spikelet

Fig. 10. Spikelet at flowering

Fig. 11. Floret in flower

Fig. 12. A flower

STRUCTURE OF GRASSES

DANTHONIA DC. **Oatgrass**

Erect perennials growing in clumps, leaves narrow, inflorescence small; spikelets several-flowered; glumes nearly equal, much longer than the lemmas, each lemma having 2 teeth at the apex with a twisted awn between them.

a. Teeth of the lemma triangular. .... ***D. spicata***
a. Teeth of the lemma tapering into long bristles. ... ***D. compressa***

D. spicata (L.) Beauv. (spiked)
Poverty Oatgrass, Poverty Grass, Moonshine Grass

Stems round, 2-7 dm high; the numerous basal leaves curly, especially in winter, those of the stems erect 2 mm or less wide; panicle 2-5 cm long, few-flowered, the few short branches erect; glumes 10-12 mm long, lemmas bearing stiff hairs, teeth triangular, the awn longer than the lemma. Flowers in June-August. Common in dry, sterile soil; an indicator or poor soil. **Numerous curly basal leaves are charteristic of this genus.**

D. compressa Aust. (compressed)
Mountain Oat Grass, Allegheny Fly-back

Stems flattened, 4-8 dm tall; leaves flat, 2-3 mm wide; panicle 5-8 cm long, the branches spreading; glumes 10-14 mm long; teeth of the lemma tapering into bristles at least 2 mm long, with a twisted awn attched between them. Flowers in June-August. Mostly in the mountains at high elevations. The dominant grass of "grassy balds" in the southern Appalachians. **Numerous curly basal leaves help identify this genus.**

DANTHONIA compressa

DANTHONIA spicata

PANICUM L. **Panic Grass**

Annual or perennial grasses, mostly weedy; spikelets with 1 perfect flower and 1 imperfect one below it; glumes unequal, the first very small, the second about equal to the sterile lemma; fertile lemma hardened, the edges inrolled; grain firmly enclosed by the lemma and palea. Many species produce an unbranched stem in the spring, called the vernal phase, which later in the year branches and becomes more or less bushy. This stage, the autumnal phase, is often quite different in appearance from the earlier form. Some species produce winter rosettes of basal leaves which remain during the spring and are usually different in shape from the stem leaves.

P. microcarpon Muhl. (small-fruited), **Small-Fruited Panic Grass**

Stems erect, in large clumps, 6-10 dm tall; nodes swollen, densely bearded, with hairs bent downwards; leaves 6-15 mm wide, thin, fringed with hairs at the base, otherwise hairless; panicles 8-12 cm long; spikelets 1.6 mm long, smooth; second glume slightly longer than the fruit. **Autumnal phase much branched, flat on the ground with densely crowded small leaves and inflorescences.** Flowers in June, July. This is the common panic grass found in wet woods and swampy places.

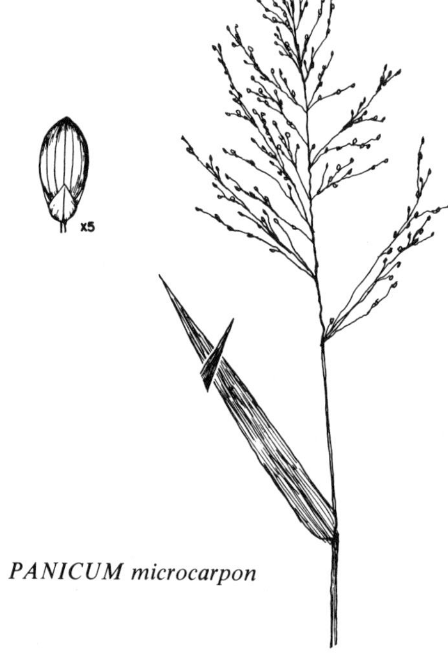

PANICUM microcarpon

CYPERUS L. Sedge

With triangular unbranched stems, leafy at base and with a whorl of leaves at the summit, beneath the inflorescence. Flowers in many-flowered, mostly flat spikelets, commonly arranged in terminal inflorescences. Scales 2-ranked. Sepals and petals none. Stamens 1-3. Style 2-3 cleft. Fruit lens-shaped or triangular.

C. strigosus L. (lean), **Galingale.**

Perennial, with hard basal rootstalks; stem 1-10 dm high; leaves flat, soft, 4-12 mm wide, the longer ones exceeding the inflorescence; most of the rays of the inflorescences elongated; spikelets elongate, appressed, several-nerved, much longer than the linear-oblong achene. Flowers in August-October. Damp or fertile soil, very common and widely distributed.

CYPERUS strigosus

SCIRPUS L. **Bulrush**

Annual or perennial with leafy stems. Spikelets solitary or in terminal clusters, commonly with a whorl of leaves. Flowers perfect. Calyx and corolla represented by 1-6 bristles or none. Stamens 2-3-cleft. Fruit lens-shaped or triangular.

S. atrovirens Muhl. (dark green)

Stems rather stout, 8-15 dm high; leaves pale green, the lower partitioned, 7-15 mm wide, the margins rough; spikelets dull greenish-brown, narrowly ovoid, 3.5-8 mm long; scales 1.5-12 mm long; bristles strongly barbed; fruit oval-oblong, 3-angled, conspicuously pointed. Flowers in June-August. In swamps, meadows, and bogs, common and widely distributed.

SCIRPUS atrovirens

CAREX L. **Sedge**

Perennial grasslike herbs with mostly **triangular stems** and 3-ranked leaves. Flowers imperfect, without a calyx or corolla, arranged in spikes; staminate flowers consisting of 3 stamens in the axil of a scale; pistillate flowers consisting of a single pistil with 2 or 3 stigmas, forming a fruit enclosed in an inflated sac borne in the axil of a scale. Staminate and pistillate flowers borne in different parts of the same spike, or in separate spikes on the same stem. This genus contains numerous species in West Virginia, many of which are difficult to determine in the field. **This genus has a characteristic inflated sac surrounding each fruit.**

C. communis Bailey (in colonies)

Stems loosely matted 1.5-5 dm high, slender, much exceeding the leaves; not stoloniferous; leaves 2.5-4 mm wide; inflorescence 1-8 cm long, the 2 or 3 pistillate spikes distinct, often remote, 4-8 mm long; staminate spike 3.5-20 mm long; inflated fruit sac hairy, oval, 3-3.5 mm long, 2-keeled, the beak broad; scales oval, sharp-pointed, greenish brown or reddish, about equaling the fruit sac. Flowers in May-July. Dry woodlands, usually on rocky ledges.

CAREX communis

ARISAEMA Martius, **Jack-in-the-Pulpit**

Perennial herbs from a tuberous rootstock bearing a simple flowering stem sheathed at the base by the petioles of the net-veined, usually compound leaves, 1-3 in number. Leaflike bract mostly enclosing and arched above the inflorescence. Male flowers above the female, each composed of 4 almost sessile, 2-4-celled anthers. Female flowers each having a 1-celled ovary. Fruit a scarlet berry.

A. triphyllum (L.) Schott (three-leaved)
Indian Turnip, Jack-in-the-Pulpit

Plants erect or nearly so, 2.4-9 dm high; leaves usually 2, compound with 3 oval, entire, pointed leaflets 6-18 cm long and 3-8.5 cm wide, sessile or very short stalked; flowering stalk simple, round, 15-30 cm high, from a fleshy and wrinkled root stalk with a very stinging taste; **leaflike bract terminating in a broad, tapering flap that arches over the top of the inflorescence;** bracts and petioles pale green, often striped or mottled with purplish lines or spots. Flowers in April-June. In rich woods and thickets.

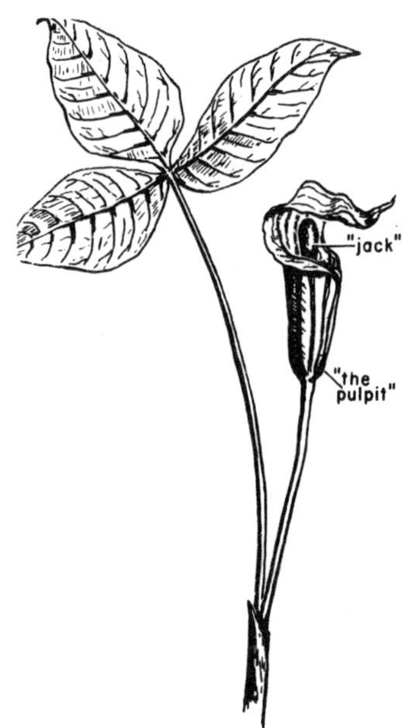

ARISAEMA triphyllum

SYMPLOCARPUS Salisb. **Skunk Cabbage**

A low perennial herb, with a thick, straight rootstock, bearing a cluster of large leaves and a short erect flowering stem that remains partly underground. Fleshy, leaflike bract completely enclosing the inflorescence, which consists of a thick stalk that is entirely covered by perfect flowers.

S. foetidus (L.) Nutt. (foul-smelling) **Skunk Cabbage**

Leaves 3 dm or more long and 2-3 dm wide; bract spotted and striped with purple and yellow-green, erect, 7-12 dm high, appearing before the leaves; inflorescence globular or oblong, about 2 cm in diameter in flower but often 5-10 cm in diameter in fruit. **Flowers in February-April.** Very common in swamps and wet soil. **Has a characteristic skunklike odor when crushed.**

SYMPLOCARPUS foetidus

JUNCUS L. **Rush**

Usually perennial plants, principally in wet soil or water, with leaf-bearing or leafless stems. Leaf-blades round or flattened. Inflorescence branched. Capsule 3-celled, sometimes imperfectly so.

J. marginatus Rostk. (margined)

Stems erect, 2-7 dm high; from the bulbous stoloniferous base; leaves flat, grasslike, 1-3 mm wide, the sheaths lobed; inflorescence of 2-20 top-shaped heads; flowers purplish and green, 2.5-3.5 mm long; sepals sharp; petals rounded, with distinct clear margins; stamens 3, about as long as the petals and sepals; capsule spherical equaling the petals and sepals. Flowers in July-September. Moist, grassy places.

JUNCUS marginatus

ALLIUM L. **Onion, Garlic, Leek, Ramp**

Odorous herbs, with solitary or clustered bulbs and sheathing leaves, basal, or sometimes also on the stem; stem simple, erect; flowers in a terminal inflorescence with 2 or 3 bracts; sepals and petals 6, colored, separate or united by their bases; stamens on the bases of petals; style persistent, threadlike; ovary sessile, 3-celled; fruit a capsule.

A. tricoccum Ait. (three-locular), **Ramp**

Bulbs slender, ovoid, 2.5-5 cm long, their outer coats fibrous net-veined; **leaves 1.5-3 dm long, 2.5-5 cm wide, erect, flower stalks 1.2-2 cm long; flowers white; flowers appear after the leaves have withered;** sepals and petals oblong, obtuse, 4-6 mm long; ovary and capsule not crested; capsule deeply 3-lobed, about 6 mm thick, 3-4 high; seeds black, smooth. Flowers in June-July. Rich woods, especially under northern hardwoods. Harvested extensively in early spring for use in local ramp suppers.

ALLIUM tricoccum

ERYTHRONIUM L. **Fawn Lily, Trout Lily Dog-tooth "Violet"**

Low herbs with 2 smooth, shining flat leaves tapering into petioles and sheathing the base of the usually 1-flowered stem that rises from a deep membranous-coated root stalk; 1-leaved, flowerless plants also occur; flowers lilylike; stamens 6; ovary sessile; 3-celled capsule.

E. americanum Ker. (American) **Yellow Fawn Lily, Trout Lily, Dog-tooth "Violet"**

Bulb deep, sending out shoots; stem 1.5-3 dm long, mostly subterranean; **leaves oblong or elongate,** 7.5-20 cm wide, sharp or short pointed at the end, **usually mottled with brown, but occasionally entirely green;** flower stalk about equalling the leaves, usually leafless; flower yellow, sometimes tinged with purple; sepals and petals 2-5 cm long, 6-8 mm wide, recurved, 3 inner ones lobed at base; style club-shaped; capsule oval, contracted into a short stalk, 1.2-2 cm long, erect. Flowers in March-May. In moist woods and thickets, especially along streams. A white species (***E. albidum*** Nutt.) also occurs.

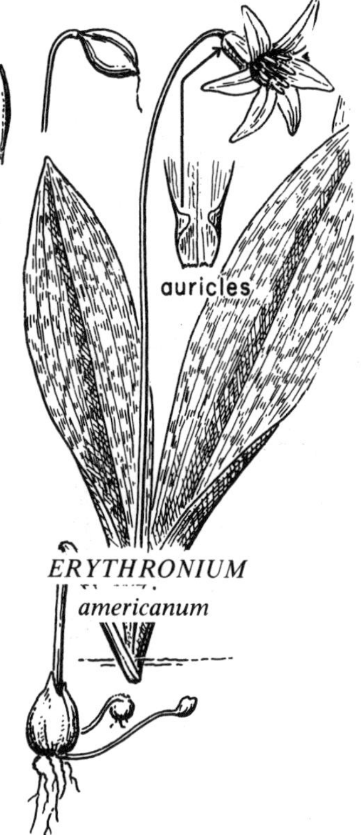

CLINTONIA Raf. **Clintonia**

Low herbs with the inflorescence on a stalk arising from the slender rootstocks; leaves few, broad, basal; fruit a berry.

C. borealis (Ait.) Raf. (northern), **Yellow Clintonia, Blue-bead Lily**

Stalk of the inflorescence and leaves 14-25 cm long; leaves 2-5, usually 3, 4-8 cm wide; inflorescence terminal, 3-8 flowered, sessile lateral inflorescences often on the same stalk; **berry blue,** about 8 mm in diameter. Flowers in May-June. In moist woods and thickets at elevations above 2,500 feet.

C. umbellata (Michx.) Morong, **White Clintonia**

Commonly found at lower elevations. **Leaves may be confused with ramps; however, in this species the leaves are persistent during flowering and fruiting stages. Does not have the typical "onion" odor of ramps.** (Not illustrated.)

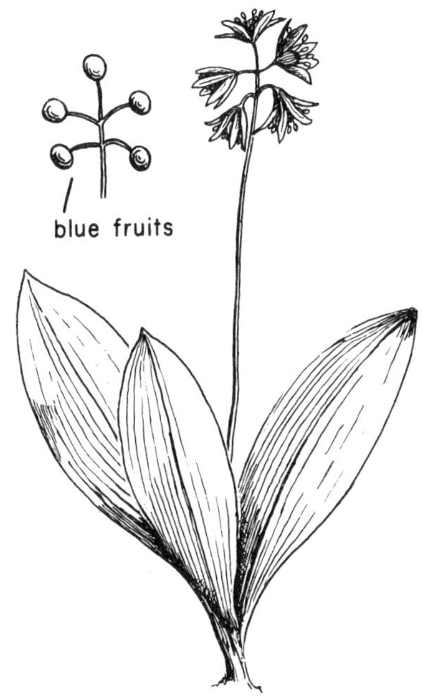

CLINTONIA borealis

SMILACINA Desf. **Plumelily**

Stem simple, from a creeping, slender or short, thick rootstock; leaves alternate; flowers white or greenish-white; small, borne in a conspicuous branched terminal inflorescence; stamens 6; fruit globular, 1-2 seeded berry, at first greenish or yellowish-white flecked with madder-brown, at length a dull ruby red.

S. racemosa (L.) Desf. (racemed)
Plumelily, False Spikenard, False Solomon's Seal

Stem 4-10 dm high; leaves numerous, 3.5-9.5 cm wide; inflorescence plumed, many-flowered, sessile, or on a stalk usually less than half its length, 0.7-1.7 dm long, 3-10 cm in diameter, flowers about 4 mm broad; berry 4-6 mm in diameter. Flowers in May-July. Moist woods, thickets, and roadsides. **Easily recognized, when flowering, by the plumed inflorescence.**

SMILACINA racemosa

MAIANTHEMUM Weber. **Mayflower**

Low perennial herbs with slender rootstocks and erect simple stems bearing 1-3 leaves and a terminal inflorescence of small white flowers; sepals and petals of 4 segments; stamens 4; fruit a berry.

M. canadense Desf. (Canadian)
Canada Mayflower, Wild Lily of the Valley

Stem 0.5-2.5 dm high, usually zigzag; leaves 1-3, finely-nerved; flower stalks mostly longer than the flowers; berry pale red, speckled. Flowers in May-July. In moist woods and thickets at high elevations. Especially common in mixed northern hardwood/red spruce forests.

MAIANTHEMUM canadense

DISPORUM Salisb., **Disporum**

Low, downy herbs from slender creeping rootstocks; stem scaly below, leafy and sparingly forked above; leaves thin, alternate, sessile, or clasping; flowers greenish-yellow, creeping on terminal stalks, solitary or few in a cluster; sepals and petals of 6 narrowly linear separate segments; stamens 6; fruit a berry.

D. lanuginosum (Michx.) Nichols. (wooly), **Hairy Disporum**

Plant finely and rather densely hairy; leaves rounded at the base, taper-pointed at the apex, minute hairs on the margins, strongly nerved, sessile; flowers solitary or 2-3 in a cluster; sepals and petals 1-2 cm long, smooth, its segments spreading; stamens half as long as the sepals and petals; ovary oblong; style slender, 3-cleft; berry red and pulpy. Flowers in May-June. In rich woods.

DISPORUM lanuginosum

STREPTOPUS Michx., **Twisted Stalk**

Low herbs with rather stout stems from creeping rootstocks, and usually forking and divergent branches; leaves membranaceous; flowers nodding, borne on slender axillary stalks that are characteristically bent or twisted at about the middle; petals keeled; fruit a berry.

*S. **roseus*** Michx. (rose-colored), **Twisted Stalk**

Plant 3-7.5 dm high; branches sparingly hairy; leaves 5-10 cm long, sharp-pointed at the apex, sessile, rounded or somewhat clasping at the base, green on both sides, finely hairy on the margin; stalk of the inflorescence 1-2.5 cm long, usually hairy, 1- (rarely 2) flowered; flowers rose-purple, 8-12 mm long; style 3-cleft; berry cherry-red, about 1 cm in diameter. Flowers in May-July. In cool moist woods, especially above 3,000 feet elevation.

STREPTOPUS roseus

TRILLIUM L. **Trillium**

Smooth, low herbs with simple, erect stems from short rootstocks, bearing a whorl of 3 net-veined leaves at the summit subtending a solitary flower; 3 green sepals and 3 colored petals; stamens 6; fruit a 3-celled berry.

a. Flower stalked; leaves subsessile; ovary and berry 6-angled or 6-lobed, purple; stigma short and stout, tapering from base to a recurved tip; petal 1.5-5.5 cm long, spreading from base. ...... b
a. Flower stalked; leaves distinctly petioled; ovary and berry globose, with 3 rounded lobes; plants 2-6 dm high. Petals white with pink or purple markings near the base. .... ***T. undulatum***

b. Flowers usually reddish-purple. .... ***T. erectum***
b. Flowers white or fading to pink. .... ***T. grandiflorum***

T. erectum L. (erect) **Ill-scented Trillium, Wake Robin**

Stem 3-6 dm high; leaves broadly rhombic; flower stalk erect or declined, 3-10 cm long; flowers ill-scented; **petals usually dark reddish-purple, sometimes pink or greenish;** filaments much shorter than the anthers. Flowers in April-June. In rich woods.

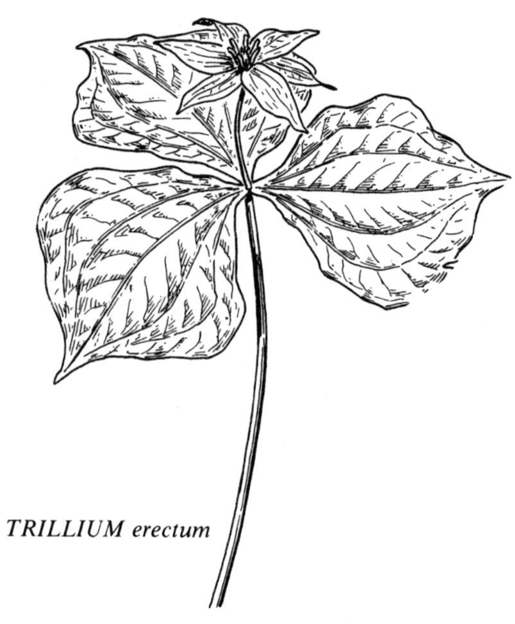

TRILLIUM erectum

T. grandiflorum (Michx.) Salisb., **Large-Flowered Trillium**

Stem 2.5 dm high; leaves 6-30 cm long; flowers showy on an erect or somewhat inclined stalk, 4-7.5 cm long; **petals much longer than the sepals, white, usually fading to rose. Berry black.** Flowers in April-June. Common in rich woods.

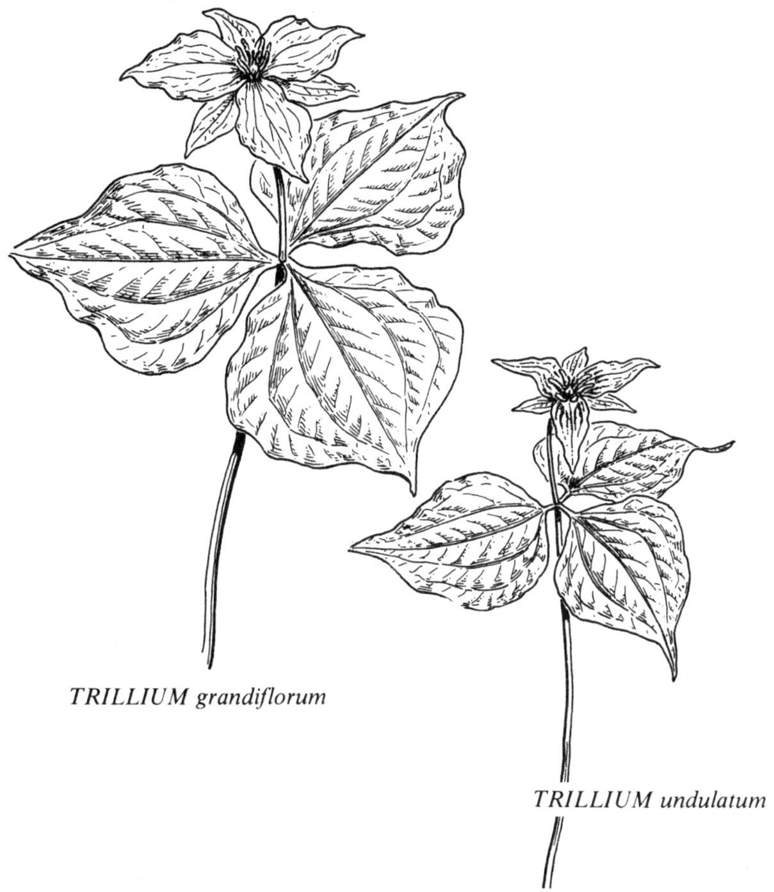

TRILLIUM grandiflorum

TRILLIUM undulatum

T. undulatum Willd. (wavy), **Painted Trillium**

Stem, 2.5 dm tall; leaves ovate, taper-pointed; **petals much exceeding the sepals, white, marked near the base with pink or purple, wavy-margined. Berry scarlet.** Flowers in May-June. Damp mountain woods at higher elevations, especially in spruce and northern hardwood stands.

SMILAX L. **Greenbrier**

Chiefly climbing plants with woody or herbaceous stems often armed with spines or prickles; leaves leathery, the petioles bearing a pair of coiling appendages (stipules) that serve in climbing as the attaching organs of the plant; flowers regular but either staminate or pistillate, borne on stout stalks; sepals and petals 3 each, greenish; stamens 6; pistillate flowers with 1-6 abortive stamens; fruit a bluish berry. **Our only woody plants having the principal veins of the leaves parallel.**

SUMMER KEY

a. Stem perennial, woody, prickly; leaves whitened on the undersurface. .... ***S. glauca***
a. Stem perennial, woody, prickly; leaves green on both sides. ..... b

b. Inflorescence stalk shorter or but little longer than the petioles; leaves 5-nerved. .... ***S. rotundifolia***
b. Inflorescence stalk 2-4 times as long as the petioles; leaves 7-nerved. .... ***S. hispida***

WINTER

Mostly woody, vinelike plants; buds 3-sided, pointed, covered by a single scale. Stems round or angular, usually with large prickles; vascular bundles scattered throughout the stem. Leaves deciduous, breaking above the broadened petiole base leaving no definite scar. Climbing by tendrils attached in pairs to the leaf petioles. Fruit a bluish or black berry, often lasting well into winter.

WINTER KEY

a. Stems not whitened. .... b
a. Stems whitened. .... ***S. glauca***

b. Prickles broadened or flattened at the base. .... ***S. rotundifolia***
b. Prickles slender, needlelike, black. .... ***S. hispida***

S. glauca Walt. (Whitened), **Saw Brier**

Stem round, usually armed with numerous prickles; **leaves mostly 5-nerved, whitened beneath and sometimes above, lower surface with minute hairs;** inflorescences with 6-12 flowers; berry bluish black. Flowers in May-June. Dry thickets and old fields.

WINTER

Stem smooth, round, whitened, with stout prickles; berries dark bluish, 6 mm in diameter. Thickets, fields, and waste places.

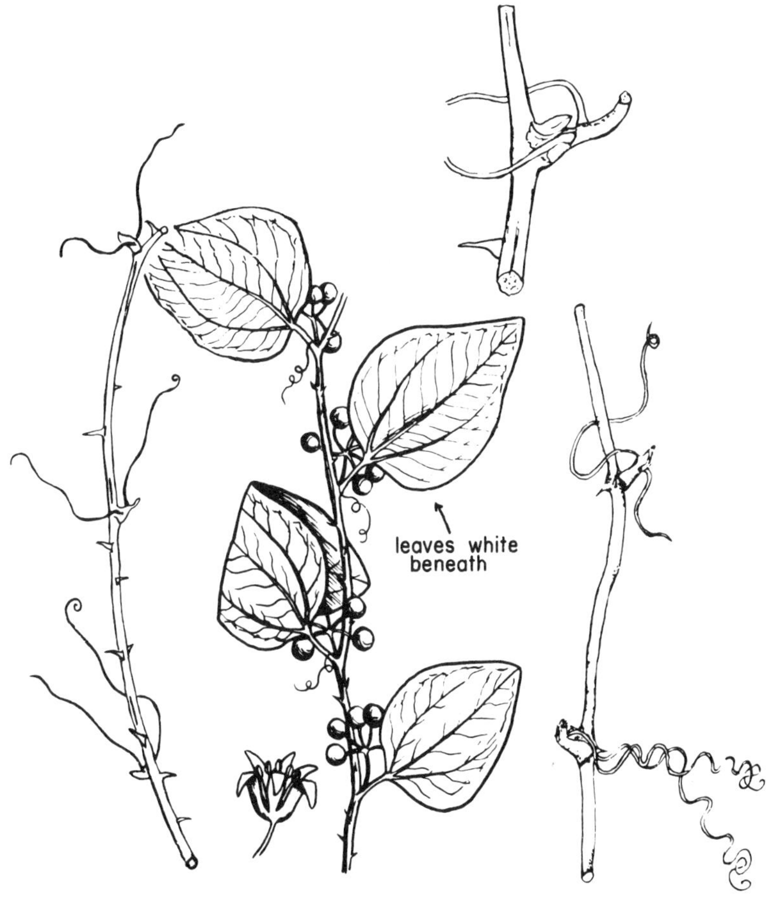

SMILAX glauca

S. rotundifolia L. (round-leaved), **Common Greenbrier**

Stem round with more or less 4-angled branches, **usually armed with stout, scattered prickles; leaves thick and shining when mature; green on both surfaces;** inflorescences with 6-25 flowers; filaments longer than the anthers; berry blue-black, covered with a whitish coating. Flowers April-June. In thickets and old fence rows.

WINTER

Older stems green, smooth, nearly round, young stems usually sharply 4-angled; prickles stout, straight or slightly curved; berries black, 6 mm in diameter, ripe in late autumn but present in winter. Old fields, thickets, and woods.

SMILAX rotundifolia

S. hispida Muhl. (with stiff hairs). **Hispid Greenbrier**

Stem round, usually thickly beset with numerous slender, black prickles; leaves thin, green on both sides, 7-nerved; inflorescences with 10-26 flowers; filaments slightly longer than anthers; berry bluish black. Flowers in May-June. In thickets, open woods, and fields.

WINTER

Stem green, climbing, smooth, round, the lower stems densely covered with black, straight, slender prickles, younger stems usually lacking these; branches angular; berries dark bluish, 6 mm in diameter. Rich woods and fields.

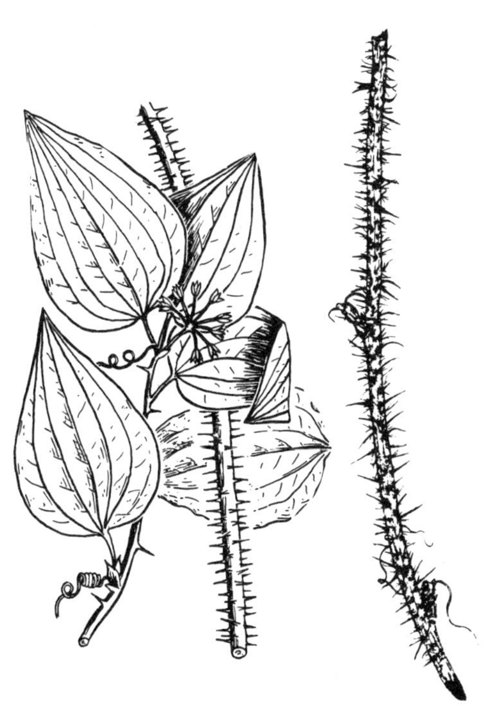

SMILAX hispida

SALIX L. **Willow**

Trees and shrubs with mostly slender, brittle twigs. Leaves alternate, mostly long and pointed with very short petioles. Flowers in catkins, the staminate consisting of 1-12 (mostly 2) stamens; the pistillate with a single ovary composed of 2 carpels. Fruit a capsule containing a number of silky seeds. Several kinds of insect galls occur on willows, including the pine cone gall, which might be mistaken for some sort of fruiting organ; it is caused by a midge.

SUMMER KEY
Based Primarily on Vegetal Organs

a. Petioles glandular; blades greenish beneath, narrowly lanceolate, finely toothed. .... ***S. nigra***

a. Petioles not glandular; leaf blades smooth, whitened beneath when expanded, toothed; twigs short, spreading or erect; yellowish brown; leaves without tiny vein-islets. .... ***S. rigida***

WINTER

Deciduous trees and shrubs. Tree trunks often clustered and leaning; shrubs often forming thickets. Buds variable in length, flattened against the stem, single, sometimes clustered, with a single exposed scale; terminal bud absent. Pith white, small, round, continuous. Leaf scars alternate shallow, narrow, curved with 3 bundle traces. Stipule scars variable. Catkins of some species appearing in late winter.

WINTER KEY

a. Trees; twigs vary in color from yellowish-green to almost black; older bark brown to black; twigs brittle; buds reddish-brown, 2-5 mm long. .... ***S. nigra***

a. Shrubs; tall, to 4 m high; not thicket-forming; twigs and buds variably hairy, not shining; buds 2-7 mm long; older bark brown. .... ***S. rigida***

S. nigra Marsh. (black), **Black Willow**

A shrub or tree to 20 m high; bark blackish, flaky; wood light, soft, brittle; twigs brown or green, becoming hairless; leaves 6.5-12 cm long, 0.4-1.8 cm wide, green, smooth, closely toothed; stipules large, somewhat heart-shaped; staminate filaments 2.5-5 cm long; capsules ovoid-conical, smooth, 3-5 mm long. Flowers in April-May. Very common along streams and in springy places. **Our only common, native, tree-sized willow.**

WINTER

A shrub or tree growing to 20 m high and 5 dm in diameter, with several trunks, often leaning. Our only common, native tree-sized willow; bark dark brownish-black, flaky; buds 2-4 mm long, reddish-brown; twigs slender, varying from greenish to dark brown, smooth, brittle at base. Abundant along streams and in low woods, often leaning over the stream.

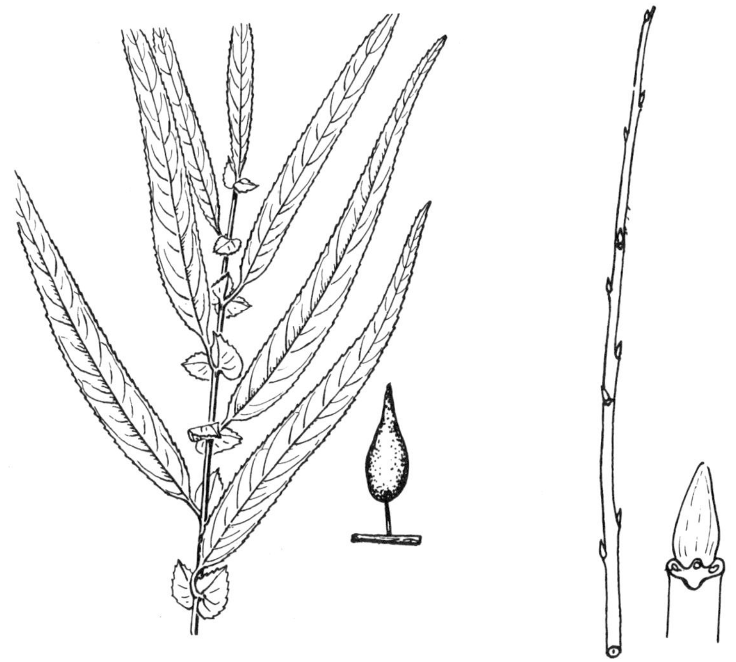

SALIX nigra

S. rigida Muhl. (stiff), **Heartleaf Willow**

A shrub to 4 m high, or, rarely, a small tree; twigs greenish, hairy or hairless; leaves oblong, lance-shaped, sharply toothed, rounded, abruptly cut off or heart-shaped at base; stipules oval, toothed, large; staminate catkins about 2.5 cm long; capsules ovoid, 4-8 mm long. Flowers in April-May. Common along streams in the mountains. **Flower scales brown to black, capsules smooth.**

WINTER

Shrub with several stems reaching 4 m high or, rarely, a small tree; buds 2-5 mm long, resembling the twigs in color. Twigs slender, 1-5 mm in diameter, varying from yellowish to dark brown, hairy when young. Common along stream banks, ditches and poorly drained areas.

SALIX rigida

POPULUS L. **Poplar, Aspen**

Trees with alternate, broad, more or less heart-shaped or oval, toothed leaves with long, often flattened petioles. Both staminate and pistillate flowers in catkins, the flowers produced from a cup-shaped disk, without nectar glands. Stamens 6-60 or more. Pistillate flowers composed of a single ovary with 2-4 stigmas. Fruit a capsule containing many hairy seeds. Younger bark usually with diamond-shaped markings.

SUMMER KEY

a. Leaves finely round-toothed. .... ***P. tremuloides***
a. Leaves coarsely wavy-toothed. .... ***P. grandidentata***

WINTER

Young bark smooth, green, whitish, or orange; older bark becoming gray and furrowed. Buds solitary, sessile, ovoid or elongated, with several scales, the lowest of which is distinct and located centrally above the leaf scar. Twigs round or somewhat angled with small, 6-angled, continuous brown pith. Leaf scars large, alternate, crescent-shaped to triangular or 3-lobed; bundle traces 3.

WINTER KEY

a. Buds shining with resin, mostly hairless. .... ***P. tremuloides***
a. Buds gray, dull (not resinous), buds silky or wooly. ....
.... ***P. grandidentata***

P. tremuloides Michx. (like *P. tremula,* of Eurasia)
Quaking Aspen, Trembling Aspen

A slender tree growing to a height of about 20 m and a diameter of 1 m; **leaves with small regular rounded teeth,** hairless on both surfaces at maturity, 2-8 cm long, **the petioles slender, flattened laterally,** permitting the leaves to quiver with the slightest breeze, hence the name; bark smooth, light green or whitish; staminate catkins 4-6 cm long. Flowers in March-May. Dry or moist soil, especially at higher elevations.

WINTER

A deciduous tree to 20 m high and 1 m in diameter; buds conical, dark brown to black, with up to 7 somewhat resinous, shiny scales, smooth or sometimes hairy on the margins; twigs slender, shiny, reddish-brown; leaf scars crescent-shaped; stipule scars elongate, dark. Bark smooth, light green to whitish. Woods or old strip mines especially, at higher elevations.

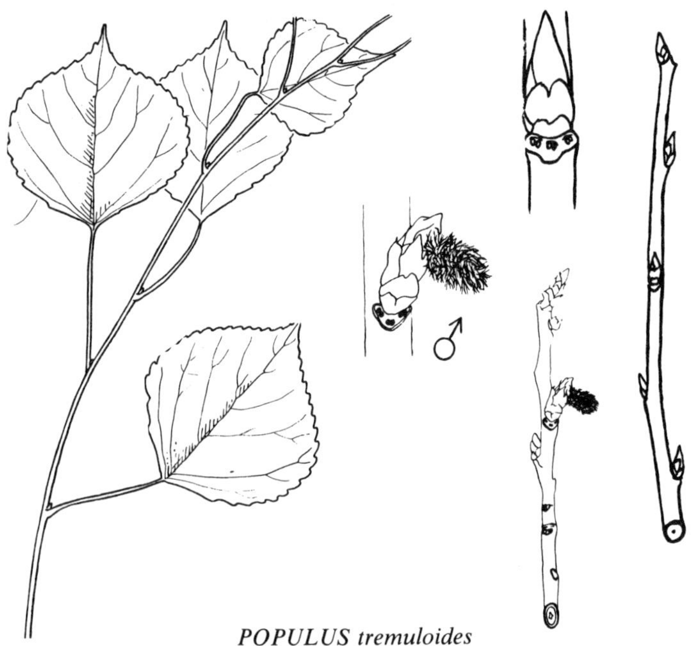

POPULUS tremuloides

P. grandidentata Michx. (large toothed). **Bigtooth Aspen**

A forest tree to 20 m high, and 6 dm in diameter; **leaves with large and irregular wavy teeth, those of very young plants densely white-wooly** sometimes 3 dm long; petioles flattened laterally; staminate catkins 5-10 cm long. Flowers in March-May. Rich woods or old fields.

WINTER

A tree growing to 20 m high and 6 dm in diameter; buds gray with small hairs, not shiny or resinous, with up to 7 scales visible; twigs thick, varying from grayish to yellowish-brown, hairless, not shiny; bark smooth, grayish-green; both kinds of flowers in catkins, appearing in late winter. Dry woods and old fields.

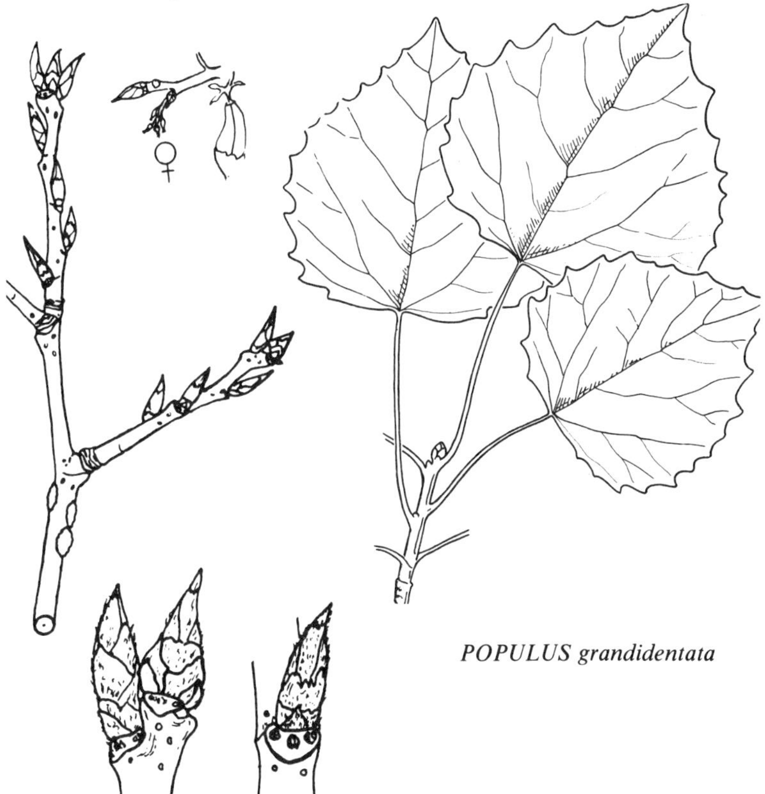

POPULUS grandidentata

COMPTONIA Banks. **Sweet-fern**

A low shrub with separate staminate and pistillate flowers on the same plant or on separate plants; with round, brown branches and narrow, deeply-divided leaves. Staminate aments oblong or narrowly cylindric, the pistillate round to oval. Ovary subtended by 8 elongate bracts which persist, surrounding the nut.

C. peregrina (L.) Coult. (foreign) **Sweet-fern**

A shrub to 6 dm high, with **sweet-scented, fernlike, lance-shaped leaves;** young branchlets and leaves with long, soft hairs; stipules semi-heart-shaped; pistillate aments burlike in fruit; 1.5-2.5 cm in diameter; nuts 4-5 mm long. Flowers in April-May. Dry soil of open sterile woodlands.

WINTER

A small shrub to 6 dm high, with erect, spreading branches; buds single, sessile, oval, with about 4 exposed scales; no terminal bud; slender, resinous-dotted twigs when young; pith small; leaf scars alternate, triangular, raised; bundle traces 3; stipule scars small. **Fruit a hard, smooth cone-shaped nut, surrounded by 8 elongate bracts that persist in winter.** Dry open woodlands and rocky banks.

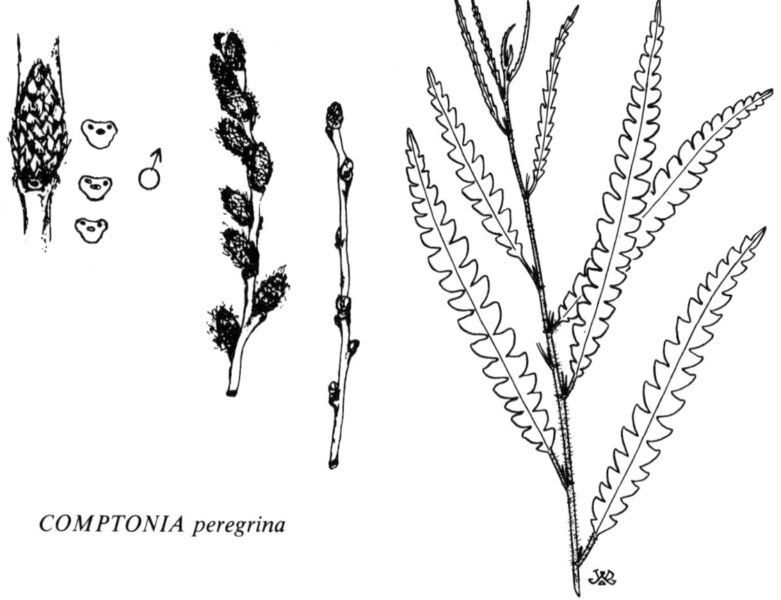

COMPTONIA peregrina

JUGLANS L. **Walnut**

Leaves alternate, pinnately compound with many leaflets. Twigs stout with terminal buds much larger than the laterals and often having superposed buds adjacent to the lateral ones. Fragrant bark. Fruit large, round or ovoid, the outer covering fleshy, fibrous, does not crack upon drying; inner covering bony, wrinkled; seed large, 4-lobed. Pith in twig chambered.

SUMMER KEY

a. Fruit oblong, pointed, sticky, inner layer of fruit with sharp corrugations; chambered pith dark brown with thick diaphragms. Leaf usually with a terminal leaflet. .... ***J. cinerea***

a. Fruit round, not sticky, inner layer of fruit with rounded corrugations; chambered pith light brown with thin diaphragms. Leaf usually without a terminal leaflet. .... ***J. nigra***

WINTER

Trees with open crowns, buds placed one above another, gray to silvery-haired, without leathery outer scales; brown chambered pith. Leaf scars alternate, large, shield-shaped, with bundle traces in 3 U-shaped groups; no stipule scars. Bark odorous. The fruit is present in winter on the ground.

WINTER KEY

a. Terminal bud oval, elongated; with a band of fine hairs across the straight top of the leaf scar; pith dark brown, chambered; bark ridged, light gray. .... ***J. cinerea***

a. Terminal bud oval to round, leaf scar U-shaped at top, without a band of fine hairs; pith light brown, chambered; bark ridged, dark brown to nearly black. .... ***J. nigra***

J. cinerea L. (ashy) **Butternut, White Walnut**

A forest tree growing to 30 m high, and 9 dm in diameter, trunk dividing into an open crown of large spreading branches; leaflets 7-17, the petioles and branchlets downy with sticky hairs; **fruit elipsoid, sticky to the touch, 5-8 cm long, pointed.** Flowers in April, May. Rich woods.

WINTER

A tree up to 30 m high and 9 dm in diameter, with a spreading crown; **leaf scars with a band of fine hairs across the top, not notched; pith dark brown.** Bark light gray, ridged on old trunks by furrows. Rich, moist woods.

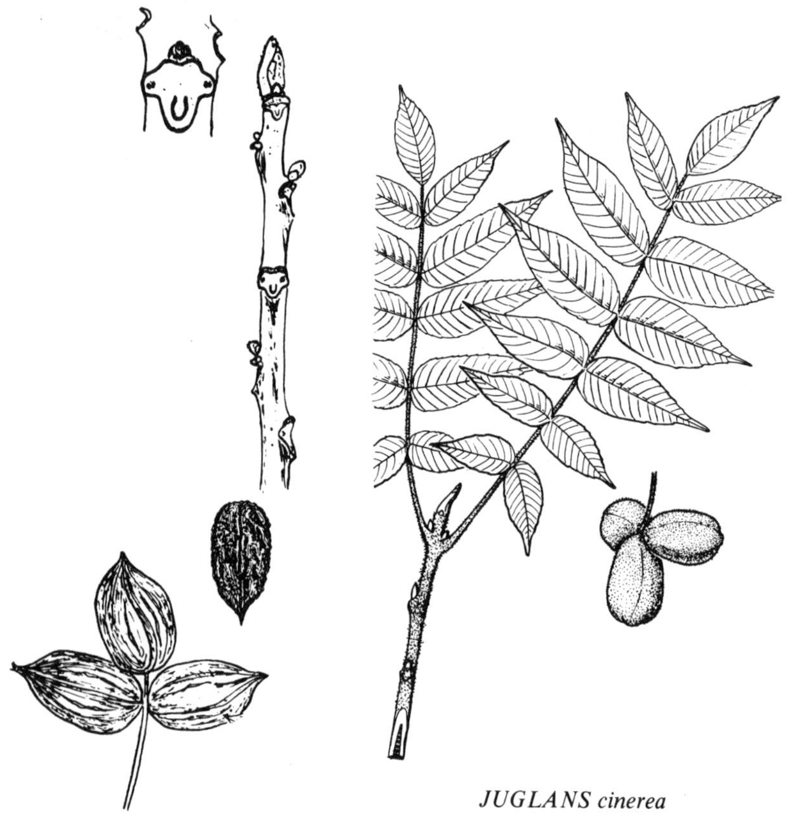

JUGLANS cinerea

J. nigra L. (black), **Black Walnut**

A handsome forest tree up to 50 m high, and 18 dm in diameter; leaflets 11-17; staminate catkins 7-13 cm long; **fruits nearly globe-shaped and not sticky to the touch, 3-8 cm in diameter.** Flowers in April, May. Rich woods, especially in coves and on well-drained bottom land and lower slopes.

WINTER

A valuable tree up to 35 m high and 18 dm in diameter; crown open, spreading; **leaf scars U-shaped at the top; pith light brown. Bark heavily furrowed, dark brown to black. Rich, moist woods.**

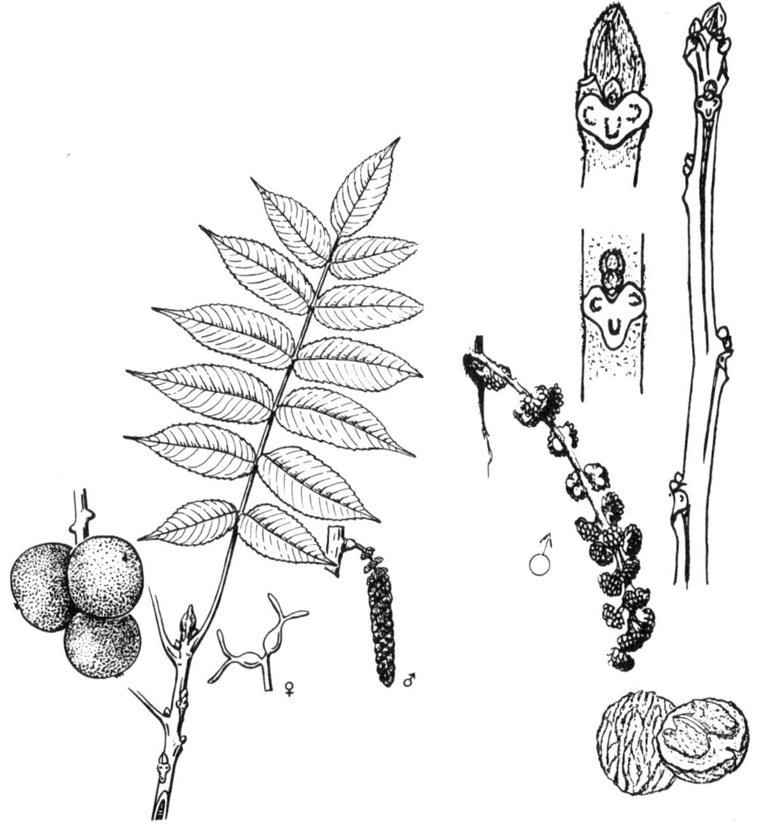

JUGLANS nigra

CARYA Nutt. **Hickory**

Trees with close or shaggy bark, alternate, odd pinnately compound leaves with toothed leaflets, and stout twigs with continuous pith. Terminal buds much larger than the lateral ones. Wood mostly hard and strong, often made into handles. Fruit a round, oblong, or oval nut, the husk separating more or less completely into 4 parts; nut woody, smooth or angled; seed sweet or bitter.

SUMMER KEY

a. Leaves with 7-11 leaflets; bud scales not overlapping, bright yellow; bark not shedding in plates, flruit husk thin with winged sutures, seed bitter. .... ***C. cordiformis***
a. Leaflets mostly 5-7; bud scales overlapping, brown or gray; bark and husk various. .... b

b. Leaflet typically 5, toothed, each tooth bearing a persistent dense tuft of hairs; bark shaggy, splitting into long plates; husk thick. .... ***C. ovata***
b. Leaflets 5-7, the teeth without dense tufts of hairs; bark and husk various. c

c. Branchlets stout, hairy; leaflets usually 7; bark and husk various. d
c. Branchlets slender, mostly smooth; bark without plates but becoming scaly in older trees; husk thin, smooth, splitting about half way down the fruit; leaflets commonly 5; fruit pear shaped. ***C. glabra***

d. Bark "shelly" (splitting into straight plates); hairs on leaf axis straight; husk thick. .... ***C. laciniosa***
d. Bark tight, ridged; hairs on leaf axis curly; husk of medium thickness. .... ***C. tomentosa***

WINTER

Trees with steel-gray, ridged, scaly or shaggy bark, stout, round twigs and continuous pith. Terminal buds large, stalked only in Bitternut Hickory; sometimes one above another. Leaf scars large, alternate, shield-shaped; bundle traces mostly in 3 groups (or sometimes scattered). The fruit persistent in winter, especially scattered on the ground under the trees.

WINTER KEY

a. Buds long and slender, stalked, bud scales not overlapping, and and occurring in pairs; buds yellow, rough; seed bitter. .... ***C. cordiformis***

a. Buds egg-shaped or nearly so, not stalked; bud scales overlapping, usually more than 2 exposed scales. .... b

b. Terminal bud, usually over 10 mm long, usually hairy; fruit with a thick husk splitting to the base. c

b. Terminal bud usually less than 10 mm long, essentially smooth (hairy if the outer bud scales have fallen); fruit with a thin husk, pear-shaped, the husk usually splits about half the way down or splits late in the season. .... ***C. glabra***

c. Outer bud scales loose at the tips and remaining on the twig causing the bud to be shaggy in appearance, bark on older trees shaggy. d

c. Outer bud scales not persistent, the bud not shaggy, the tight inner bud scales, hairy, somewhat silvery green. Bark not shaggy or platy. .... ***C. tomentosa***

d. Younger twigs dark, reddish brown, fruit oval, 3-6 cm long. .... ***C. ovata***

d. Young twigs lighter, orange-brown or buff-colored; fruit oval, 4-6.5 cm long. .... ***C. laciniosa***

C. cordiformis (Wang) K. Koch (heart-form), **Bitternut Hickory**

A slender tree growing to 30 m high, and 7 dm in diamter; leaflets 7-11 mostly more than 7); fruit oval, narrowly 6-ridged, 2-2.5 cm long, the husk thin, eventually splitting into 4 parts, the 4 sutures winged above the middle, nut spherical, thin-walled; **seed extremely bitter.** Flowers in May, June. Rich soil in woods and along streams. **Leaflets usually more numerous than in our other native hickories. The only tree of the region having bright, sulfur-yellow buds.**

WINTER

A tree up to 50 m high, and 7 dm in diameter; bud scales in pairs, not overlapping, bright yellow. Bark gray, tight with flat-topped ridges and very shallow fissures. Rich soil in woods and along streams.

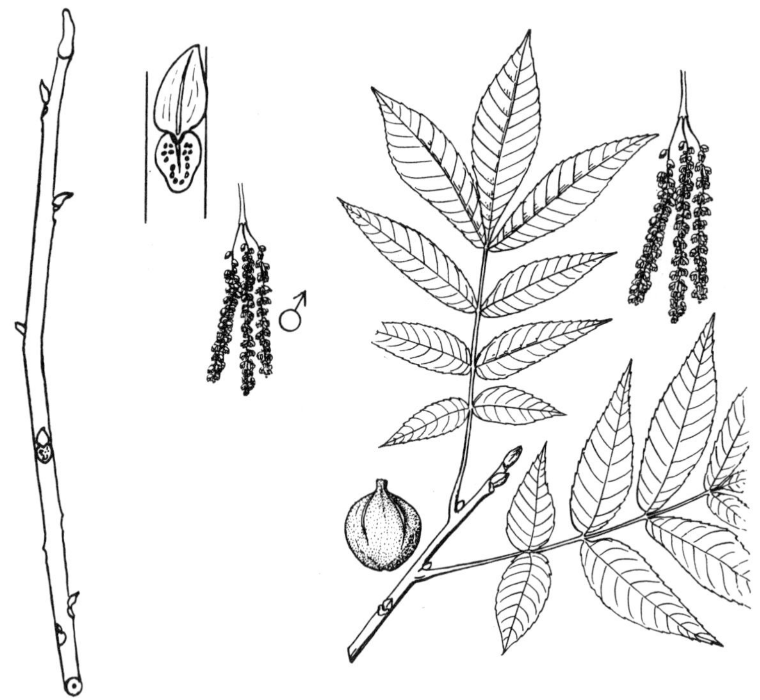

CARYA cordiformis

C. ovata (Mill.) K. Koch (ovate), **Shagbark Hickory**

A handsome tree up to 40 m high, and 6 dm in diameter; **bark on older trees splitting in plates that curl away from the trunk; leaflets mostly 5, each tooth of the leaflets with a tuft of hairs;** downy beneath when young; fruit subspherical, 2.5-6.5 cm long, the husk thick, splitting into 4 parts when mature; nut angled, thin-shelled; seed sweet. Flowers in May. Rich soil along streams and on hillsides.

WINTER

A tree up to 40 m high, and 6 dm in diameter; bud scales more than 2, **overlapping scales loose at apex gives bud shaggy appearance.** Twigs gray or brown, young twigs with very small hairs or smooth; **bark on older trees splitting in plates that curl away from the trunk giving a shaggy appearance.** Rich woods.

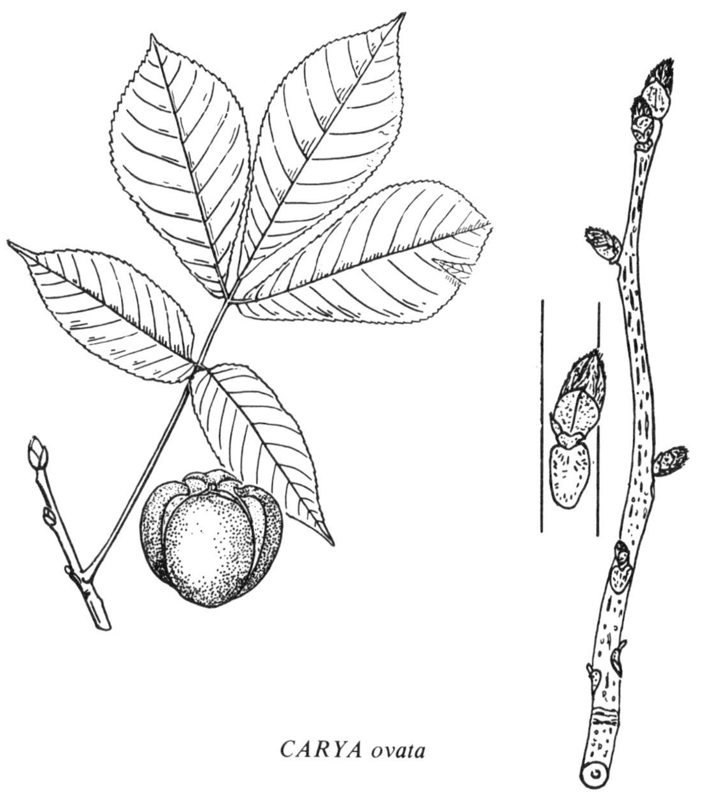

CARYA ovata

C. laciniosa (Michx. f.) Loud. (full of flaps; from the plates of bark)
Shellbark Hickory, King Nut

A tree to 40 m high, and 6 dm in diameter with bark splitting into long straight plates but not curling away from the trunk; leaflets usually 7, velvety beneath and with straight hairs on the leaf axis; fruit oblong, 5-8 cm long, the largest hickory fruit, the husk thick, splitting to the base at maturity; nut oblong, thick-shelled; seed sweet, no larger than that of shagbark. Flowers in May. Rich damp bottom lands and coves.

WINTER

A tree up to 40 m high, and 6 dm in diameter; **terminal bud** similar to that of Shagbark but **a little larger than that of any other native hickory;** twigs light tan or orange; **bark splitting into long narrow plates loose but not curling as in Shagbark.** Bottomlands and along streams.

CARYA laciniosa

C. tomentosa Nutt. (tomentose), **Mockernut Hickory**

A tree to 30 m high, 7 dm in diameter; leaflets 7-9 (mostly 7), aromatic, hairy beneath and with curly hairs on the central axis; fruit globe-shaped, 3.5 cm long, the husk freely splitting; **inner wall of nut globe-shaped, very thick (hence the common name Mockernut);** seed sweet. Rich soil, especially on hillsides.

WINTER

A tree up to 30 m high, and 7 dm in diameter; **outer bud scales not persistent, the bud neat in appearance; exposed inner bud scales hairy, silvery-green;** twigs wooly-hairy; bark tight with flat-topped ridges and shallow fissures, but not shaggy or splitting in plates. Rich woods.

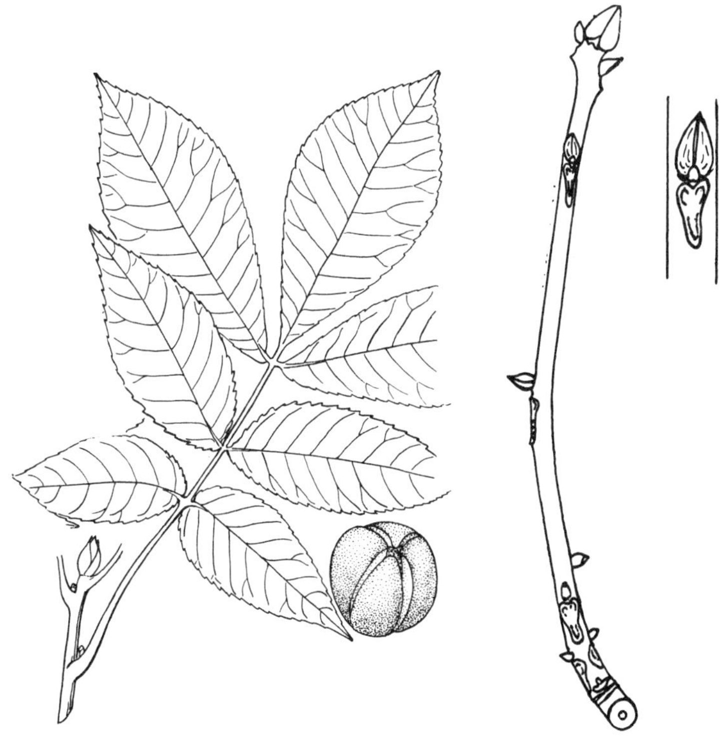

CARYA tomentosa

C. glabra (Mill.) Sweet (smooth) **Pignut Hickory**

A tree to 30 m high and 10 dm in diameter; leaflets mostly 5, not hairy (hairy below in var. ***hirsuta*** Ashe); **fruit pear-shaped, 1.5-3.5 cm long, the husk thin, splitting only part way to the base; inner wall of fruit very thick and not ridged;** seed sweet or slightly bitter. Flowers in May-June. Dry woods.

WINTER

A tree up to 30 m high, and 10 dm in diameter; **terminal bud less than 10 mm long; outer bud scales usually persistent through winter; twigs hairless or almost so; bark tight,** ridged with flat-topped ridges and shallow fissures, scaly on older trees. Dry woods.

CARYA glabra

CORYLUS L. **Hazelnut**

Shrubs with simple, alternate, thin, broad-toothed leaves. Staminate catkins expanding before the leaves; calyx none. Pistillate flowers clustered at the ends of short branches, each consisting of an ovary with a short style and 2 stigmas, subtended by 2 bractlets which enlarge to form a leaflike covering of the nut.

SUMMER KEY

a. Leaves toothed; covering of the nut of 2 broad ragged appearing bracts; twigs with pinkish, gland-tipped hairs (become black and brittle in winter). .... ***C. americana***

a. Leaves rough-lobed-toothed; covering of nut prolonged into a tubular beak, twigs without pinkish, gland-tipped hairs. . ***C. cornuta***

WINTER

Shrubs. Buds sessile, oval, rounded, with about 4-6 scales. Twigs round, zigzag; with continuous, 3-angled, light brown pith. Leaf scars alternate, more or less 3-sided, small; bundle traces 3 or multiples of 3; stipule scars present, elongated.

WINTER KEY

a. Bud scales present throughout the winter, outer short; twigs with brittle blackish gland-tipped hairs. .... ***C. americana***

a. Bud scales often not present throughout winter, outer elongated; twigs without brittle, blackish, gland-tipped hairs. ... ***C. cornuta***

C. americana Walt. (American), **Hazelnut**

A shrub up to 3 m high, the young shoots russet-brown, densely bristly with pinkish hairs which become darker and may fall during the winter; leaves ovate or broadly oval, heart-shaped, hairless, finely wooly beneath, 7-15 cm long; staminate aments 7-10 cm long; **covering of the nut composed of 2 broad, almost distinct downy bracts that are ragged on the ends;** nut light brown, striped, 1-1.5 cm high, sweet. Flowers in March, April. Common in thickets.

WINTER

A shrub up to 3 m high. Buds 4 mm long, gray-hairy; young twigs reddish brown, densely bristled with pinkish hairs when young, becoming darker with age, mostly gone by spring. Thickets and forest borders.

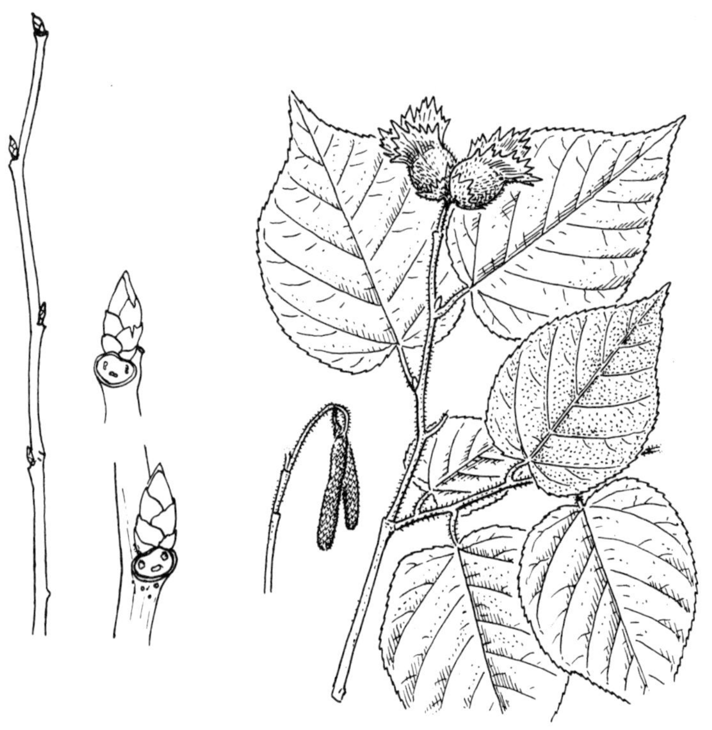

CORYLUS americana

C. cornuta Marsh. (horned), **Beaked Hazelnut**

A shrub to 3 m high, the twigs not glandular-bristly; leaves ovate or oval, sharp-pointed, heart-shaped or rounded at the base, rough-lobed-toothed, nearly hairless above, sparingly hairy beneath, 6.5-10 cm long; **covering of the nut bristly-hairy, united at the summit, prolonged into a tubular beak, about 2-3 cm long; nut ovoid,** striped, 1-1.4 cm high, sweet. Flowers in April, May. In thickets; less common than the preceding species.

WINTER

Shrub up to 3 m high, outer bud scales elongate, often shedding; twigs not glandular-bristly. Thickets and woodland borders.

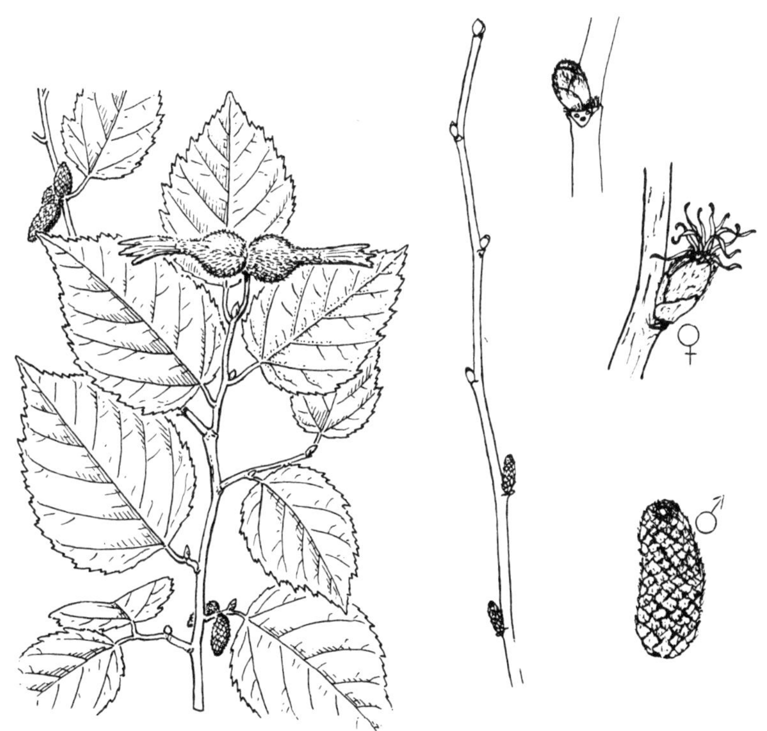

CORYLUS cornuta

CARPINUS L. **American Hornbeam, Muscletree**

Deciduous trees with smooth dark blue-gray bark, the trunk with irregular longitudinal ridges, suggesting the common name, Muscletree. Leaves very finely toothed, simple, alternate, straight-veined (resemble those of Hop Hornbeam and Yellow and Black Birch). Staminate catkins long-cylindrical, sessile at the ends of short branches. Pistillate flowers in short terminal clusters, each subtended by a flat bractlet which becomes enlarged and leaflike in fruit. Fruit a nutlet attached to the base of the bract.

C. caroliniana Walt. (Carolinian)
American Hornbeam, Blue-beech, Water-beech, Muscletree

A small tree to 12 m high, the **trunk short, often leaning, furrowed and ridged with dark bluish-gray bark, smooth, thin, tight bark;** wood very hard; leaves ovate-oblong; sharply and finely doubly-toothed, 6-10 cm long, hairless above, slightly hairy beneath; staminate catkins 2.5-4 cm long; bractlet of the pistillate flower lobed or incised; **nutlet 4 mm long and attached to the base of the usually 3-lobed bract.** Flowers in April, May. Moist soil along streams.

WINTER

Trees with smooth bluish-gray bark, with irregular ridges running lengthwise giving a musclelike appearance. Buds single, small, oval, sessile, inclined to one side of the leaf scar, with about 12 scales in 4 rows, buds somewhat 4-angled. Twigs slender, zigzag, round; pith pale, small, round or angled, continuous. Leaf scars alternate, small, sickle-shaped; bundle traces 3; stipule scars unequal in length.

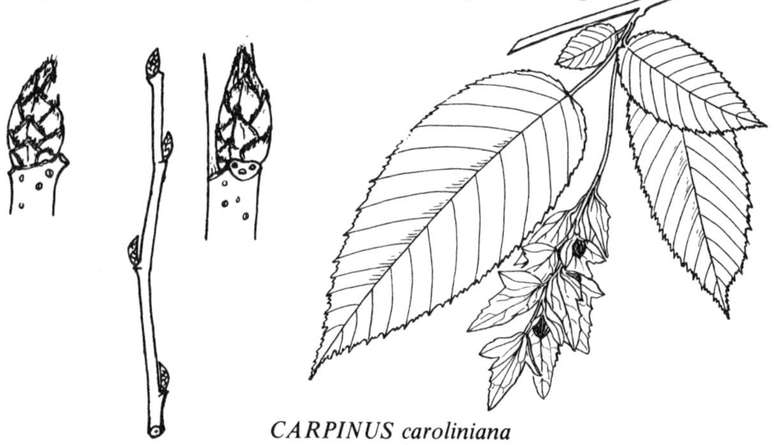

CARPINUS caroliniana

OSTRYA Scop. **Ironwood, Hop Hornbeam**

Deciduous trees with rough, scaly bark, very hard wood, and alternate, simple, finely and sharply doubly-toothed leaves. Staminate catkins sessile, appearing with leaves. Pistillate flowers in short, terminal erect spikes, each subtended by a tubular bractlet which enlarges to form a bladderlike sac enclosing the fruit. Fruit a nutlet.

O. virginiana (Mill.) K. Koch (Virginian), **Hop Hornbeam, Ironwood**

A slender tree up to 15 m high and 6 dm in diameter, with very hard wood, and brownish finely scaly bark; leaves oblong-ovate, sharply doubly-toothed, downy beneath, 6-10 cm long; (resemble those of American Hornbeam and Black and Yellow Birch); **covering on fruits 1.2-1.6 cm long, hairy, loosely overlapping to form pendant clusters somewhat resembling those of hops;** nutlets 5 mm long compressed. Flowers in April, May. Rich open woods of slopes and ridges.

WINTER

Trees with rough, finely scaled bark. Buds usually single, sessile, oval, somewhat inclined to one side of the leaf scar, with about 6 scales in spiral arrangement, with faint longitudinal grooves; no terminal bud. Slender, round zigzag, twigs, pith continuous, small, pale green, round or somewhat angled. Leaf scars alternate, crescent-shaped or oval, small; bundle traces 3; stipule scars unequal in length. Rich open woods.

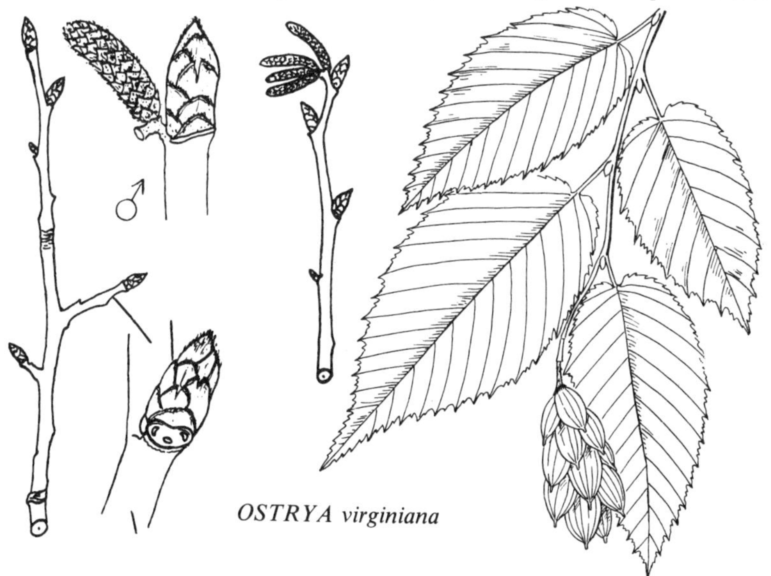

OSTRYA virginiana

BETULA L. **Birch**

Deciduous trees with round slender twigs and minute compressed green continuous pith. Buds moderate with 2 or 3 visible scales. Leaves alternate, simple, singly or doubly-toothed, on older twigs usually 2 or more leaves on the ends of spurlike branches. Staminate flowers in drooping catkins, each usually with a 4-toothed calyx. The pistillate flowers in erect catkins, naked. Fruit a small laterally winged nutlet.

SUMMER KEY

a. Fruiting catkins sessile. .... b
a. Fruiting catkins stalked, wooly; inner bark reddish, peeling in thin layers, leaves coarsely and often double-toothed. .... ***B. nigra***

b. Leaves mostly heart-shaped at base, margin finely single-toothed; fruiting bracts 4-5 mm long, smooth. .... ***B. lenta***
b. Leaves rounded at base, margin finely double-toothed; fruiting bracts 7-10 mm long, hairy with long hairs on the margins. .... ***B. alleghaniensis***

WINTER

Deciduous trees and shrubs. Buds single, spindle-shaped, sessile on the twig of young growth and on spurlike branches on older twigs and branches, with 2 or 3 visible scales. Twigs slender, may be aromatic, round; lenticels elongated around the twig similar to Cherry; pith small, flattened, continuous, green. Leaf scars alternate, oval, 3-angled or crescent-shaped; bundle traces 3. Staminate catkins often clustered in the winter; pistillate catkins oval or cylindrical.

WINTER KEY

a. Twigs with an odor of wintergreen. .... b
a. Twigs without an odor of wintergreen, reddish-brown, hairy; buds tapering from base to apex; inner bark on old trunks light pink to greenish brown, the older dark gray, shedding in thin strips.. .... ***B. nigra***

b. Bark on old trunks very dark; scaly to platy; buds sharply pointed, not tight against the twig; mostly hairless; twigs dark brown to black, very aromatic with odor of wintergreen. .... ***B. lenta***

b. Barks on old trunks bronze, platy; buds tight against the twig along the lower bud half, often hairy; twigs greenish brown, somewhat aromatic with the odor of wintergreen. .... ***B. alleghaniensis***

B. lenta L. (tough or flexible) **Sweet Birch, Black Birch, Cherry Birch**

A forest tree to 30 m high and 12 dm in diameter; wood hard, close-grained; **young twigs with a very sweet wintergreen taste; lenticels horizontal, prominent;** leaves ovate, sharply but finely single-toothed, green and shiny above, 6-10 cm long; staminate catkins clustered, 6-10 cm long; pistillate catkins sessile, dense, oblong, 2.5 cm long, 1.5 cm in diameter in fruit; fruit oblong, with narrow wings. Flowers in April-May. Rich moist woods.

WINTER

A tree up to 30 m high, and 12 dm in diameter; twigs smooth, slender and flexible, reddish-brown; **bark tight, dark brown, smooth, becoming platy on older trees, not peeling in layers, the young bark with a conspicuous wintergreen taste and odor; lenticels prominent.** Rich woods, especially at lower elevations.

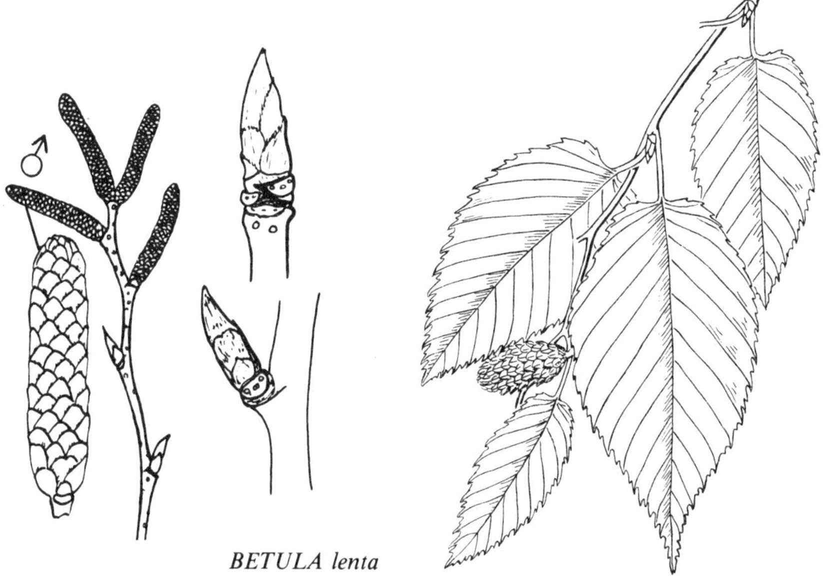

BETULA lenta

B. alleghaniensis Britt. (of the Alleghenies) **Yellow Birch**
(***B. lutea*** Michx. f.)

A forest tree up to 30 m and 12 dm in diameter, **bark on younger trees and larger branches of older trees, yellowish or silvery gray, detaching in thin layers, curling at edges, giving a ragged appearance; twigs less aromatic than Black Birch;** leaves oval or oblong-oval, sharply and finely double-toothed, dark green above, 3-10 cm long; staminate catkins usually 2-4 together; pistillate catkins 4 cm or less long, 1.4-1.8 cm thick in fruit; fruit broadly oblong. Flowers in April-May. Moist rich soil at higher elevations.

WINTER

A tree up to 30 m high, and 12 dm in diameter; buds often hairy; twigs greenish-brown with a slight odor of wintergreen; catkins in fruit oblong, 2-4 cm long, the scales hairy. **Bark of younger trees and larger branches on older trees yellowish or silvery gray, detaching in thin filmy layers.** Rich cool woods at higher elevations.

BETULA alleghaniensis

B. nigra L. (Black), **River Birch. Red Birch.**

Tree to 30 m high and 9 dm in diameter, with **greenish brown or reddish inner bark exposed by the deeply furrowed and broken outer bark peeling in thin layers, which turn up at the edges;** twigs reddish, not aromatic, leaves ovate-oval, sharp-pointed at the end, downy beneath when young, coarsely single or double-toothed or lobed, not toothed at the wedge-shaped base, 4-8 cm long; staminate catkins 6.5-9 cm long, pistillate catkins oblong-cylindric at the base, nutlet wider than its wings, hairy. Flowers in April, May. Moist soil along banks of streams and bottomland.

WINTER

A tree up to 30 m high, and 9 dm in diameter; buds hairy, the outer scales elongated; twigs reddish, not aromatic; **bark light reddish brown, outer bark deeply furrowed and splitting into thin irregular layers, exposing the orange-red inner bark,** catkins in fruit thick-cylindric, 2.5-3 cm. long, scales wooly; bottom lands and stream banks.

BETULA nigra

ALNUS B. **Alder**

Deciduous shrubs with smooth, gray bark and small continuous 3-sided pith. Buds usually stalked, rather large, solitary with two or three scales. Leaves toothed. Both staminate and pistillate flowers in catkins. Fruit a small, laterally-winged nutlet.

SUMMER KEY

a. Leaves whitened beneath; fruiting catkins bent downwards. .... ***A. rugosa.***
a. Leaves green on both sides; fruiting catkins erect. ***A. serrulata.***

WINTER

Shrubs with smooth, gray bark. Buds usually stalked, large, single, with 2 or 3 non-overlapping scales. Leaf scars alternate, raised, semi-circular; bundle traces 3 or compound. Pith small, 3-sided, continuous. Both staminate and pistillate flowers in catkins, next season's staminate flowers usually present in winter, along with the previous year's cone-like fruiting catkins and the small immature pistillate catkins of the next season.

WINTER KEY

a. Buds stalked; stems with long horizontal lenticels; fruiting catkins drooping. .... ***A. rugosa.***
a. Buds stalked; lenticels shorter, fewer, darker than above; fruiting catkins upright. .... ***A. serrulata.***

A. rugosa (Du Roi) Spreng. (wrinkled), **Speckled** or **Hoary Alder**

A shrub or rarely a small tree to 6 m high; **leaves oval, fine-toothed (often double-toothed), rounded at the base, dark green above, downy or whitened beneath,** 5-13 cm long; catkins expanding much before the leaves, the staminate 4-8 cm long, the pistillate oval, about 1.2 cm long in fruit; winged nutlet round. Flowers in April, May. Wet soil, common in the mountains above the 2,600-foot contour. Often forming vast thickets in glady regions.

WINTER

A shrub up to 6 m high, with hairless twigs; marked (speckled) with light elongate lenticels; fruiting catkins oval, 12 mm long, drooping. Blooms very early, often in March. Wet soil and stream banks at higher elevations.

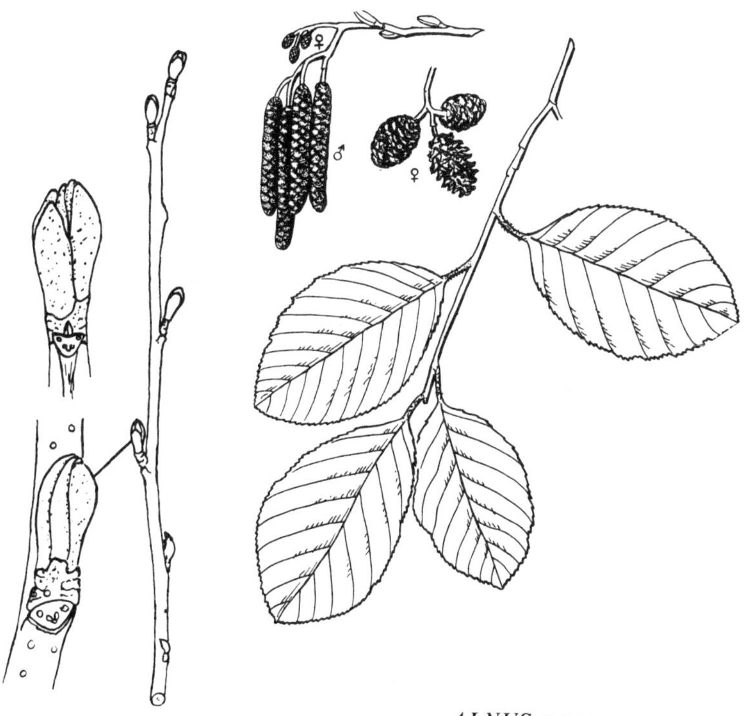

ALNUS rugosa

A. serrulata (Ait.) Willd. (finely saw-toothed), **Smooth Alder. Brookside Alder.**

A shrub or rarely a small tree to 7 m high, the bark smooth; **leaves green on both sides,** oval, usually sharply single-toothed, smooth above, hairy at least on the veins beneath; catkins unfolding much before the leaves, the staminate 5-10 cm long, the pistillate ovoid, 1.2-1.8 cm long in fruit, persistent and cone-like in winter; winged nutlet oval. Flowers in March, April. In wet soil along stream.

WINTER

A shrub up to 7 m high, with smooth bark; fruiting catkins upright, oval, 12-18 mm long; winged nutlet oval. Blooms as early as February or March. Stream-margins at lower elevations.

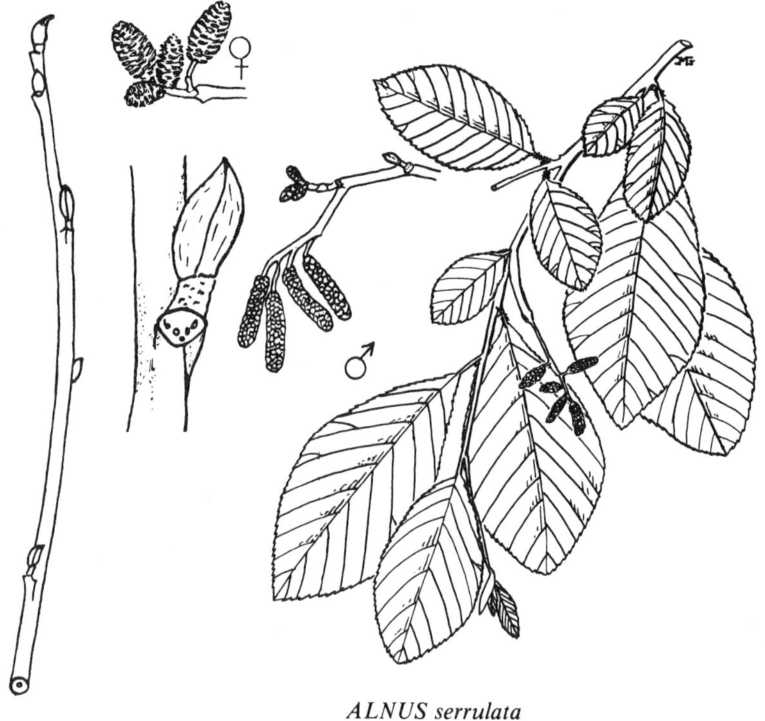

ALNUS serrulata

FAGUS L. Beech

Deciduous trees with smooth, tight, gray bark. Twigs slender, round, zig-zag, pith continuous. Buds elongate, spindle-shaped, the lateral ones almost at right angles to the twig, with 10 or more scales. Leaves alternate, simple, strongly straight-veined, the veins forming prominent ridges on the lower side of the leaf. Staminate flowers in small heads on drooping stalks. Pistillate flowers usually in pairs at the ends of short stalks, surrounded by numerous bractlets which fuse to form a 4-part bur. Fruit a triangular nut with two or three fruits per bur.

F. grandifolia Ehrn. (large-leaved), **American Beech.**

A forest tree to 36 m high with a diameter of 9 dm; **bark smooth, close, light gray, often with included woody nodules;** twigs hairless, **buds long, red-brown;** leaves oval, firm, papery in texture, 5-12 cm long, densely silky when young, smooth or somewhat silky at maturity, coarsely to slightly toothed; heads of staminate flowers 1.2-1.8 cm in diameter, hanging on stalks 2.5-7.5 cm long; bur 1.2-2 cm high, prickly; nut brown and triangular; seed sweet. Flowers in April, May. Rich soil.

WINTER

Trees with distinctive **smooth, light gray bark, even on old, mature trees.** Buds usually single, sessile or short-stalked, elongate spindle-shaped, standing at nearly right angles to the twig, positioned to the side of the leaf-scar, reddish brown with 10 or more scales spirally arranged. Twigs round, zigzag; with small, round, continuous pith. Leaf scars alternate, small, semicircular; bundle traces 3 to many; stipule scars elongate, nearly encircling the twig. **Buds very similar to those of serviceberry but differ in having many more scales and in their right angle position to the twig.**

FAGUS grandifolia

CASTANEA Mill. **Chestnut**

Large deciduous trees with furrowed bark. Twigs grooved, pith continuous, angled. Leaves alternate, simple, sharp-toothed, straight-veined. Staminate flowers in erect or spreading yellowish catkins. Fruit a one-seeded nut, with 2-3 nuts in a bur covered with very sharp, branched spines.

C. dentata (Marsh.). Borkh. (toothed), **American Chestnut**

A forest tree formerly to 30 m high, and 2 m in diameter, with brown bark in longitudinal plates; **leaves oblong lance-shaped, hairless, firm, coarse-toothed with very sharp-pointed teeth,** 1.2-3 dm long; **burs very sharp-spiny,** 4-10 cm in diameter, **enclosing 2 or 3 nuts; 1-2.5 cm wide, very sweet. Flowers in June, July. Rich, sandy loam; now occurs mostly as root sprouts.**

WINTER

Formerly large deciduous trees but found now mostly as root sprouts. Buds single, ovoid, placed obliquely over the leaf scar, sessile, 2 or 3 scales visible, the terminal bud sometimes missing. Twigs grooved, chestnut brown; pith continuous, angled. Bark brown in longitudinal plates. Leaf scars alternate, semicircular; with 3- to many bundle traces; stipule scars of unequal length. **Nuts usually 3 contained in a prickly bur.** Common as root sprouts in woods. **Bark on sprouts somewhat shiny and almost black (or blackish gray).**

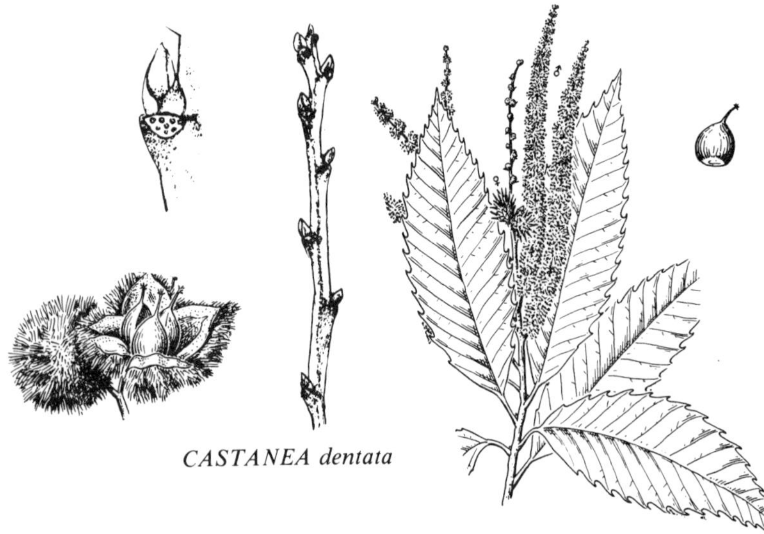

CASTANEA dentata

QUERCUS L. **Oak**

Deciduous (our species) trees or shrubs with alternate, simple leaves; **multiple terminal buds,** twigs with star-shaped pith, and deciduous stipules. Staminate flowers in catkins. Pistillate flowers solitary or somewhat clustered, enclosed by scales which become a hardened cup around the base or the fruit (a nut commonly called an acorn).

SUMMER KEY

a. Fruit maturing in one growing season; lobes of the leaves rounded to sharp, but never having bristle-tipped lobes. (**White Oaks**) .. b

a. Fruit maturing at the end of the second growing season; leaves pinnately lobed with bristle-tipped lobes. (**Red or Black Oaks**) d

b. Leaves more or less deeply lobed. Mature leaves smooth on both surfaces, deeply and evenly lobed, the sinuses narrow; acorn 2-3 cm long, having a cup with warty scales covering about ¼ of the acorn. Bark ashy gray and somewhat platy. .... ***Q. alba***

b. Leaves coarsely wavy toothed or shallowly lobed (**Chestnut Oaks**) c

c. Acorn long-stalked; cup very thin and having indistinct warty scales, cup covering about ½ of the acorn; leaves with rounded teeth or shallowly lobed, eliptical or nearly so; bark hard, very deeply and coarsely furrowed. .... ***Q. prinus***

c. Acorn sessile or nearly so; leaves oblong, lance-shaped, coarsely toothed (teeth not as rounded as in ***Q. prinus***; bark like that of ***Q. alba***) .... ***Q. muehlenbergii***

d. Mature leaves green on both sides. .... e

d. Mature leaves whitish or grayish beneath, straggling shrub 1-5 mm high. .... ***Q. ilicifolia***

e. Lateral lobes of the leaves about as long as the undivided portion of the blade. .... f

e. Lateral lobes of the leaves usually much longer than the undivided portion of the blade; cup strongly convex on the bottom covering ¼ to ½ of the acorn, all the cup scales tight; acorn usually with one or more concentric rings below the apex; (rings appear as fine hairline cracks at the acorn tip) leaves hairless except for tufts of hairs in the angles of the veins underneath. .... ***Q. coccinea***

f. Leaves thin; acorn 2-3 cm long, the scales of the cup tight throughout, the cup forming a shallow "saucer" and covering very little of the acorn. Terminal buds essentially hairless and round in cross section. .... ***Q. rubra***

f. Leaves firm; acorn 1.5-2.5 cm long, the scales at the rim of the cup loose, the cup coverig ½ or a little more of the acorn. Terminal buds usually hairy and 5-sided in cross section. ...... ***Q. velutina***

WINTER KEY

a. Fruit maturing the first season; shell of acorn smooth on the inner surface. (**White Oaks**). .... b

a. Fruit maturing the second season; shell of acorn hairy on the inner surface; acorn cups sessile or short-stalked. (**Black or Red Oaks**) .... d

b. Buds broadly ovoid, rounded; mostly 2-4 mm long, reddish brown; twigs gray to purple; bark of young branches not peeling off in scales; bark thick, light gray or white, mostly with shallow fissures and irregular flat scales or sometimes with scaly ridges; acorn cups thick with raised warty scales, bowl-shaped, sessile or on short stalks. .... ***Q. alba***

b. Buds narrow, pointed or blunt, lateral divergent, terminal ones mostly 5 mm long or more; twigs orange to reddish brown; branchlets without corky ridges; acorn cups not fringed by sharp extensions of the scales. c

c. Twigs slender or stout, hairy or hairless; bark thick with irregular fissures and grayish or brownish scales; (bark greatly resembling that of ***Q. alba***) acorn cups thin, shallow, cup-shaped, sessile or nearly so; bud scales chestnut brown with white, scarious margins. .... ***Q. muehlenbergii***

c. Twigs stout, hairless; bark "steel" gray to dark brown to black, thick, with broad continuous fissures and solid sharp-angled ridges without scales; acorn cup thin, hemispheric, with indistinct warty scales; cup with a short stem. .... ***Q. prinus***

d. Buds large, terminal ones usually over 4.5 mm long. .... e

d. Buds small; terminal ones usually less than 4.5 mm long. Twigs dull and hairy during the first winter; buds hairless; bark gray to dark brown; acorn cups saucer-shaped or with rounded base. .... f

e. Buds usually covered with dense wool, yellowish gray, prominently angled; bark of trunk black, rough, with deep fissures and irregular ridges which are broken crosswise, inner bark yellowish-orange; twigs glabrous; acorn cups top-shaped to hemispheric; covering ½ or a little more of the acorn; cup scales loose at the rim. ***Q. velutina***

e. Buds not covered with dense wool, not prominently angled, blunt or rounded, reddish brown, smooth or wooly above the middle; acorn cups top-shaped to hemispheric, covering about ½ of the acorn, cup scales all tight. One or more concentric rings, appearing as hairline cracks usually present at the tip of the acorn. ***Q. coccinea***

f. Buds blunt, hairless or hairy; shrubs. .... ***Q. ilicifolia***

f. Buds acute, slightly hairy above the middle or not; trees; inner bark pinkish to whitish. .... ***Q. rubra***

Q. alba L., **White Oak**

A forest to 35 m high, and 2 m in diameter; **mature leaves pale and whitened beneath, lobes rounded and base of indentations rounded,** oblong, obliquely cut into 5-9 lobes; **acorn ovoid, 2-3 cm long, the cup bowl-like, with raised warty scales, much shorter than the acorn.** Flowers in May, June. Rich moist soil. The most economically important species of the white oak group.

WINTER

An important timber tree up to 35 m high and 2 m in diameter; twigs gray to purplish, often with a whitish coating, buds spherical to oval, hairless, about 5 mm long; bark dark gray, very rough; **acorn oval, 2-3 cm long, the cup bowl-shaped, with raised warty scales, much shorter than the nut.** Rich woods, the most important hardwood tree in many areas.

QUERCUS alba

Q. muehlenbergii Engelm. **Yellow Oak, Chinquapin Oak.**

A tree up to 25 m high and 9 dm in diameter; **leaves somewhat resembling those of chestnut oak but with sharp lobes,** the bark resembles that of white oak; sun leaves lance-shaped, shade leaves oval, the margin coarsely toothed with gland-tipped teeth; **acorn spherical or oval, 1.2-2 cm long, the cup thin, enclosing about ½ the acorn.** Flowers in May, June. Dry hillsides, generally on limestone soils (not common).

WINTER

A tree up to 25 m high and 9 dm in diameter; with tight gray bark, becoming flaky on mature trees; twigs dark orange-brown; **acorn spherical or ovoid, 1-2 cm long, sessile or almost so, the cup enclosing about ½ the nut;** buds 3 mm long, oval, smooth or with brown wool, the bud scales often with pale margins. Dry slopes especially in limestone regions.

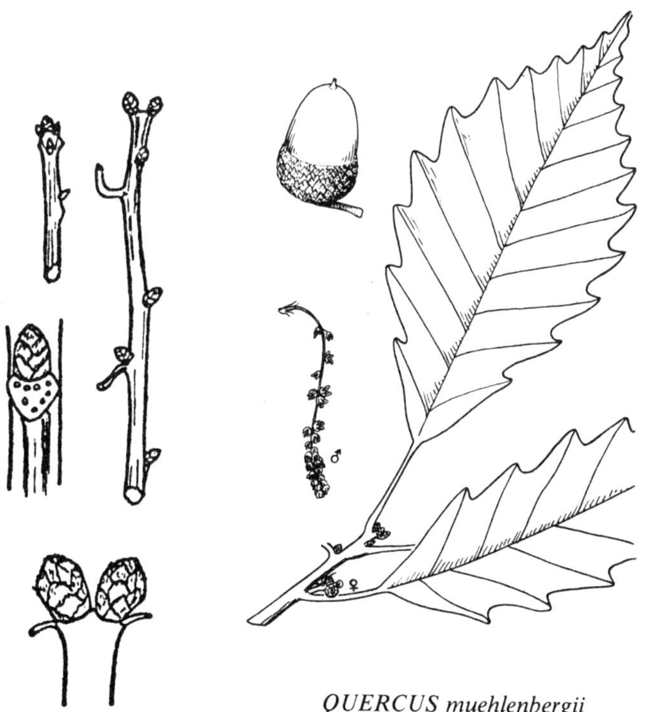

QUERCUS muehlenbergii

Q. prinus L. (*Q. montana* Willd.), **Chestnut Oak, Rock Oak**

A tree to 30 m high and 2 m in diameter; wood hard, strong; **leaves thick, oblong or lance-shaped, wavy round-toothed, pale and finely downy beneath; acorn 2.5-3.5 cm long, ovoid enclosed by a thin cup having indistinct warty scales, covering one third to ½ of the acorn.** Flowers in May, June. Dry shaly hillsides and ridges.

WINTER

A tree up to 30 m high and 2 m in diameter; buds cone-shaped, 6 mm long, dark brown, dull, outer scales with pale margins; twigs brown; bark steel-gray to blackish, thick and deeply grooved, hard; acorn 2.5-3.5 cm long; oval, the thin cup covering one third or more of the nut. Dry woods.

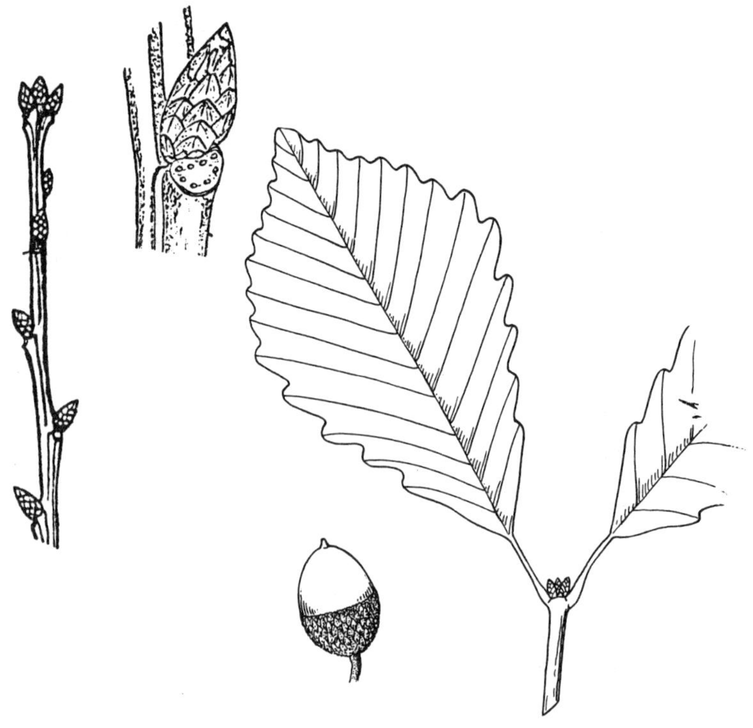

QUERCUS prinus

Q. rubra L. **Northern Red Oak**
(*Q. borealis* Michx.)

A forest tree to 30 m high and 2 m in diameter; wood heavy, strong; leaves thin, turning red in autumn, moderately lobed; **acorn 2-3 cm long, ovoid (usually) or ellipsoid, the cup shallow and saucer-shaped with tight scales,** 1.8-3 cm broad. Flowers in May, June. A characteristic species of the cove hardwood community.

WINTER

A large tree up to 30 m high and 2 m in diameter; buds reddish, slightly hairy above the middle, about 5 mm long; twigs smooth; bark smooth, greenish brown, becoming broken into flat-topped usually grayish ridges on older trees; inner bark pinkish to white; acorn 2-3 cm long, oval with a shallow, saucer-shaped cup. An important tree in coves and moist woods.

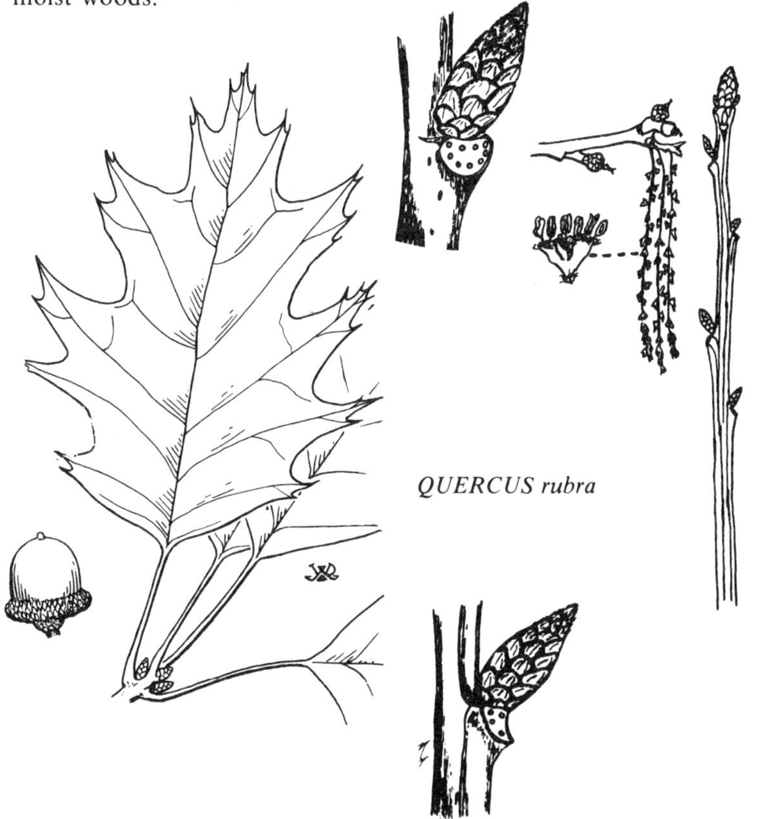

QUERCUS rubra

5. *Q. coccinea* Muench. **Scarlet Oak**

A tree to 30 m high and 9 dm in diameter; wood hard, strong; leaves oval, the margin deeply 5-9-lobed, with wide, nearly circular angles, brilliant scarlet in autumn; **acorn 1.5-2.2 cm long, sub-spherical or oval, usually with a few concentric rings about the apex, acorn one third to ½ enclosed in a bowl-like cup, the scales tight.** Flowers in May, June. Dry sandy soil of hillsides and ridges.

WINTER

A tree up to 30 m high and 9 dm in diameter; buds silky, brownish red, 5-6 mm long; twigs hairless; bark rough, dark gray, to black (resembling northern red oak in younger trees and black oak in older trees); younger trees usually with dead, drooping lower branches, the inner bark reddish; **acorn 1.3-2 cm long, spherical or oval, usually with concentric rings about the apex; cup bowl-like, enclosing one third to one half of the nut, the scales tight.** Dry ridges.

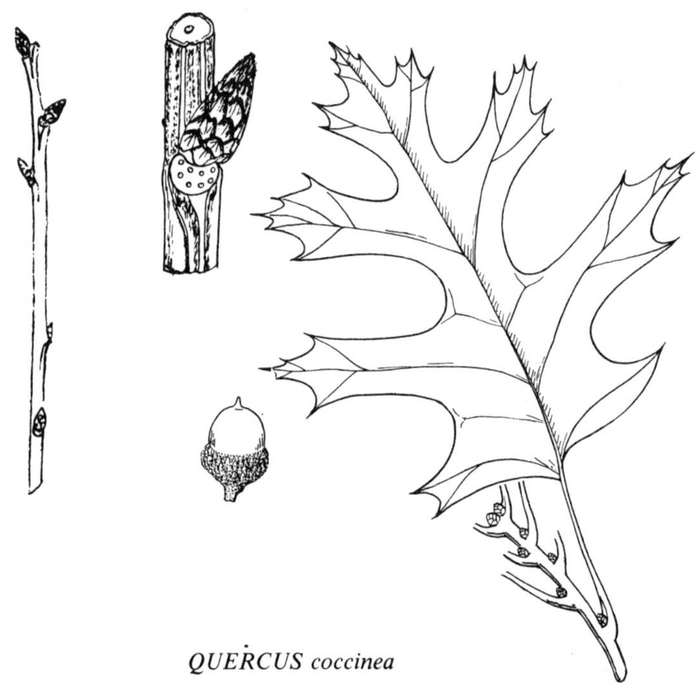

QUERCUS coccinea

6. ***Q. velutina*** Lam. **Black Oak**

A forest tree to 35 m tall and 12 dm in diameter; wood hard, strong; leaves firm, oval, with 5-7 lobes separated by angles of variable depth, some leaves in upper part of crown with very deep sinuses resembling those of scarlet oak, shade leaves in lower part of crown with shallow or no sinuses; **leaves lustrous and dark green on top, scurfy-hairy beneath;** acorn 1.2-2.2 cm long, often hairy, 1/4 to 1/3 enclosed in a bowl-like cup, the scales loose at the rim. Flowers in May, June. Dry soil of slopes or ridges.

WINTER

A tree to 35 m tall, with a diameter up to 12 dm; buds 7-10 mm, hairy, terminal buds angled in cross section; bark dark brown to black, rough with low ridges, **with bright orange-yellow inner bark;** acorn oval to round, 1-2 cm long, brown, often hairy; cup deeply bowl-shaped. Dry ridges and hillsides.

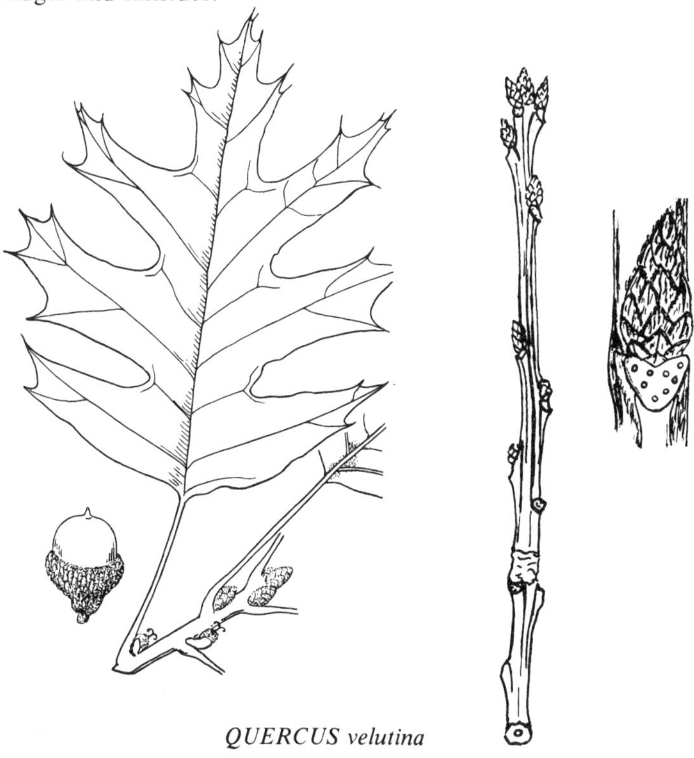

QUERCUS velutina

Q. ilicifolia Wang. **Scrub Oak, Bear Oak, Turkey Oak**

A straggling shrub or low tree to 6 m high and 15 cm in diameter, **often forming dense thickets; leaves firm, oval, wedge-shaped at base, about 5-lobed, downy white beneath, the lobes short and triangular;** acorn spherical-ovoid, 1-1.2 cm long, about half enclosed by the saucer-shaped cup. Flowers in May. Dry soil of slopes and mountain tops.

WINTER

A low, straggling shrub 6 m high, usually forming dense thickets; buds 4 mm long, hairless; twigs hairless; acorn round to oval, 1-1.2 cm long, the cup bowl-shaped. **The red-brown, dry leaves often persist through winter and locally called "red brush."** Dry soil of slopes and mountain tops.

QUERCUS ilicifolia

ULMUS L. **Elm**

Trees with zigzag twigs, continuous pith and 2-ranked, alternate double-toothed leaves (our species), oblique or unequally heart-shaped at base; buds oblique over the leaf scar. Leaf scar with 3 dotlike bundle scars that are sunken. Flowers without petals, appearing before the leaves; ovary flattened. Calyx 4-9 lobed. Fruit a flat, round or oval winged structure with the seed in the center (a samara).

SUMMER KEY

a. Leaves very rough above; flowers short-pedicelled; fruit hairy on the seed cavity but not on the edges of the wing; shallowly notched at apex; young twigs rough to the touch. .... 1. ***U. rubra***

a. Leaves smooth to slightly rough above; flowers long-pedicelled; fruit densely hairy on the edges of the wing but not on the seed cavity, fruit deeply notched at apex, young twigs not rough to the touch. .... 2. ***U. americana***

WINTER

Large deciduous trees with simple, alternate leaves. Buds single or clustered, oval, sessile, not centered over the leaf scar, no terminal bud; scales usually 6, in 2 rows. Twigs slender, zigzag, round; with small round continuous pith. Leaf scars alternate, sickle-shaped or semicircular; bundle traces 3 or more, in sunken pits; stipule scars of unequal length.

WINTER KEY

a. Buds with fine hairs, dark gray to nearly black; twigs rough, light gray, cross sections of outer bark do not show alternating white and brown layers. .... ***U. rubra***

a. Buds reddish brown, smooth or with pale hairs; twigs reddish brown, smooth or with few hairs; cross sections of bark show alternating brown and white layers. .... ***U. americana***

U. rubra Muhl. (red), **Slippery Elm, Red Elm**

A tree to 24 m high and 7 dm in diameter with tough, reddish wood; wood hard; young twigs rough-hairy; **leaves oblique at the base, rough above and somewhat rough below,** 1-2 dm long; flowers nearly sessile; **fruit 1.2-1.8 cm long, hairy over the seed, otherwise hairless, the margins not hairy.** Flowers in March, April. On lower slopes and bottomlands, and dry, limy upper slopes.

WINTER

A tree up to 24 m high and 7 dm in diameter. Buds nearly black with fine red hairs; twigs gray to tan; rough, hairy; tough reddish wood; **outer bark corky, rough; gray to brownish, without white layers, the inner bark very mucilaginous** (whence the name slippery elm); flowers appear very early in March; sessile with several in a group. Moist soil of lower slopes and dry, limy, upper slopes.

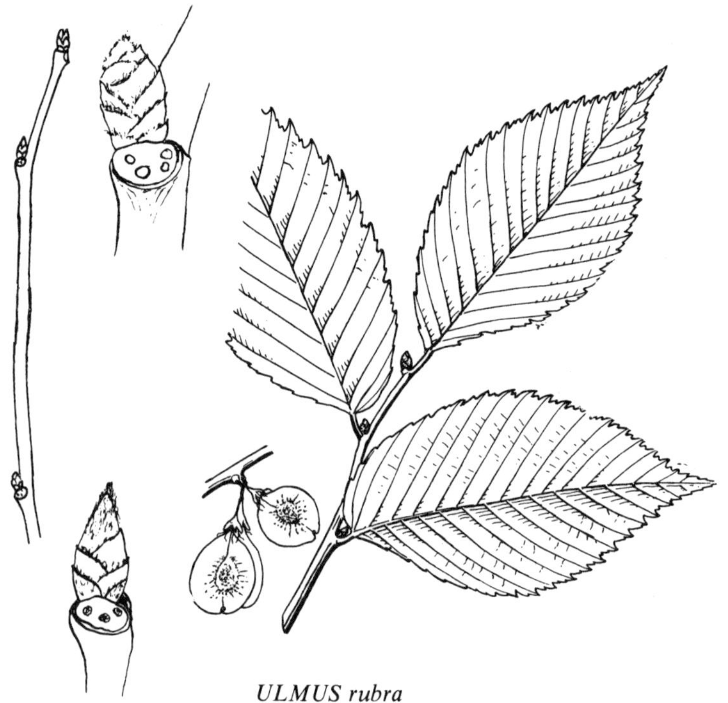

ULMUS rubra

U. americana L. (American), **American Elm**

A handsome tree to 35 m high and 18 dm in diameter, usually with a very distinctive spreading vase-shaped crown in somewhat open situations and with somewhat drooping branchlets; wood hard; **leaves oblique at the base, smooth above, velvety below,** 5-10 cm long; flowers in close clusters, on slender drooping stalks; **fruit 1.2 cm long, hairy on the margin of the wing.** Flowers in March, April. Moist rich woods, especially on river bottomlands.

WINTER

A large spreading tree, vase-shaped, to 35 m high and 18 dm in diameter; buds brown, hairless or somewhat hairy; reddish brown twigs smooth or sparsely hairy; branchlets drooping, **bark gray, flaky, cross sections of the ridges with alternating white and brown layers;** flowers appear in March, long-stalked, in small groups of 3 or 4. Mostly on river bottomlands and rich lower slopes.

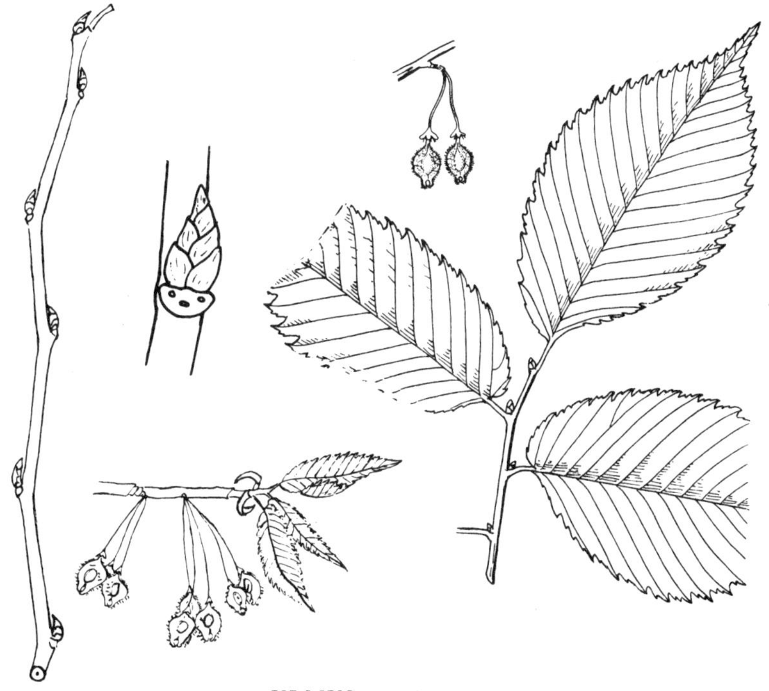

ULMUS americana

CELTIS L. **Hackberry**

Deciduous trees with alternate, simple leaves and rounded slender twigs with small white pith, finely chambered at the nodes and continuous in the internodes. Leaves toothed or nearly entire. Flowers without petals, calyx of 4-6 parts, separate or united. Two stigmas. Fruit one-seeded with a thin fleshy covering.

C. occidentalis L. (western), **Hackberry**

A tree to 28 m high and 7 dm in diameter, the **bark dark, rough, corky-ridged or warty;** wood heavy, soft; buds, small 3-4 mm long, closely appressed against the twig; leaves oval-lance shaped, usually conspicuously taper-pointed, more or less oblique at base, sharply toothed, 3-12 cm long; staminate flowers numerous, the pistillate usually solitary; fruit round or oval; black when mature, 8-10 mm in diameter, wrinkled in drying, the flesh sweet and edible but very thin, the pit conspicuously lined. Flowers in April, May. Most common on limestone soils at lower elevations.

WINTER

A tree up to 28 m high and 7 dm in diameter. Bark very dark, rough, warty, with corky ridges. Buds 3-4 mm long, sessile, solitary, ovoid, with about 4 scales lying close against the twig. Twigs rounded, slender; pith small, white, round, finely chambered at the nodes. Leaf scars alternate, crescent-shaped or eliptical; bundle traces 1 or 3; stipule scars narrow. **Trees often with clusters of deformed branches called "witch's brooms."**

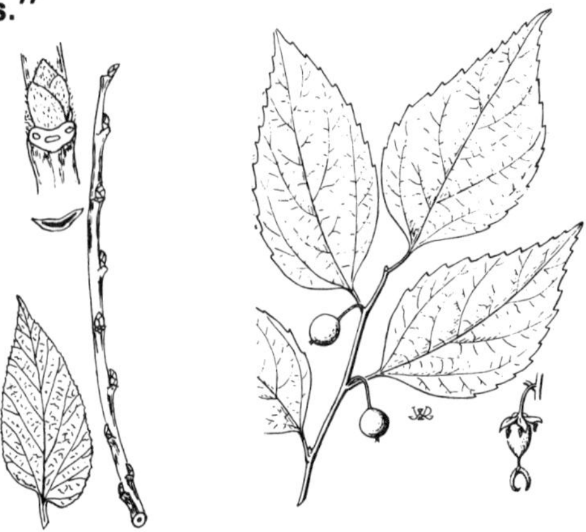

CELTIS occidentalis

MORUS L. **Mulberry**

Trees with alternate, simple, 2 or 3 lobed or unlobed, toothed leaves. Flowers without petals. Fruit an edible multiple of drupes (resembles a blackberry).

M. rubra L. (red), **Red Mulberry**

A tree up to 20 m high and 2 m in diameter; bark brown and rough; wood light, soft; **leaves heart-shaped oval or (especially on young trees) 2-3 lobed, toothed, rough above, downy beneath;** fruit dark purple, 2.5-4 cm long, delicious. Flowers in April, May. Rich woods. May be dying out because of disease.

WINTER

Trees up to 20 m high and 2 m in diameter. Buds 6-8 mm long, sessile, single, or in clusters, oval, oblique over the leaf scar, with 3-6 scales; no terminal bud; bud scales brown, on the margin. Twigs round with fine hairs; pith round, continuous. Leaf scars alternate, roundish; bundle traces many, scattered or in 3 groups; stipule scars narrow. Bark rough, dark brown. Rich slopes.

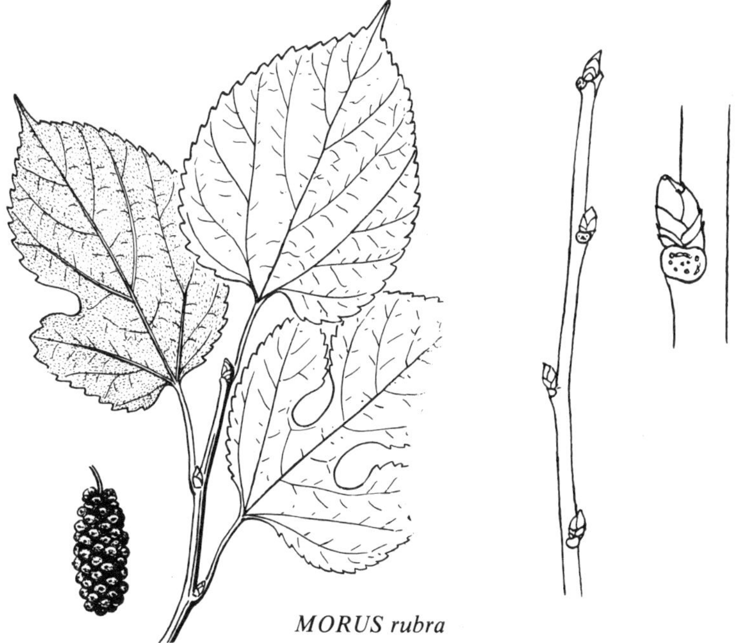

MORUS rubra

LAPORTEA Gaud. **Nettle**

Perennial herbs with stinging hairs, the leaves broad, alternate, toothed. Flowers in loose branched inflorescences. Staminate flowers with 5 sepals and 5 stamens. Pistillate flowers with 4 unequal sepals and a pistil with a single style. Fruit oblique.

L. canadensis (L.) Wedd. (of Canada), **Wood Nettle**

Stem 6-9 cm high; **leaves alternate,** oval, pointed, 7-15 cm long, **long-petioled;** flower clusters large and loose, the pistillate divergent. **Upper stems, leaves and petioles with numerous stinging hairs.** Flowers in July, August. Rich woods.

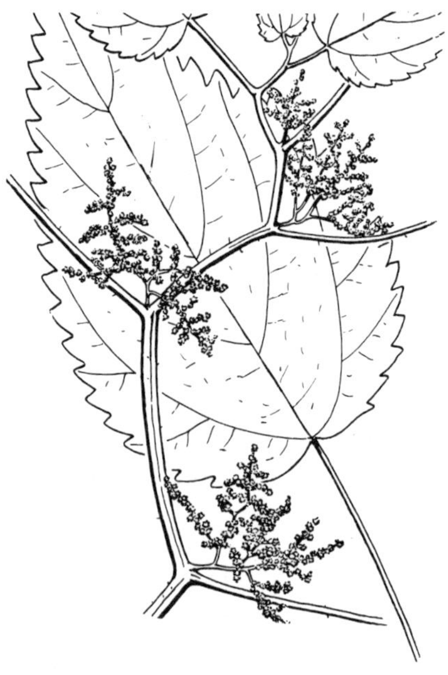

LAPORTEA canadensis

URTICA L. **Nettle**

Annual and perennial herbs with stinging hairs, opposite, toothed or cut stipulate leaves and numerous small flowers. Staminate flowers with a 4-parted calyx and 4 stamens. Pistillate calyx 4-parted, the segments unequal.

a. Leaves broadly oval, heart-shaped at base, coarsely toothed; staminate and pistillate flowers chiefly in separate inflorescences many times longer than the petioles. .... ***U. dioica***

a. Leaves elongate to long-oval, rounded at base. .... ***U. gracilis***

U. dioica L. (dioecious), **Stinging Nettle**

Common Nettle. A very bristly and stinging perennial, 6-20 dm high; **leaves opposite 5-15 cm long, oval, heart-shaped at the base, pointed-toothed, downy beneath, with numerous stinging hairs on both surfaces and the internodes,** the petioles less than half the width of the leaves; inflorescences much branched, staminate and pistillate flowers on the same or separate plants. flowers in July-September. Introduced from Europe, perhaps for use as greens and now occasionally established along roadsides, fence rows, or about old homesteads.

URTICA dioica

U. gracilis Ait. (slender), **Wild Nettle**

(Includes ***U. procera*** Muhl.). **Leaves opposite** typically lance-shaped, rounded at base; **upper internodes nearly without stinging hairs.** Flowers in July-September. Moist ground along streams.

URTICA gracilis

PYRULARIA Michx. **Buffalonut**

Shrubs with thin deciduous leaves and small flowers. Pistillate and perfect flowers with the calyx attached to the oval ovary. Fruit a drupe.

P. pubera Michx. (pubescent) **Buffalonut, Oilnut**

A straggly shrub to 4 m high, downy when young; leaves alternate, simple, oval-oblong, sharp-pointed, entire margined, soft, 8-13 cm long; flowers greenish, in few-flowered spikes; calyx 5-cleft; **fruit pear-shaped,** 2.5 cm long, **with a very acrid oil.** Flowers in May. Rich woods especially in the southern counties.

WINTER

Small shrubs partially parasitic on roots of other woody plants. Buds oval, brown. Leaf scars alternate, rounded with 3 bundle traces, stipule scars none. Twigs comparatively large, round with conspicuous lenticels in the bark, hairy when young; pith large, round. Conspicuous branch scars are also present. These contain numerous bundle traces in an oval. **The soft leaves are very frost hardy and persist into early winter as green leaves after most other species have dropped their leaves.** Rich woods, not common except locally.

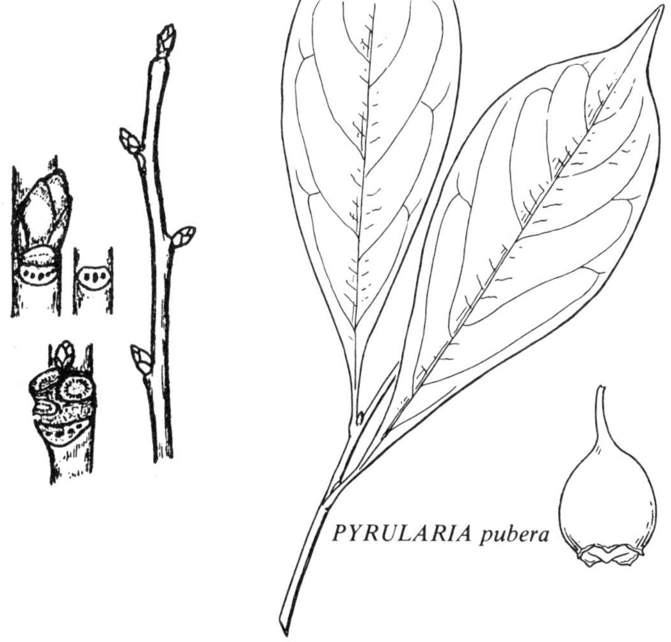
PYRULARIA pubera

ARISTOLOCHIA L. **Pipevine**

Perennial herbs or twining vines. Leaves alternate, entire, heart-shaped. Flowers irregular. Calyx 3-6-lobed. stamens mostly 6. Ovary inferior, 6-celled; style 3-6-lobed. Fruit a many-seeded capsule.

A. macrophylla Lam. (large-leaved) **Pipevine, Dutchman's Pipe**
(***A. durior*** Hill)

A twining vine, the stem sometimes 10 m or more long and to 5 cm in diameter, **climbing high into trees; leaves round heart-shaped, thin, hairless, 1-4 dm broad; flowers 3 cm long, curved like a Dutch pipe, yellowish green or brown-purple;** capsule oblong-cylindric, 5.5-8 cm long. Flowers in May, June. Rich woods, especially in northern hardwood forests.

WINTER

Large deciduous vine, climbing into the treetops. Buds small, rounded, growing on a silky scar-like area, covered by finely haired scales; no terminal bud. Stems round, smooth, green, with swollen nodes; pith large, round, continuous, light colored. Leaf scars alternate, thinly U-shaped; with 3 bundle traces; no stipule scars. Common in northern hardwood forests. **may be distinguished from grape by the smooth, green stems.**

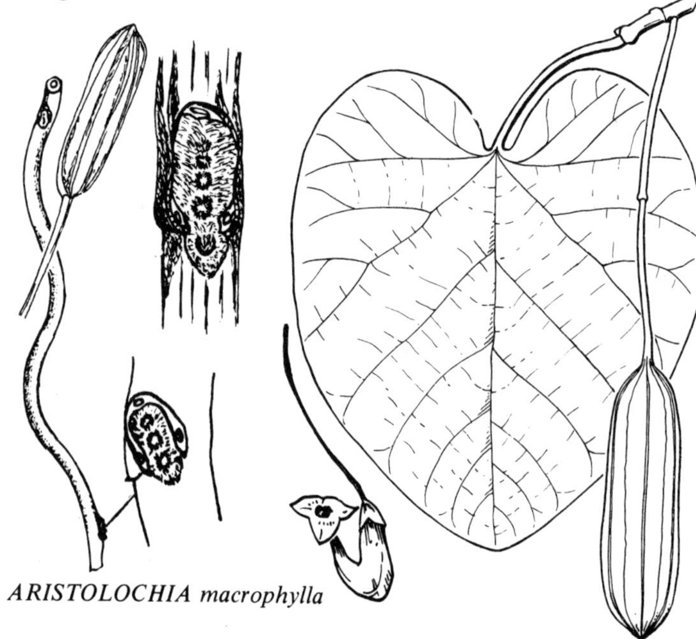

ARISTOLOCHIA macrophylla

RUMEX L. **Dock**

Annual or perennial herbs with grooved, mostly erect stems and entire or wavy margined leaves; thin, brittle sheath on the stem above the nodes. Flowers green, perfect or imperfect. Calyx 6-parted, the outer 3, unchanged in fruit, the 3 inner ones develop into wings, one or all often bearing a grain-like nodule. Stamens 6. Style 3-parted; fruit 3-angled.

R. obtusifolius L. (blunt-leaved), **Broadleaf Dock, Bitter Dock**

Perennial, smooth, dark green, 1-2 m high, somewhat scurfy above; lower leaves oblong, lance-shaped, 1.5-3.5 dm long, blunt at the base, the veins often red, the upper lance-shaped, smaller, sharp-pointed; flowers loosely whorled in branched inflorescences; **calyx wings arrow-shaped, fringed with spreading teeth, one of them bearing a nodule.** Flowers in June-August. A common weed.

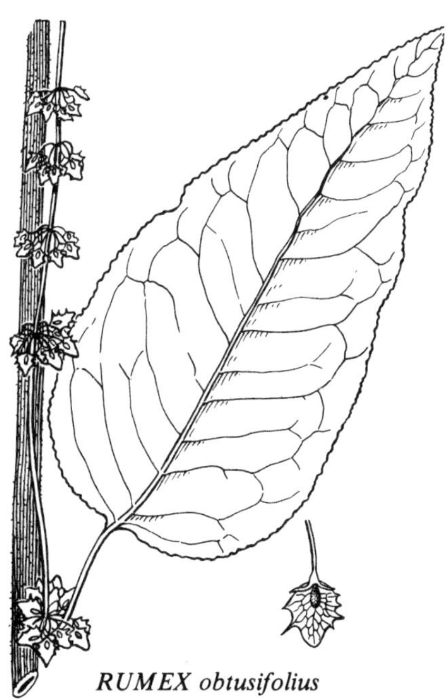

RUMEX obtusifolius

POLYGONUM L. **Bindweed**

Herbaceous erect or twining plants. Leaves alternate; leaf sheaths arising above the swollen nodes. Calyx 4-6 parted, the divisions often petal-like. Stamens 3-9. Styles or stigmas 2 or 3. Fruits lens-shaped or triangular. The plants often are infected with smut.

P. scandens L. (climbing), **Climbing False Buckwheat**

Perennial, stem smooth, to 6 m long, striped, rough on the ridges; leaves heart-shaped or lance-shaped, pointed, 5-13 cm long; inflorescences interrupted, leafy; **flowers greenish yellow; calyx 5-parted, the outer lobes strongly keeled and broadly winged in fruit,** 8-10 mm long, the wings often crisped; fruit smooth and shining, 3.5-6 mm long. Flowers in August-September. Moist, open woods.

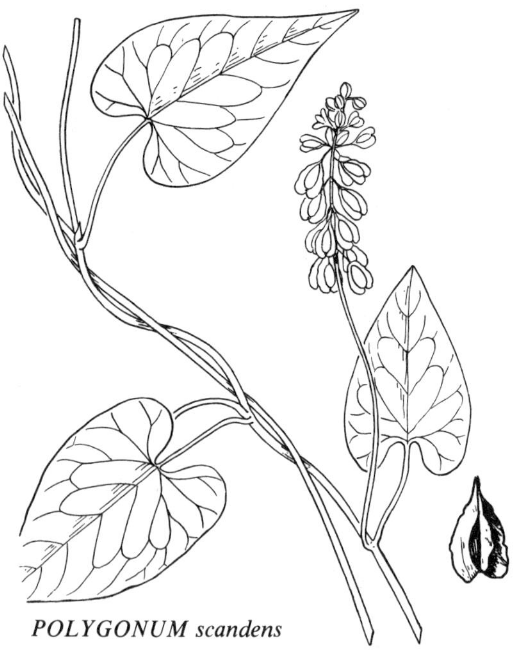

POLYGONUM scandens

PHYTOLACCA L. **Pokeweed**

Tall perennials with alternate leaves and small flowers. Calyx petal-like. Ovary of 5-15 cells. Fruit a 5-15-celled juicy berry.

P. americana L. (American), **Pokeweed**

A smooth, unpleasantly-scented plant 1.2-3.6 m high, arising from a **thick poisonous root; calyx white,** 4-6 mm broad; ovary green, 10-celled; **berries in long racemes, dark purple,** 10-12 mm in diameter; **ripe in autumn.** Flowers in July-September. A common weed in low ground and rich soil.

PHYTOLACCA americana

CLAYTONIA L. **Spring Beauty**

Perennials with simple stems arising from deep tubers, leaves two, opposite; flowers in loose-branched inflorescences. Sepals 2, oval, persistent. Petals 5. Stamens 5. Style 3-cleft at the apex. Capsule 3-6-seeded.

a. Leaves oval. .... ***C. caroliniana***
a. Leaves elongate, lance-shaped. .... ***C. virginica***

C. caroliniana Michx. (of Carolina), **Carolina Spring Beauty**

Stems 0.3-3 dm long; **its two leaves oval or oblong, 2.5-5 cm long, 0.5-3.3 cm wide; flowers white or pink with deeper stripes.** Flowers in March-May. Rich moist woods.

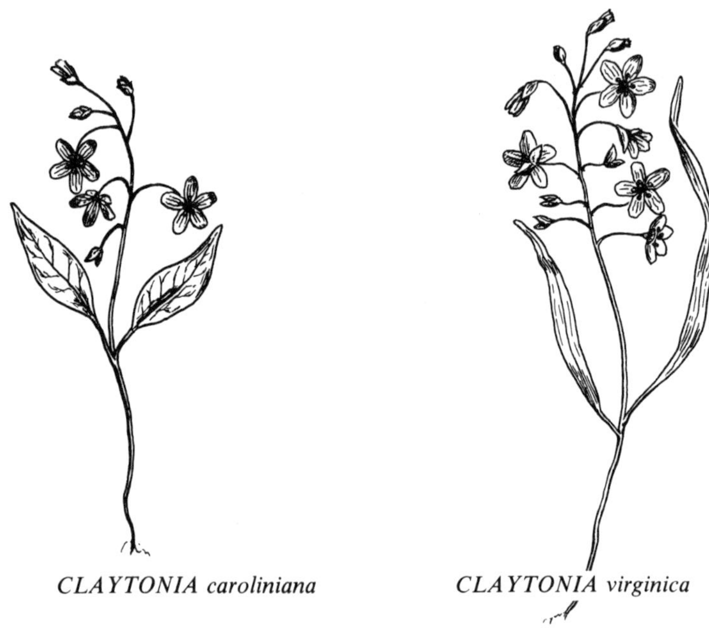

CLAYTONIA caroliniana *CLAYTONIA virginica*

C. virginica L. (of Virginia), **Spring Beauty**

Stems upright or trailing 1.5-3 dm high; **its two leaves narrow, elongated, 7-15 cm long, 0.2-1 cm wide;** raceme terminal; **flowers** 1.2-2 cm broad, **white or pink, with darker pink veins.** Flowers in March-May. Rich moist woods. **Distinguished from the preceding by the slender leaves.**

RANUNCULUS L. **Crowfoot, Buttercup**

Annual or perennial herbs, with alternate leaves and yellow or white flowers. Sepals 5. Petals usually 5, with a small nectar-bearing pit at the base. Stamens numerous. Pistils numerous.

R. recurvatus Poir. (bent backward, referring to the styles)
Hooked Crowfoot

Stem long, hairy, 3-6 dm high, basal leaves and stem leaves nearly alike, long-stalked, deeply 3-cleft, the divisions again variously cleft, 5-7.5 cm wide, flowers 8-10 mm broad; petals pale yellow, shorter than the sepals; **fruit beak strongly hooked.** Flowers in May-June. Common in rich woods.

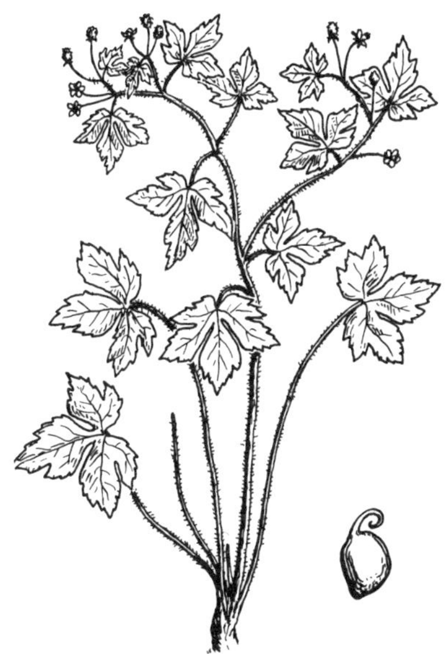

RANUNCULUS recurvatus

ACTAEA L. **Baneberry**

Erect, perennial herbs with tri-compound leaves and small flowers in terminal clusters. Sepals 3-5, petal-like, falling off quickly. Petals 4-10, small, narrow. Stamens numerous. Pistil single.

A. pachypoda Ell. (having thick pedicels), **White Baneberry, Doll's Eyes**

Erect, 3-6 dm high; leaves tri-compound, the leaflets generally deeply incised; petals slender, abruptly cut off at the end; **flower stalks red, thickened in fruit, as large as the stalk of the inflorescence; berries spherical, white, with a dark spot.** Flowers in April-June. Frequent in rich woods.

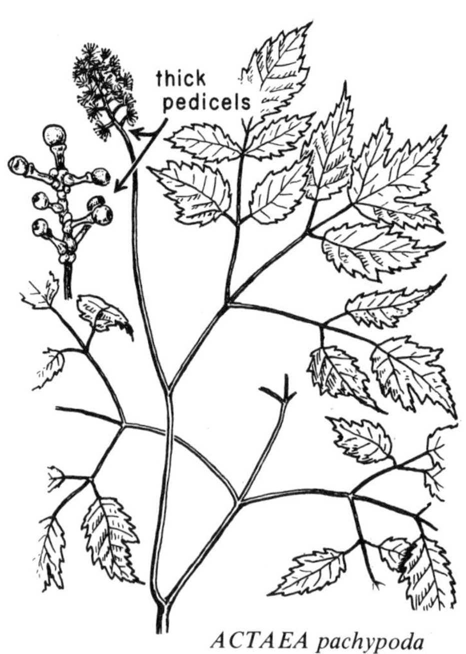

ACTAEA pachypoda

PODOPHYLLUM L. **Mayapple**

Erect, perennial herbs with horizontal rootstocks, each stem bearing 2 large umbrella-like lobed leaves and a solitary flower. Sepals 6, with a slender point. Petals 6-9, oval, longer than the sepals. Stamens twice the number of the petals; stigma large, sessile, thick and wavy; ovary oval-shaped; fruit a large fleshy berry (the May "apple"). Seeds numerous, each one enclosed in a fleshy covering.

P. peltatum L. (shield-shaped), **Mayapple**

Plant 3-4 dm high; basal leaves long-petioled, deeply 5-9-lobed, lobes 2-cleft and toothed at the apex; flowerless stems terminated by a leaf; **flowering stems bearing 2 lopsided leaves, and a nodding white flower from the fork;** fruit ovoid, 2.5-5 cm long, yellow when mature; ripe in July, sweet and slightly tart, edible, slightly poisonous to some persons. Flowers in May. Rich woods, thickets, and old pastures.

PODOPHYLLUM peltatum

MAGNOLIA L. **Magnolia**

Trees or shrubs. Leaves large, alternate, simple, and entire. Flowers large, fragrant. Sepals 3, petals 6-12. Pistils united, forming a cone-like fruit, each carpel when ripe opening on the back from which the 1 or 2 scarlet seeds hang by a thread.

SUMMER KEY

a. Leaves unlobed, hairy beneath, at least when young. .... b
a. Leaves lobed at the base, hairless. .... ***M. fraseri***

b. Leaf buds silky-haired; leaves scattered along the branches. .... ***M. acuminata***
b. Leaf buds hairless; leaves clustered at the ends of the flowering branches. .... ***M. tripetala***

WINTER

Large trees with deciduous leaves (all our native species). Buds single, oval, or spindle-shaped, with a single scale; twigs relatively thick, round; pith large, continuous, round, with periodic firmer plates. Leaf scars alternate, roundish or U-shaped; usually with a leaf scar at the base of the terminal bud; bundle traces several, scattered; stipule scars linear, conspicuous, completely encircling the twig.

WINTER KEY

a. Leaf buds with silvery, silky hairs. .... ***M. acuminata***
a. Leaf buds not hairy. .... b

b. Terminal buds over 3 cm long. .... ***M. tripetala***
b. Terminal buds less than 3 cm long. .... ***M. fraseri***

M. acuminata L. (acuminate), **Cucumber Tree, Cucumber Magnolia**

A tree to 30 m high, with a trunk to 18 dm in diameter; wood light, soft, close-grained (almost identical to that of Yellow Poplar); leaves 15-25 cm long, 7.5-10 cm wide, thin, oval, sharp-pointed; flowers greenish yellow, 5 cm wide; petals oval or oblong, much exceeding the sepals; fruit conelike, (cucumber-like when immature) upright, cylindric, 7.5-10 cm long, about 2.5 cm in diameter. Flowers in May, June. In rich soil of bottoms, coves and hillsides. **Leaf buds silvery, silky-haired; leaves scattered along the branches.**

WINTER

A tall tree up to 30 m high and 18 dm in diameter; twigs moderately large; **leaf buds silvery silky,** 10-20 mm long; leaf scars horseshoe-shaped. Bark brown, furrowed, soft and flaky; remains of fruit commonly found on the ground under the tree in winter. Rich coves and slopes. **Our only forest tree having silvery-haired buds.**

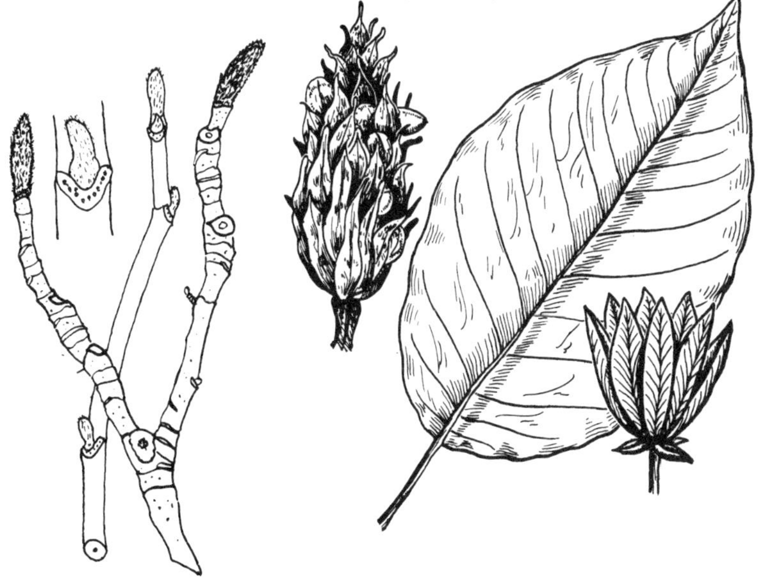

MAGNOLIA acuminata

M. tripetala L. (with 3 petals, alluding to the 3 petal-like sepals), **Umbrella Tree, Umbrella Magnolia**

A tree to 18 m high, with a trunk 4 dm in diameter; **leaves** 3-4.5 dm long, 1-2 dm wide, oval, sharp-pointed, **crowded in umbrella-like clusters on the ends of the branches;** flowers 2-2.5 dm in diameter, white, fragrant; sepals early-deciduous; conelike fruit 1-1.5 dm long. Flowers in May. Rich woods.

WINTER

A small tree up to 18 m tall and 4 dm in diameter; leaf buds smooth, purplish, 2.5 cm long, very large and sharp-pointed; leaf scars comparatively large, oval. Rich woods at lower elevations.

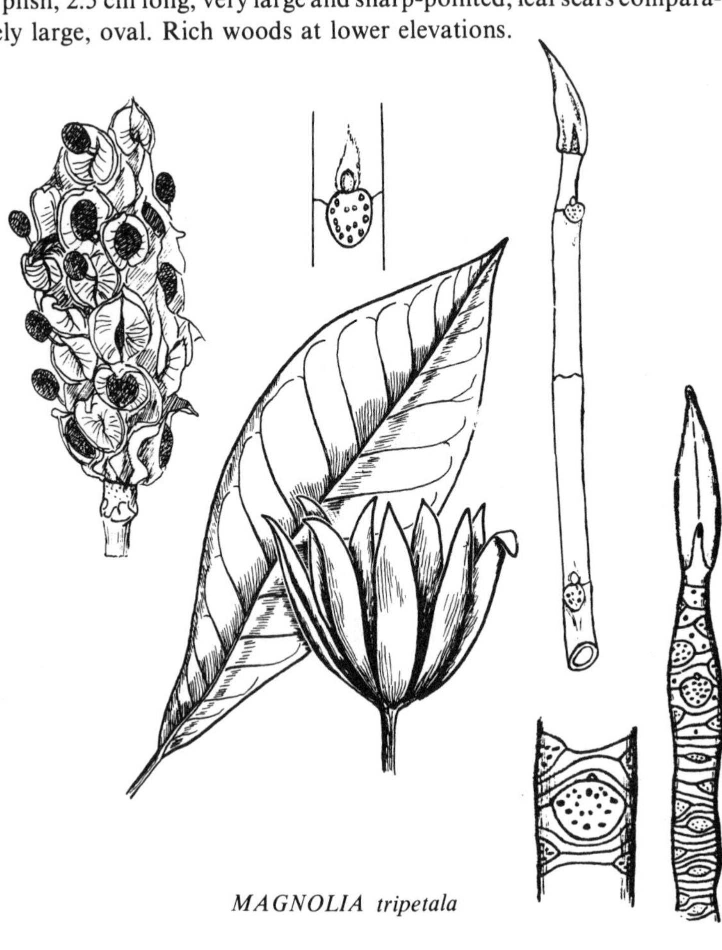

MAGNOLIA tripetala

M. fraseri Walt. (for John Fraser, 1750-1811),
Mountain Magnolia, Fraser Magnolia

A small tree to 15 m high, with trunk up to 6 dm in diameter, and branches widely spreading; **leaves lobed at the base** 1.5-5 dm long, 7.5-20 dm broad; petals much exceeding the sepals; fruit 7.5-20 cm long, the seeds bright rose color. Flowers in May, June. Common in rich woods in the mountains, especially along streams.

WINTER

A tree up to 15 m tall and 6 dm in diameter; **leaf buds smooth, purplish,** small up to 5 cm long; twigs smooth and whitened, slender; leaf scars alternate, somewhat rounded; bark smooth, dark brown. Rich woods, especially in northern hardwoods and along mountain streams.

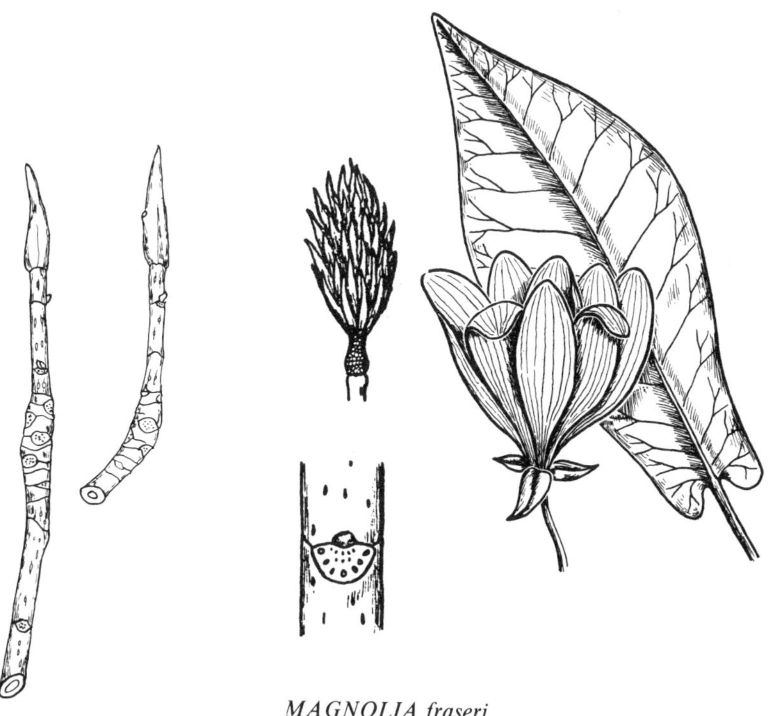

MAGNOLIA fraseri

LIRIODENDRON L. **Tuliptree, Yellow-poplar**

A large tree with simple, alternate, 4-6-lobed, entire leaves. Flowers; large, greenish yellow, fragrant. Sepals 3, petal-like. Petals 6. Fruit an aggregate of winged fruitlets on an elongated receptacle.

L. tulipifera L. (tulip bearing) **Tuliptree, Yellow-poplar, Tulip-poplar**

A beautiful tree 18-60 m high, with a trunk 1-3 dm in diameter, and a conical crown; wood light, soft; **leaves broadly notched at the apex,** 7.5-15 cm long, with 2 apical and 2 basal lobes; **flowers about 5 cm wide, erect, tulip-like, greenish yellow, orange within. Fruit an upright aggregate of winged fruitlets, 7.5 cm long.** Flowers May-June. Rich soil. An important tree, especially in cove hardwoods.

WINTER

Large, important trees. Buds single or superposed, the **terminal buds large, oblong, stalked, flattened, duckbill-shaped; with 2 non-overlapping scales.** Axilliary buds small, sessile. Twigs round with rounded, whitish continuous pith with periodic firmer plates. Leaf scars alternate, large, almost round; bundle traces several, scattered; stipule scars conspicuous, encircling the twig. Bark smooth with whitish spots or lines on young trees. On older trees, strongly ridged and without the whitish spots or lines. **Fruits cone-like, persistent in winter and visible in the tops of the tallest trees.** An important tree in rich coves and slopes.

LIRIODENDRON tulipifera

ASIMINA Adans. **Pawpaw**

Shrubs or small trees, usually aromatic buds naked; leaves alternate, entire, pinnately veined. Flowers solitary in the axils, corolla attached below the ovary, calyx of 3 sepals; corolla of 6 thickish petals in 2 rows. Stamens indefinite. Pistils several or many, separate, or coherent, fleshy or pulpy in fruit.

A. triloba (L.) Dunal. (three-lobed) **Pawpaw**

Shrub or tree, with an unpleasant odor when bruised; to 14 m high and 25 cm in diameter; **leaves acute at apex,** 1.5-3 dm long, gradually tapering from near the apex to the base; **flowers axillary, appearing with the leaves,** 2.5-4 cm in diameter, **at first greenish yellow, turning to a dark wine-red color; corolla of 6 thickish petals in two rows,** outer petals spreading, almost circular, slightly longer than the oval inner ones; stamens numerous; **fruit a pulpy berry, 3-15 cm long, 2.5-5 cm thick, sweet, edible, brown when ripe.** Flowers in March, April. Mature fruit in September and October. Moist rich soils at lower elevations. The long slender feather-like terminal buds are without leathery scales and are reddish brown in summer.

WINTER

Small trees up to 14 m high and 25 cm in diameter. The feather-like terminal buds without scales; leaf buds oblong, flower buds spherical. Buds are chocolate brown in winter. Twigs round, moderate-sized; pith in young twigs round, white, continuous, in two-year-old twigs firmer with greenish plates at intervals, and often brown and chambered in older twigs. **Leaf scars alternate, half-round or U-shaped; bundle traces 5,7, or more; no stipule scars.** Rich woods, often forms thickets.

ASIMINA triloba

SASSAFRAS Nees. **Sassafras**

Trees with rough bark, greenish branchlets, and variably shaped leaves, the entire plant spicy aromatic. Trees with staminate and pistillate flowers on separate plants, with a 6-parted spreading calyx, staminate flowers with 9 stamens in 3 rows, the 3 inner having a pair of stalked glands at the base of each; pistillate flowers bearing 6 rudimentary stamens and an oval ovary.

S. albidum (Nutt.) Nees. (whitish) **Sassafras**

May form a tree to 30 m high and 1.8 m in diameter but usually a small scraggly tree, **the young shoots yellowish green; wood soft, aromatic; leaves oval, entire, unlobed or 2-3-lobed, some of them mitten-shaped, aromatic;** flowers greenish yellow, about 6 mm broad, appearing with the leaves, drupe oval, blue, borne on a cone-shaped, rather fleshy, reddish stalk. Flowers in April. Woods and thickets especially common in old fields.

WINTER

Usually small trees, rarely large. Buds usually single, oval, sessile, circular; scales usually 4. **Twigs bright green,** hairless, rounded; bark very aromatic, pith white, continuous. Leaf scars alternate, small, semicircular or sickle-shaped; bundle trace a single horizontal line sometimes appearing as 3; stipule scars none. **The upward curve of the outer branches usually distinctive. Bark gray on young trees turning quite reddish on older ones.** Usually very common in old fields.

SASSAFRAS albidum

LINDERA Thunb. **Spicebush**

Shrubs with alternate, entire leaves and perfect or imperfect yellow flowers in lateral, sessile clusters surrounded with bracts, appearing before the leaves; entire plant with a spicy odor. Calyx 6-parted; staminate flowers with 9 stamens in 3 rows, the inner filaments gland-bearing at base; pistillate flowers with 15-18 rudimentary stamens in 2 forms, and a spherical ovary. Drupe oval, the stalk not thickened.

L. benzoin (L.) Blume (old name for some member of this family)
Spicebush or **Spicewood**

Hairless shrub with a spicy odor, up to 5 m high and 6 cm in diameter; **drupe red when ripe,** 8-10 mm long, about 6 mm in diameter. Flowers in March-May. In damp woods and along streams. The fruits mature in August and September. Small, stalked, co-lateral flower buds are green in late summer and fall.

WINTER

Small shrubs up to 5 m high and 6 cm in diameter. Buds small, superposed; flower buds co-lateral, green to reddish; round, stalked; no terminal bud. Twigs hairless, rounded, slender, greenish, with relatively large, round, white, continuous pith. Leaf scars small, alternate, sickle-shaped or semi-round, small, with 3 bundle traces; stipule scars none. **Fruit a smooth oval or oblong drupe turning from green to scarlet and wrinkled and blackish with frost. Leaves, fruit and twigs with a distinct, spicy odor.** Moist woods especially along streams.

LINDERA benzoin

DICENTRA Bernh.

Low herbs with dissected leaves, nodding flowers. Petals 4, in 2 pairs, slightly cohering into a heart-shaped or 2-spurred corolla. Stigma 2-crested or 2-horned. Style slender. Capsule oblong or elongate; seeds crested.

a. Inflorescence simple, few flowered; flowers white or whitish. .... b
a. Inflorescence compound, clustered; flowers pink (rarely white. .... ***D. eximia***

b. Spurs widely divergent, inner petals slightly crested. ***D. cucullaria***
b. Spurs short, rounded; inner petals conspicuously crested. .... ***D. canadensis***

D. cucullaria (L.) Bernh (hoodlike) **Dutchman's Breeches**

Delicate, smooth herb, arising from a scaly bulbous base; leaves basal, pale beneath, slender-petioled, thrice compound; stalk of the inflorescence slender, 12.5-25 cm high; inflorescence one-sided, 4-10 flowered; flowers 12-16 mm long, 16-20 mm broad at base, white or faintly pink, yellow at the summit. Flowers in April, May. Common in rich woods.

DICENTRA cucullaria

D. canadensis (Goldie) Walp. (Canadian) **Squirrel Corn**

Delicate herbs arising from subterranean shoots bearing scattered grain-like yellow tubers the size of peas; corolla narrowly heart-shaped, greenish white, tinged with pink, spurs very short and rounded; crest of the inner petals conspicuous, projecting. Flowers in April, May. Common in rich woods. **May be distinguished from the preceeding species by the grain-like tubers and the shorter rounded petal spurs.**

DICENTRA canadensis

DICENTRA eximia

D. eximia (Ker) Torr. (choice) **Wild Bleeding Heart**

Smooth, slightly whitened, weak herb, 2.5-6 dm high; leaves basal, thrice parted; stalk of the inflorescence slender, about equaling the leaves; flowers pink, nodding, about 1.6-2 cm long, 6-8 mm broad at base. Flowers in May-September. Rocky places in the mountains.

SEDUM L. **Stonecrop**

Mostly smooth, fleshy-leaved perennials, erect or trailing, with alternate, entire or toothed leaves, and perfect flowers in terminal, often one-sided inflorescences. Stamens 8-10. Fruits many-seeded.

S. ternatum Michx. (in threes) **Stonecrop**

Stem creeping, with flowering branches 7.5-20 cm high; **leaves fleshy;** lower leaves and those of the sterile shoots flat, oval, 1.2-2.4 cm long, upper leaves oblong, alternate, sessile; **inflorescence 2-4-forked, its branches spreading or recurved in flower;** petals elongate sharp-pointed, 8-10 mm long, nearly twice the length of the sepals; fruits 5 mm long. Flowers in April-June. Damp rocky places.

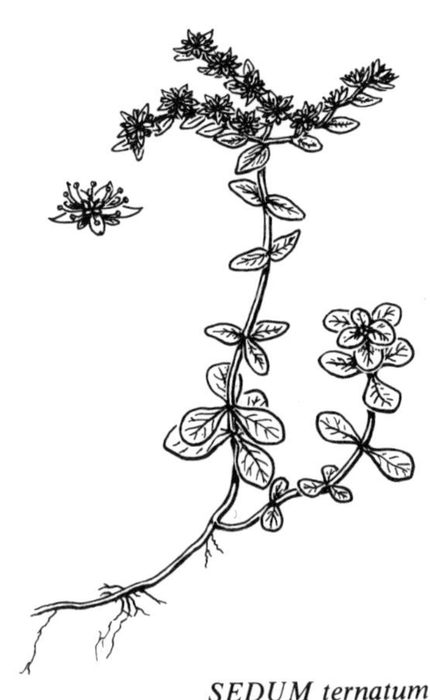

SEDUM ternatum

TIARELLA L. **Foamflower**

Low perennial herbs with mainly basal leaves and flowers in an open inflorescence. Calyx bell-shaped, 5-parted. Petals 5, clawed. Stamens 10, long and slender. Ovary one-celled, styles 2. Capsules thin, one-celled.

T. cordifolia L. (heart-leaved) **Foamflower, False Miterwort**

1.5-3 dm high, slender, hairy; leaves broadly ovate or nearly round, heart-shaped at base, 3-7-lobed, sparsely hairy above, downy beneath, 5-10 cm long, toothed; inflorescence glandular, minutely hairy; flowers white, about 6 mm broad; petals oblong, entire or somewhat toothed, clawed, slightly exceeding the calyx lobes; capsules bend downward, about 6 mm long. Flowers in April-July. In rich woods.

TIARELLA cordifolia

HYDRANGEA L. **Hydrangea**

Shrubs with opposite simple petioled leaves and flowers in a flat-topped inflorescence, usually sterile, consisting merely of a showy white calyx. Perfect flowers small. Calyx tube hemispherical, attached to the ovary, the blade 4-5-toothed; petals 4 or 5, ovate. Stamens 8-10. Ovary 2-4-celled. Capsule thin, 15-ribbed, 2-celled below, many-seeded.

H. arborescens L. (becoming tree-like) **Wild Hydrangea**

Shrub up to 3 m high; **leaves oval, thin, 7.5-15 cm long, sharp or long-pointed at the tip, heart-shaped or broadly wedge-shaped at the base, sharply toothed; inflorescences flat-topped** 5-12.5 cm broad. Flowers in June, July. In woods, rocky slopes, or stream banks.

WINTER

Small shrubs up to 3 m high. Buds single, sessile or short-stalked, spherical to oblong, with 4 to 6 scales. Twigs round, relatively light, thick, smooth; pith large, round, continuous. Leaf scars opposite, crescent-shaped, large, often continuous by lines around the stem; bundle traces 3, 5, or 7; no stipule scars. Fruit a tiny, thin-walled capsule, persistent in winter. Rich woods and borders.

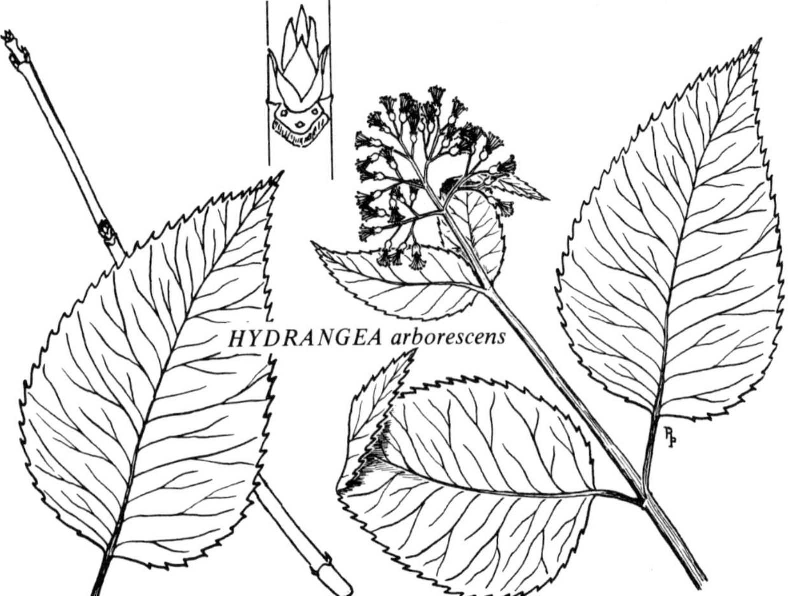

HYDRANGEA arborescens

RIBES L. **Gooseberry, Currant**

Low, sometimes prickly shrubs with alternate leaves, often clustered on the branches. Inflorescences few-several-flowered; the flower stalks joined beneath the ovary, usually with a pair of bractlets just below the joint. Calyx 5-lobed, often colored, the tube attached to the ovary. Petals 5, small, inserted in the throat of the calyx. Stamens 5. Ovary 1-celled, with 2 placentas on the sides of the ovary. Fruit a fleshy, edible berry. All native members of this genus are alternate hosts for white pine blister rust.

SUMMER KEY

a. Inflorescences few-flowered (1-5); stems usually bearing spines at the base of the leaf clusters (gooseberries). .... b
a. Flowers several in elongated inflorescences; stems unarmed; ovary and fruit glandular, bristly (currants). .... ***R. glandulosum***

b. Calyx-lobes much shorter than the tube; berries unusually prickly. .... ***R. cynosbati***
b. Calyx lobes equaling or exceeding the tube, 5-7 mm long; stamens much exceeding the calyx lobes; flowering stalks elongate; spines none or single (rarely 3). .... ***R. rotundifolium***

WINTER

Shrubs with peeling outer bark. Buds small, single, sessile or short-stalked, oval or spindle-shaped, covered with about 6 scales. Twigs round, spiny in some species, ridged lengthwise below the nodes; pith large, whitish, round, continuous but becoming porous when mature. Leaf scars alternate, U-shaped with 3 bundle traces; stipule scars absent.

WINTER KEY

a. Stems erect or arching. .... b
a. Stems trailing, with a skunk-like odor. .... ***R. glandulosum***

b. Buds elongate, spindle-shaped, 3 mm long, downy, dull brown; leaf scars very narrow; nodal prickles 2-5 mm long. ***R. rotundifolium***
b. Buds elongate, spindle-shaped, 5-6 mm long, dull brown; leaf scars very narrow; nodal prickles 5-10 mm long. .... ***R. cynosbati***

R. cynosbati L. (dogberry) **Prickly Gooseberry**

Nodal spines slender, 0.5-1 cm long; prickles of the branches few; weak or none; leaves round-ovate, rounded or heart-shaped at base, 2.5-5 cm broad, deeply 3-5-lobed, inflorescences loose, 2.5-6 cm long; flowers 1-3, green, 6-8 mm long; stamens not extended beyond the corolla; **berry large, armed with long prickles (rarely smooth),** 8-12 mm in diameter. Flowers in May, June. In rocky woods.

WINTER

Erect shrub; branches with slender spines, 5-10 mm long; bud scales silky, keeled. Rocky woods and pastures.

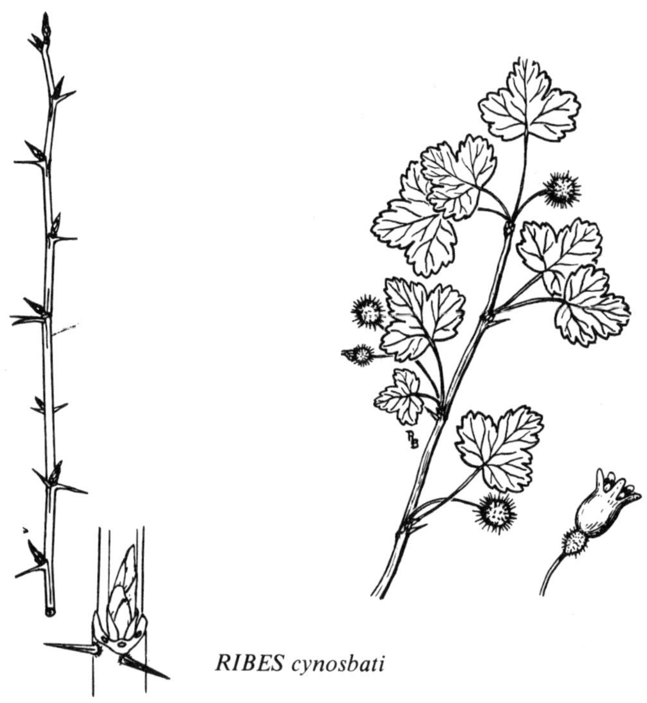

RIBES cynosbati

R. rotundifolium Michx. (round-leaved) **Smooth Gooseberry**

Nodal spines short or none, when present 2-5 mm long; leaves rather firm, subcircular, mostly rounded at base; stalks of the inflorescences short, flowers 1-3, greenish purple, 6-8 mm long; filaments slender, 4-7 mm long; **berry spherical, smooth, purplish, about 8 mm in diameter.** Flowers in April-June. Rocky woods.

WINTER

Erect shrub with short **spines 2-5 mm long;** buds downy; 3 mm long. Rocky woods and pastures.

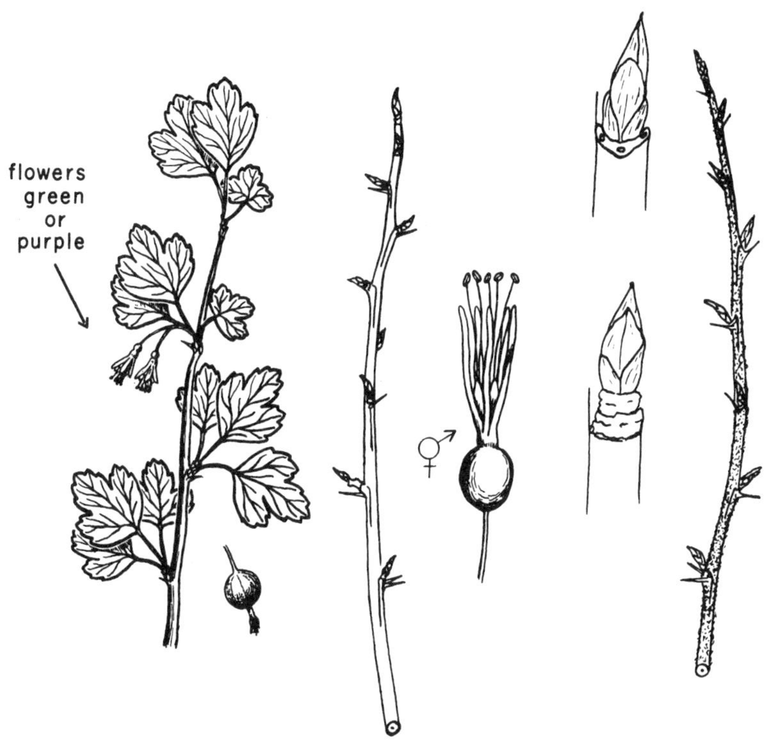

RIBES rotundifolium

R. glandulosum Grauer (glandular) **Skunk Currant**

Branches reclining and spreading, unarmed; leaves subcircular, deeply heart-shaped, 5-7-lobed, smooth, 2.5-7.5 cm wide, the lobes oval, sharp, double-toothed; inflorescences erect, slender; flowers about 5 mm broad; flower stalks 4-5 mm long, glandular; fruit red, glandular, bristly, about 6 mm in diameter. Flowers in May-August. Wet woods, clearings and rocky slopes, especially in northern hardwoods. **Foliage has a distinct skunk-like odor when bruised.**

WINTER

A trailing, very ill-scented shrub; bark blackish; twigs unarmed, smooth. Branches often rooting. Wet woods, particularly in northern hardwoods.

RIBES glandulosum

HAMAMELIS L. **Witch Hazel**

Tall shrubs or small trees, with alternate simple leaves and yellow flowers in small axillary clusters. Calyx 4-5-parted, persistent. Petals 4, strap-shaped, long and narrow. Anther-bearing stamens 4, alternating with 4 scale-like knobs. Capsule woody.

H. virginiana L. (Virginian) **Witch Hazel**

Shrub or rarely a small tree attaining a height of 7 m; twigs smooth or somewhat scaley; leaves simple, short-petioled, oval, wavy toothed, 5-12.5 cm long, usually asymmetrical with left and right sides of the leaf of different shape; **flowers appearing very late in the season when the leaves are falling;** calyx lobes spreading or recurved; the yellow petals about 1.2-1.8 cm long; the two-seeded capsule maturing the second season, beaked with the 2 persistent styles, densely hairy, 6-8 mm long, opening suddenly and throwing out the two black seeds when mature. Flowers and mature fruit occur in September-November. Dry or moist woods and borders of fields. **Our only late fall flowering shrub.**

WINTER

Erect shrubs. **Buds stalked, oblong, densely hairy, rusty, reddish brown,usually with one long and one short bud adjacent at the tip of the twig.** Twigs rounded, zigzag, slender densely hairy with branched hairs to smooth; pith round, small, green continuous. Leaf scars alternate, semicircular or 3-lobed with 3 bundle traces, often compound; stipule scars dissimilar, one rounded, one elongated. the petioles fall normally in autumn and leaving a layer on the leaf scar which falls in spring. Woods, thickets, and borders of fields.

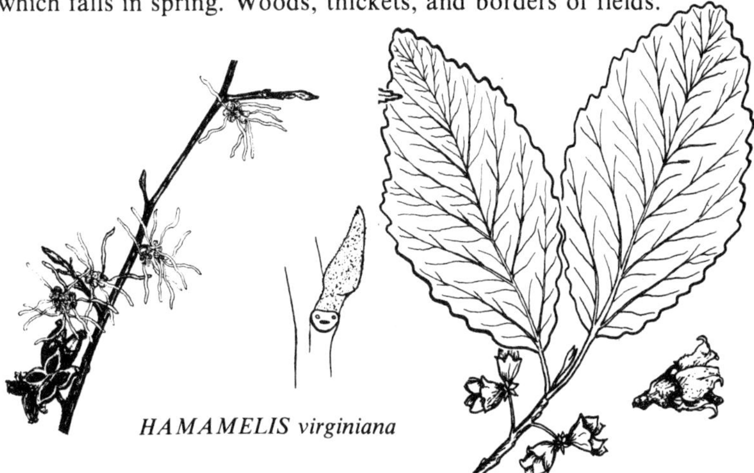

HAMAMELIS virginiana

PLATANUS L. **Sycamore**

Staminate flowers of numerous stamens. Pistillate flowers in separate heads, consisting of inversely pyramidal ovaries. Ripened fruiting heads composed of numerous leathery fruits containing a single seed.

P. occidentalis L. (western) **Sycamore**

A large tree attaining a height of 50 m and trunk diameter of 4 m or more; bark peeling off in thin plates exposing the white to greenish inner layers; wood heavy, hard; leaves mostly truncate at base, 1-2.5 dm wide, 3-5-lobed, densely loose wooly-pubescent with whitish branched hairs when young, less so above and becoming nearly smooth when old; stipules conspicuous on young shoots; **buds completely enclosed within the swollen base of the petiole;** fruiting heads 2.5 cm in diameter, persistent throughout the winter. Flowers in May. Along streams and in low, wet woods. **Easily recognized by the whitish bark exposed by the peeling outer bark.**

WINTER

Large trees. Buds single, rather large, sessile, with a single cone-shaped scale enclosing the bud, green turning reddish brown in winter; no terminal bud. Twigs rounded, hairless, light tan, zigzag; pith round, white or brownish, continuous. **Leaf scars alternate, encircling the buds as a ring;** bundle traces 5-9, stipule scars very narrow, ringing the twig. **Bark sheds in broad scales exposing the smooth, whitish inner bark. Balls of fruits remain most of the winter hanging on long stems.** Characteristic of low moist soil along streams.

PLATANUS occidentalis

SPIRAEA L. **Spiraea**

Shrubs with simple leaves and compound inflorescences. Calyx 5-cleft, short, persistent. Petals 5. Stamens 10-50. Fruits 5-8, not inflated, few-several-seeded.

S. alba DuRoi (white) **Meadowsweet, Pipestem**

Stem hollow, erect, to 2 m high; twigs tough, yellowish brown, more or less angled, hairy at least in the inflorescence; leaves finely toothed, lance-oblong, 5-7 cm long; flowers 6-8 mm broad; petals subcircular, white. Flowers from June-September. Common in wet soil. Used by the Indians for pipestems.

WINTER

Low shrubs with erect, usually hollow branches. Buds small, single or grouped, sessile, spherical to spindle-shaped, covered with about 6 scales. **Twigs tough, rounded, slender, yellowish brown; pith in young twigs, small, round, continuous.** Leaf scars alternate, half-round or crescent-shaped, small with 1 bundle trace. Remains of inflorescence present in the winter.

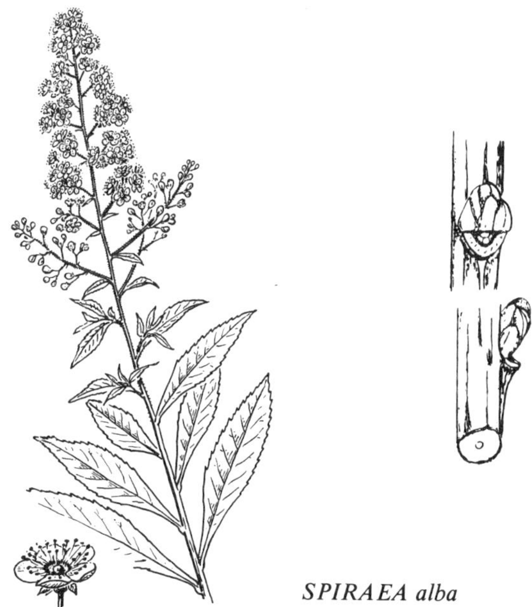

SPIRAEA alba

PYRUS L. **Crab Apples, Chokeberries, Mountain-ash**

Trees or shrubs with alternate, simple or compound leaves and often showy flowers in terminal inflorescences. Calyx tube urn-shaped. Calyx 5-lobed. Petals 5. Stamens usually numerous. Styles 2-5. Fruit apple-like.

SUMMER KEY

a. Leaves simple. .... b
a. Leaves pinnate. .... ***P. americana***

b. Trees or large shrubs, often with spine-like branches; leaves toothed, mostly sharp, hairless when mature; calyx hairless when mature. .... ***P. coronaria***
b. Shrubs with slender ascending to spreading branches. c

c. Lower surface of leaves, young shoots, and flower stalks soft, hairy. .... ***P. arbutifolia***
c. Lower surface of leaves, new shoots, and flower stalks hairless. ... . ***P. melanocarpa***

WINTER

Shrubs or small trees with rounded twigs, ending in sharp points in some species. Buds single, sessile with 4 scales. Pith continuous, angled. Leaf scars alternate, elongated with 3 bundle traces; no stipule scars.

WINTER KEY

a. Shrubs to 3 m tall, growing in patches or clumps; fruits 1 cm in diameter or less, bright red, purple or black, persistent through most of the winter. .... b
a. Trees; trunks not in clumps; over 4 m tall when mature. c

b. Twigs and buds wooly; fruit 4-7 mm in diameter; stalked glands present on sepals of persistent fruits. .... ***P. arbutifolia***
b. Twigs and buds nearly hairless. .... ***P. melanocarpa***

c. Terminal bud large; all buds sticky; twigs with odor of almond when crushed; pith light brown with orange tint. .... ***P. americana***
c. Buds 2-3 mm long, the terminal much longer, the bright, red scales hairy, rough with long hairs on the darker margins or tips; twigs reddish brown, hairless or slightly hairy. .... ***P. coronaria***

P. coronaria L. (suitable for a wreath) **Wild Crab Apple**

A small tree to 9 m high and 3.5 dm in diameter, forming a wide, open crown; branchlets at first white, hairy, later hairless and bright red-brown with thorn-like twigs; buds blunt; leaves oval, sharp, coarsely toothed, 5-7 cm long, 2.5-6.5 cm wide, turning yellow in the autmumn; flowers 3-4 cm broad, white or rose color; styles 5, fruit yellow-green at maturity, 2-2.5 cm in diameter. Flowers in April, May. Slopes, thickets and clearings.

WINTER

Small tree, up to 9 m high and 3.5 dm in diameter; buds cone-like, with hairy scales, sharp-pointed; twigs usually thorn-like, linear leaf scars with 3 bundle traces. Thickets and old pasture fields.

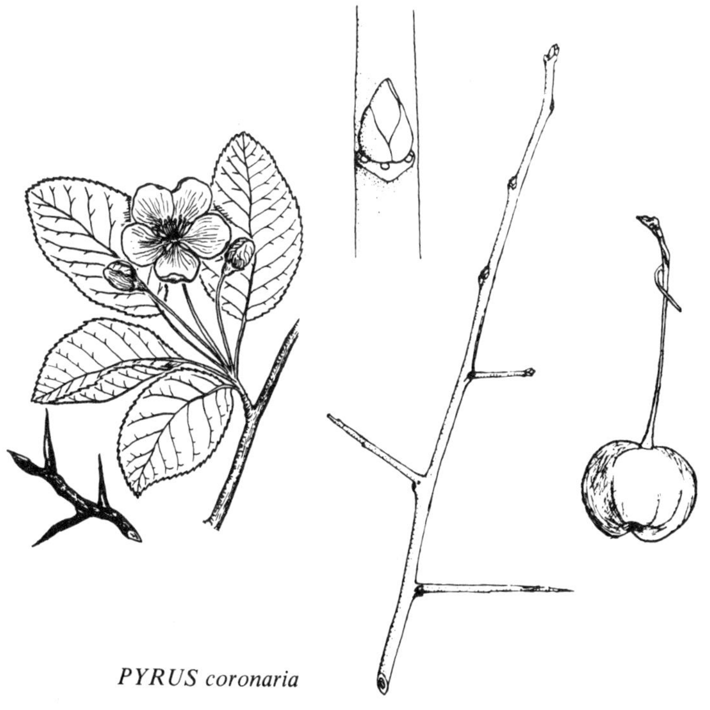

PYRUS coronaria

P. arbutifolia (L.) L.f. (with leaves like Arbutus) **Red Chokeberry**

A shrub to 4 m high, **leaves oblong-elongate, pointed, glandular-toothed, densely hairy beneath,** 2.5-7.5 cm long, red in autumn; flowers white or purplish-tinged, 8-12 mm broad; sepals with stalked glands; fruit red, 5-7 mm in diameter, astringent. Flowers from March-May. Swamps and wet woods especially in the margins of glades and swamps.

WINTER

A small shrub to 4 m high; with wooly buds and twigs; leaf scars with 3 bundle traces; **fruits red, present in early winter.** Edges of swamps and thickets.

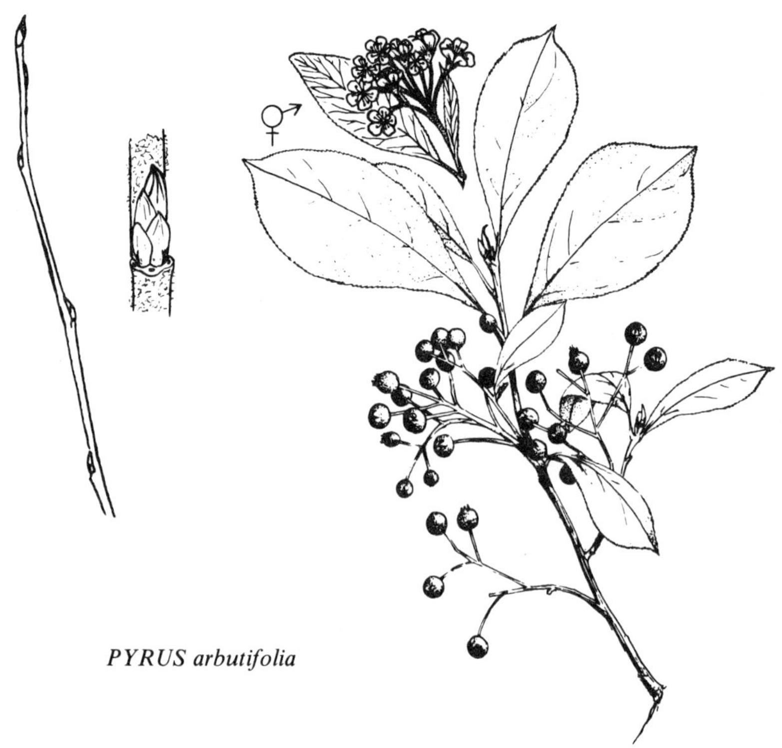

PYRUS arbutifolia

P. melanocarpa (Michx.) Willd. (black fruited) **Black Chokeberry**

A shrub generally somewhat shorter than *P. arbutifolia;* leaves broadly oblong to spoon-shaped, sharp-pointed to scarcely pointed, hairless or nearly so beneath when mature; flowers white or purplish, 8-12 mm broad; fruit spherical, purplish black or essentially black, 6-8 mm in diameter. Flowers in March-June. Moist woods especially in the margins of swamps and glades. Sometimes in rocky uplands.

WINTER

A shrub usually less than 3 m high, buds and twigs hairless; leaf scars with 3 bundle-traces; **fruits black, present in early winter.** Moist thickets and swamp edges.

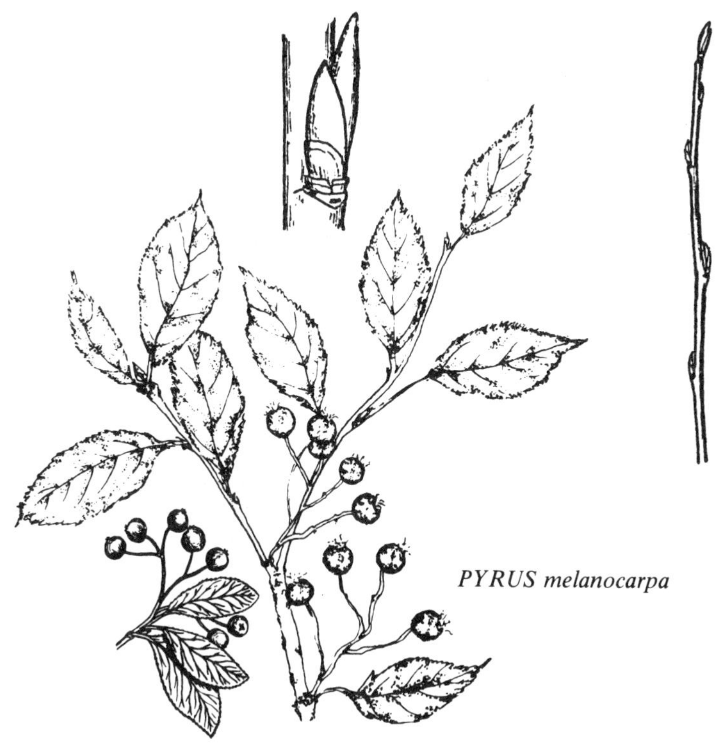

PYRUS melanocarpa

P. americana (Marsh.) DC. **Mountain-ash**

Trees to 10 m tall and 3 dm in diameter; buds oblong, gummy; twigs stout, with prominent lenticels; **leaves pinnately compound,** leaflets 13-15, lanceolate, sharply toothed; **inflorescences large and flat; flowers white, 4-6 mm broad; fruit spherical, orange-red, 4-6 mm in diameter.** Flowers in May-June. Woods and barrens at elevations above 2,500 feet.

WINTER

A small tree up to 10 m tall, and 3 dm in diameter; buds oval, the terminal bud much larger than the lateral buds; buds single, sessile, with long hairs matted in gum; twigs stout, with conspicuous lenticels; leaf scars raised, crescent-shaped or elongate; with 3-5 bundle traces, **fruits clustered, orange-red, 4-6 mm in diameter, persistent through the winter, but becoming faded.** Woods and barrens at high elevations.

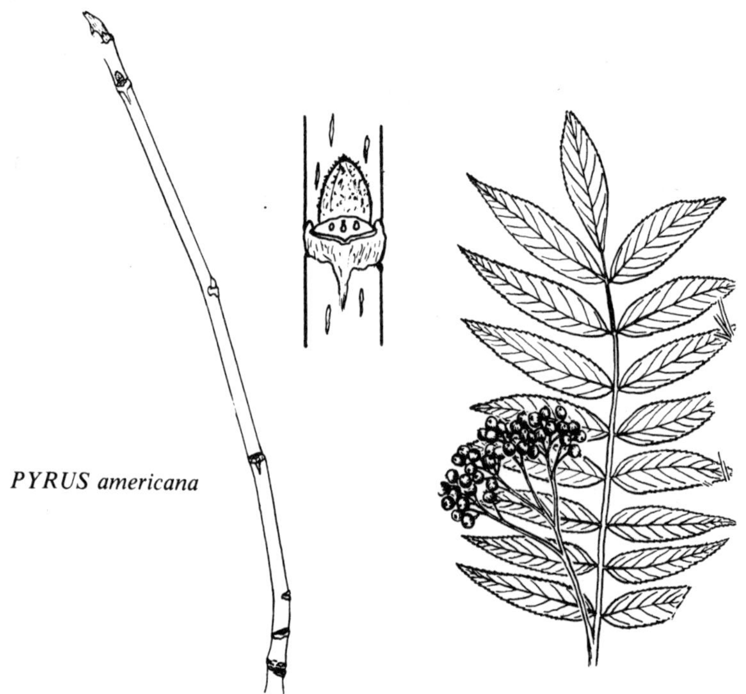

PYRUS americana

AMELANCHIER Medic. **Sarvice. Service Berry**

Shrubs or trees with alternate simple leaves, white (or pinkish) flowers. Flowers in early spring, calyx tube bell-shaped, calyx 5-lobed. Petals 5, white. Stamens numerous. Styles 5. Ovary wholly or partly inferior, the cavities by false partitions becoming twice as many as the styles. Fruit small, apple-like.

SUMMER KEY

a. Inflorescences 3-14 flowered; fruits red to deep purple; leaf tips blunt; leaves with 15-32 teeth on each side; petals more than 10 mm long; inflorescence 4-8 cm long. A low shrub. .... ***A sanguinea***
a. Inflorescences 3-14 flowered; fruits red to deep purple; leaf tips sharp-pointed; leaves with 20-75 teeth on each side, small trees. b

b. Leaves wooly to long-haired when unfolding. .... ***A. arborea***
b. Leaves almost hairless when unfolding. .... ***A. laevis***

WINTER

Small trees or shrubs. Buds sessile, single, elongated, cigar-shaped, greenish turning pale tan in winter (similar to the buds of Beech but fewer scaled, smaller, and the lateral buds appressed against th twig), with about 6 somewhat twisted scales. Twigs slender, round, zigzag; pith somewhat 5-angled, continuous, whitish. Leaf scars alternate, sickle-shaped or U-shaped with 3 bundle traces; stipule scars absent. (Good winter characters are not evident).

WINTER KEY

a. Low shrubs, up to 8 m high; not stoloniferous; stems single or few in a clump. .... ***A. sanguinea***
a. Trees, up to 20 m high. .... b

b. Leaves densely hairy when young. .... ***A. arborea***
b. Leaves hairless or only slightly hairy when young. .... ***A. laevis***

A. sanguinea (Pursh) DC. (blood-red) **Roundleaf Serviceberry**

Straggling or arching slender shrub, not forming colonies, the stems solitary or few in a clump; leaves oval to subcircular, tips blunt, 2.5-7 cm long; flowers many; fruit ripe in July, August, spherical, purplish black, 6-8 mm in diameter, sweet, juicy. Flowers in May, June. Dry, rocky or gravelly soil in open woods.

WINTER

A slender shrub up to 2.5 m high and 3 cm in diameter, **not forming extensive colonies, the stems single or few in a clump;** buds slender, dull, russet, 6-7 mm long; smaller branches reddish or russet. Woods or rocky hillsides.

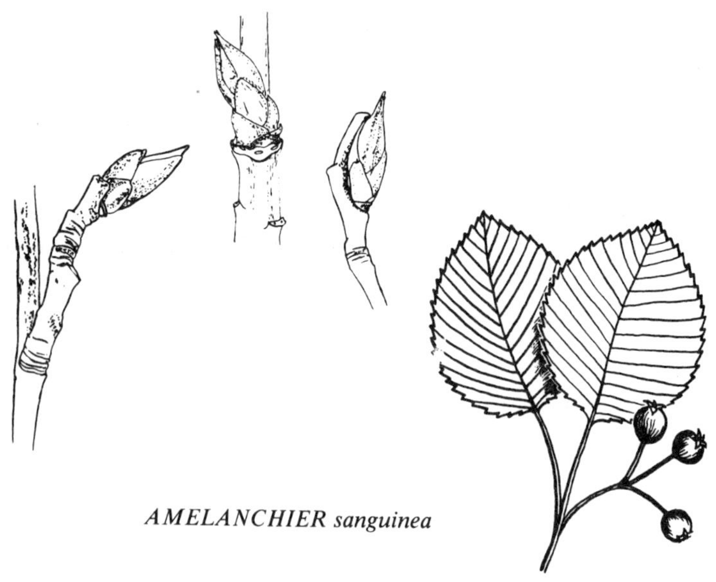

AMELANCHIER sanguinea

A. arborea (Michx. f.) Fernald. (tree-like) **Common Serviceberry**

Small trees to 20 m tall with a diameter to 4 dm; bark smooth, gray; **leaves 4-10 cm long, oval, toothed; wooly to long-haired when unfolding;** flowers showy, fragrant, usually appearing as the leaves unfold or before; fruit ripe in June-July, spherical, reddish, sweet, 6-10 mm in diameter. Flowers in March-May. Dry woods, open ground and wooded hillsides.

WINTER

A small scraggly tree up to 20 m high and 4 dm in diameter; buds 6-13 mm long; **leaves densely hairy when young.** Rich woods and slopes.

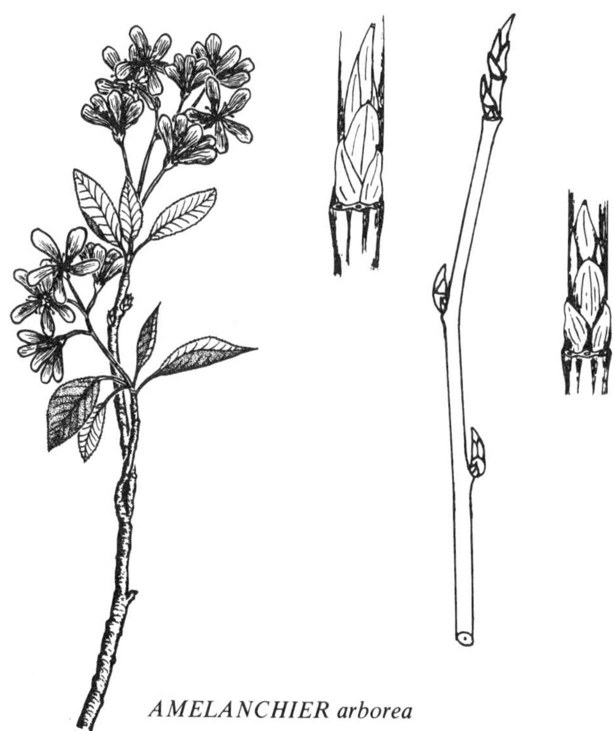

AMELANCHIER arborea

A. laevis Wiegand (smooth) **Smooth Serviceberry**

Juneberry

Small tree to 13 m tall; **leaves 4-6 cm long, oval, pointed at the apex, half-grown at flowering time; almost hairless when unfolding,** flowers large and showy, in many-flowered drooping inflorescences; petals 12-22 mm long; fruit abundant, ripe in June-July, spherical, dark purple to black, 6-8 mm long, sweet. Flowers in May. Dry open woodlands, damp shady slopes or at the edge of swamps, frequent at high elevations (mostly above 2,500 ft).

WINTER

A small tree up to 13 m tall; buds 0.9-1.7 cm long. Thickets and open woodlands especially above 2,500 feet.

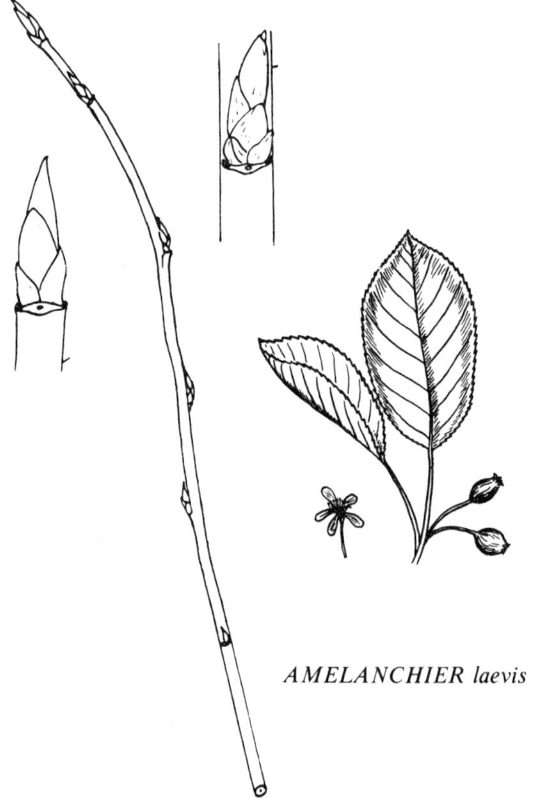

AMELANCHIER laevis

CRATAEGUS L. **Hawthorn**

Shrubs or small trees, usually spiny, with alternate simple leaves and white flowers. Calyx tube cup-shaped. Calyx 5-lobed. Petals usually 5. Stamens 5-25. Ovary inferior, 1-5-celled; styles 5. Fruit a small apple containing 1-5 bony seeds, utilized by numerous species of wildlife. The plants often form almost impenetrable thickets in abandoned fields. A very variable genus with many species and forms most of which are difficult to identify.

C. macrosperma Ashc (large-seeded) **Variable Hawthorn**

Tree-like shrub or tree up to 8 m high, with usually fluted trunk and larger branches, thin scaly bark, and **slender branchlets armed with curved thorns 2-7 cm long;** leaves mostly oval, more or less sharply lobed, thin, smooth except for short, rough hairs on the upper surface while young; flowers 13-15 mm wide in hairless inflorescences; stamens 10 or less; anthers pink or red; seeds 3-5. Common in pastures and abandoned fields.

WINTER

Deciduous shrubs or small trees. Boles and larger branches fluted, not round or symmetrical in cross section. **With stout strongly curved thorns, 2-7 cm long.** Buds small, rounded and red in winter, single or clustered, sessile, roundish, or oval, with about 6 scales. Twigs slender, round, pith small, round, continuous. Leaf scars alternate, sickle-shaped with 3 bundle traces and small stipule scars. Has many species and forms most which are difficult to identify. Common in open woods and pastures.

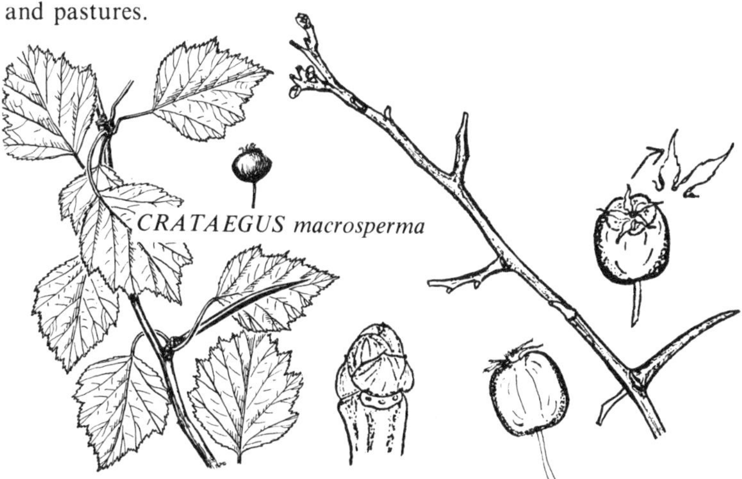

RUBUS L. **Raspberry, Blackberry, Dewberry**

Perennial herbs, shrubs or trailing vines, often prickly, with alternate leaves. In most species the aerial stem lives two years, the **primocane** (the shoot in its first year) usually sterile and with foilage unlike the **floricane** (the shoot in its second year), which bears flowers and fruits; identification of such species is usually impossible without collections of both stages, and careful notes as to the habit. Flowers variously clustered, usually perfect, mostly white in color. Calyx persistent, deeply 5-parted. Petals 5. Stamens numerous, attached to a convex or elongate receptacle, ripening into drupelets, forming an aggregate fruit, usually edible. The leaves are often discolored with an orange rust. A very variable genus with numerous species and forms, many of which are difficult to identify.

SUMMER KEY

a. Plants without prickles, shrubby, the stem becoming woody, with flaky bark; stipules on petioles; flowers large, purple, 2-5 cm across; no definite primocane-floricane succession. .... ***R. odoratus***
a. Plant usually with prickles; definite primocane-floricane succession. .... b

b. Fruit thimble-like, the dry receptacle remaining on the bush. **Raspberries.** c
b. Fruit not separating from the fleshy receptacle. **Blackberries, Dewberries.** .... d

c. Stems arching, rooting at the tips; primocanes not bristly or glandular, armed with rather stout, hooked prickles; primocane leaves 3-7-foliate; fruit normally black. .... ***R. occidentalis***
c. Stems erect, not rooting at the tips; primocanes bristly and glandular, without hooked prickles; primocane leaves 3-7-foliate; fruit red. .... ***R. strigosus***

d. Plant trailing or mounding, at least the terminal third of the mature stem prostrate, usually rooting at the tip; prickles mostly hooked; plants glandless; primocane leaflets soft-haired beneath. .... ***R. michiganensis***
d. Plant erect or arching, only occasionally tip rooting. .... e

e. Inflorescence decidedly glandular, branched, cylindrical, or narrowed upward; inflorescences short, less than three times as long as wide; prickles well separated; branches not drooping; primocane leaflets not overlapping, the central one mostly less than two-thirds as wide as long. .... ***R. allegheniensis***

e. Inflorescence glandless, or rarely with a very few glands on some flower stalks; primocanes unarmed, or with straight slender prickles; leaves shiny, smooth or nearly so beneath; mountain species. .... ***R. canadensis***

WINTER

Arching shrubs or vines, usually with prickles. Stems often angled with round or angled continuous pith. Buds sessile, oval. Alternate leaf scars with the persistent base of the petiole often present. Bundle traces obscure; stipules prominent, often present in winter.

WINTER KEY

a. Without true prickles; bark shredding in strips on older stems; stems weak, 1-2 m long, densely bristled with dark red or purplish, nonglandular hairs. .... ***R. odoratus***

a. True prickles usually present, even though sparse; bark not shredding; bristles seldom present. .... b

b. Stems low, weak, trailing or prostrate, often rooting at tips, smooth between prickles; stems red or greenish, firm-woody in winter, to 6 mm in diameter at the base; prickles curved, small but stout. .... ***R. michiganensis***

b. Stems upright or arching, not trailing; mostly 1 m tall or more. c

c. Stems round, heavily blue glaucous (bright purplish when wax is rubbed off), arching and tip rooting. .... ***R. occidentalis***

c. Stems not glaucous, often angled or grooved. .... d

d. Stems with coarse bristles and also prickles; stems erect; spreading by underground stems; bristles not red and glandular. ***R. strigosus***

d. Stems not coarse bristly; prickles usually present and prominent. e

e. Prickles nearly absent in its natural range at high altitudes; stem glabrous, angled, green to reddish. .... ***R. canadensis***

e. Prickles present, stout and broad-based, straight or curved; sparse fine hairs sometimes present between prickles; glandular hairs present on stalks and parts of the old fruit clusters and sometimes near tips of primocanes. .... ***R. allegheniensis***

R. odoratus L. (fragrant) **Flowering Raspberry**

Vigorous, erect-spreading; leaves large, often 4 dm across, palmate and variously 3- or 5-lobed; inflorescence irregular, flowers few or many, rose-purple, fragrant, 3-5 cm across; fruit rose-purple, juicy. Flowers in June-September. Abundant in shady places along woods, roads, thickets and margins of fields.

WINTER

Erect shrubs, stems thickly glandular-hairy, but unarmed, 1-1.5 m tall, with flaking bark. Rocky places along roads and fields.

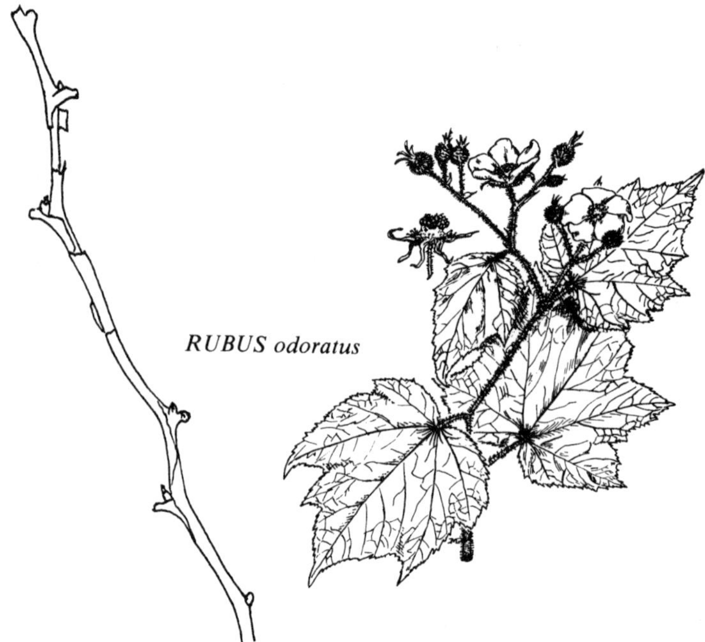

RUBUS odoratus

R. strigosus Michx. (with straight, stiff hairs) **Red Raspberry**

Slender erect plant to 2 m tall; primocane leaves 3-5-parted, the leaflets long-oval, gray, hairy to wooly beneath; flowers in clusters of about half a dozen, about 1 cm broad; corolla white; fruit conic, red; flowers in May-July. Rather common in the mountains above 3,000 feet.

WINTER

Shrub 1-2 m high, the stems with stiff hairs close to the stem or bristly spreading; older stems may have small, hooked prickles. Thickets, waste places.

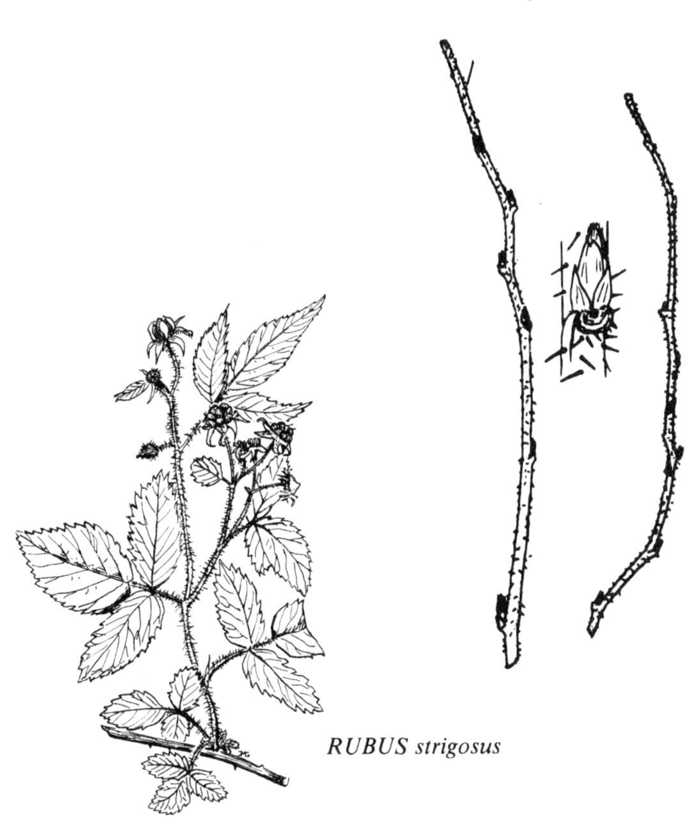

RUBUS strigosus

R. occidentalis L. (Western) **Black Raspberry**

Strong, upright, glandless plant, 1-2.5 m tall, overarching and strongly rooting at the tip, **stems whitened;** prickles few, stout, curved; primocane leaves 3-parted, white-hairy underneath, leaflets oval; flowers terminating lateral shoots; corolla 12-15 mm wide, whitish; fruit 15 mm or less broad, black, of high quality. Flowers from May-July. Common in woods, borders, fields, fence-rows and thickets.

WINTER

Shrub with arching **stem, with a conspicuous whitish covering,** rooting at the tip. Armed with few small prickles. Rich thickets and woodland borders.

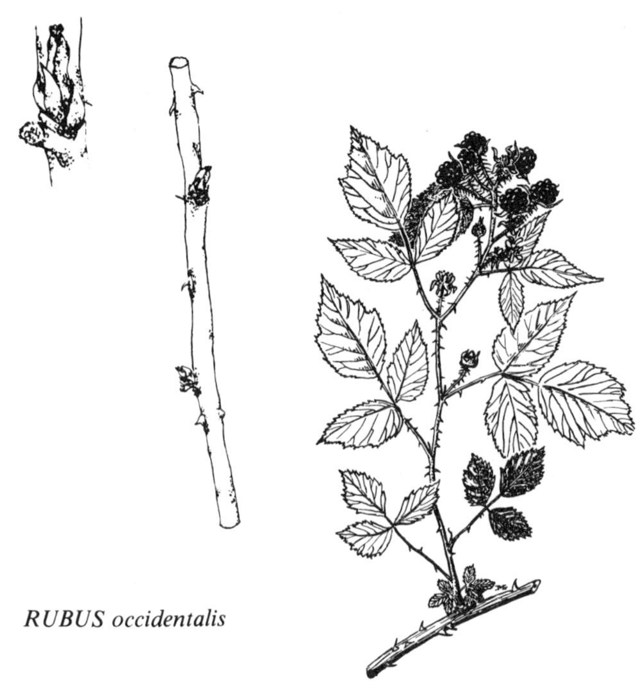

RUBUS occidentalis

R. michiganensis (Card) Bailey (of Michigan) **Dewberry**

Stems with few bristly prickles; leaflets toothed; flowering shoot with long hairs; inflorescence leafy; flower stalks long-haired; fruit spherical, of good quality, one of our most productive dewberries. Flowers in May-June. Sandy and light soil.

WINTER

Primocanes slightly angled up to 6 mm in diameter at base, **trailing to prostrate in winter,** up to 6 m long, usually rooting at the tips; green to reddish; armed with few to many small usually curved, broad-based prickles; smooth between prickles, never bristly; buds oval, reddish, 3-5 mm long.

RUBUS michiganensis

R. allegheniensis Porter (of the Allegheny Mountains)
Allegheny Blackberry

A robust, prickly, highbush plant, in many forms in different locations; primocane leaflets 5, hairy, narrow, sharp-pointed, usually very long-pointed; flower clusters glandular, elongated, with spreading flower stalks; flowers 2 cm and more across; fruit abundant, delicious, spicy, thimble-shaped, 2 cm or more long. Flowers in May-July. Common in dry places from lowlands to hills and mountains, open places in woodlands, along roadsides, on old fields, in fence-rows, clearings and thickets.

WINTER

Stems coarse, erect, angled, 1-3 m tall, usually armed with stout, broad-based, nearly straight prickles (these rarely lacking). Stems brownish green to deep red; the glandular hairs of the old fruit clusters on dead canes are useful winter characters.

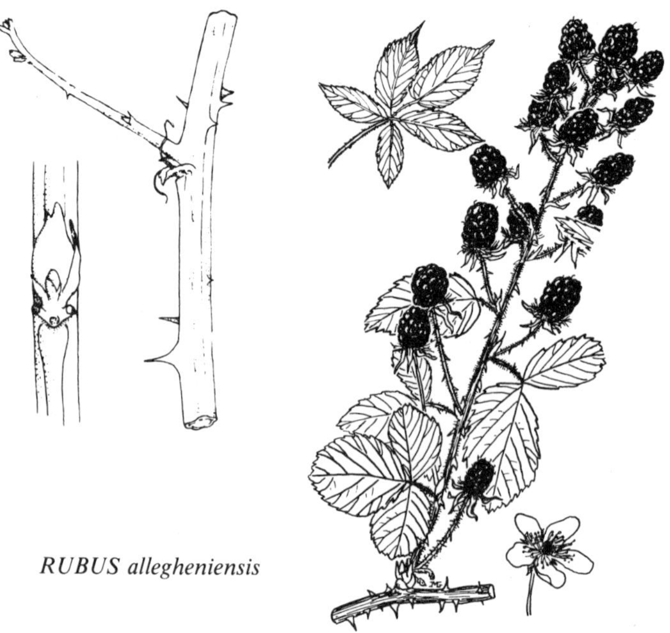

RUBUS allegheniensis

R. canadensis L. (Canadian) **Thornless Blackberry**

Vigorous spineless or very weakly armed, large, upright, glandless, essentially hairless bush, commonly 2 m tall, sometimes much more than that, often growing in large colonies; leaves thin and bright green, often shining, nerves rusty-prominent underneath; primocane leaflets 5, narrow and long-petioled; main flower-clusters long, but secondary clusters indefinite; flowers large, 2-3.5 cm broad; fruit widely variable, commonly oblong and 2 cm or less long, solid; a variable and dominant blackberry. Flowers in June-July. One of the later-flowering species, the fruits remaining until late August or September. Common in woods, old fields, cool hollows, and along roadsides.

WINTER

Stems erect or high arching, 1-3 m tall, almost without prickles; buds oval, sharp-pointed, about 9 mm long with several scales; stems smooth, somewhat angled, greenish to purplish, with only an occasional small prickle. Roadsides and old fields especially at higher elevations.

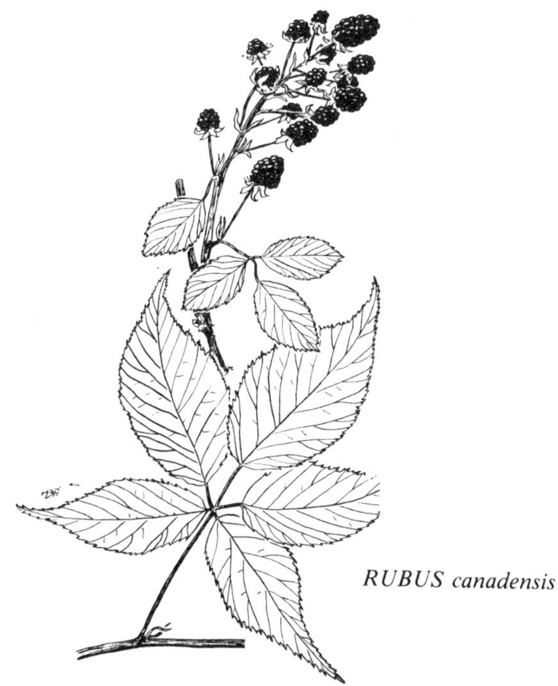

RUBUS canadensis

ROSA L. **Rose**

Erect or climbing shrubs, usually bristly or prickly, the prickles scattered or below the stipules, with pinnate leaves and clustered or solitary flowers. Calyx tube cup-shaped or urn-shaped, constricted at the throat, becoming fleshy in fruit. Calyx 5-lobed. Petals 5, spreading. Stamens numerous, inserted on the edge of a disk lining the calyx tube. Fruits numerous, enclosed by the red or yellow fleshy, enlarged calyx tube ("rose hip").

R. carolina L. (Carolinian) **Pasture Rose**

Stems often tall and stout, to 20 dm high, with stout, usually straight prickles; stipules more or less flattened; leaflets mostly 7, dark green, thick, smooth and shining above; flowers few or solitary, 3-5.5 cm broad, pink; sepals frequently lobed; fruit spherical, glandular, hairy, 8 mm high. Flowers in May-July. Dry sandy or rocky places or thin woods.

WINTER

Shrub with erect stems to 20 dm tall. Numerous straight, needle-like prickles. Sepals fall from the fruits before winter. Dry soil in thickets and borders.

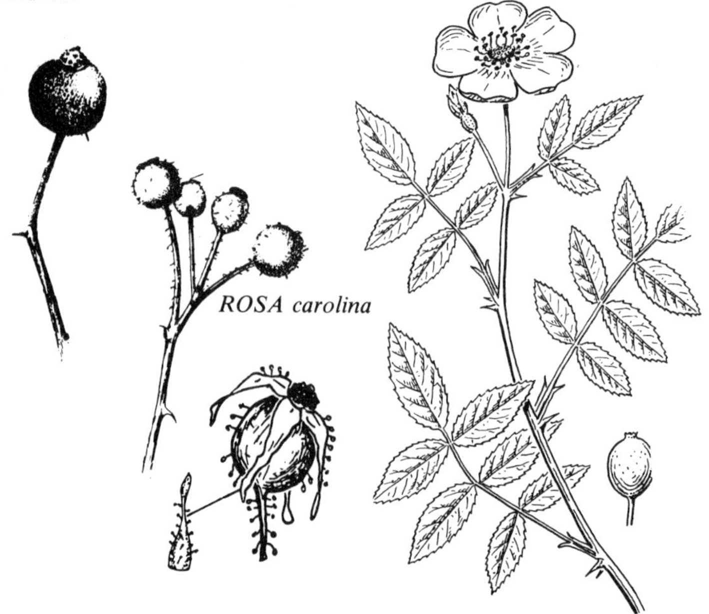

ROSA carolina

PRUNUS L. **Cherry**

Shrubs or trees, mostly with edible fleshy fruits, alternate, simple leaves and clustered flowers. Calyx free from the ovary, 5-lobed. Petals 5. Stamens numerous. Pistil 1. Fruit fleshy, one-seeded. Seeds and wilted leaves poisonous.

SUMMER KEY

a. Flower clusters short, flattened; leaves lance-shaped. .... ***P. pensylvanica***
a. Flower clusters elongate. .... b

b. Leaves oblong, round-toothed, the teeth incurved. ..... ***P. serotina***
b. Leaves oval, sharp-toothed, the teeth spreading. ..... ***P. virginiana***

WINTER

Trees or shrubs with slender, rounded twigs somewhat angled at the nodes, sharp-pointed in some species; buds single or clustered, sessile, almost spherical or oval, with 6 scales. Pith round or angled, whitish or brown, continuous. Leaf scars alternate, semicircular or oval, small with 3 bundle traces, stipule scars present.

WINTER KEY

a. Buds dull brown, oval; scales rough; twigs hairless, brown or gray. .... ***P. virginiana***
a. Buds shiny brown or glossy. .... b

b. Buds 4 mm long; scales deep-brown, keeled. .... ***P. serotina***
b. Buds 2 mm long; scales red-brown, hairs on the margin. .... ***P. pensylvanica***

P. pensylvanica L. f. (of Pennsylvania) **Bird, Fire, or Pin Cherry**

Tree to 12 m high, with light red-brown bark; **leaves oval or elongate, pointed, finely toothed, shining, hairless on both sides;** flowers white, many in a cluster, on long stalks; **fruit red, ripe July-September, spherical, 4-6 mm in diameter, the flesh thin and sour.** Seeds and wilted leaves poisonous. Flowers in April-June. Rocky woods and clearings. Common on old strip mines or burned over areas.

WINTER

A tree up to 12 m high, with reddish brown bark; **buds 2 mm long; scales red-brown, hairs on the margins.** Twigs hairless, slender, reddish, glossy. Woods, old strip mines, recent burns, and clearings.

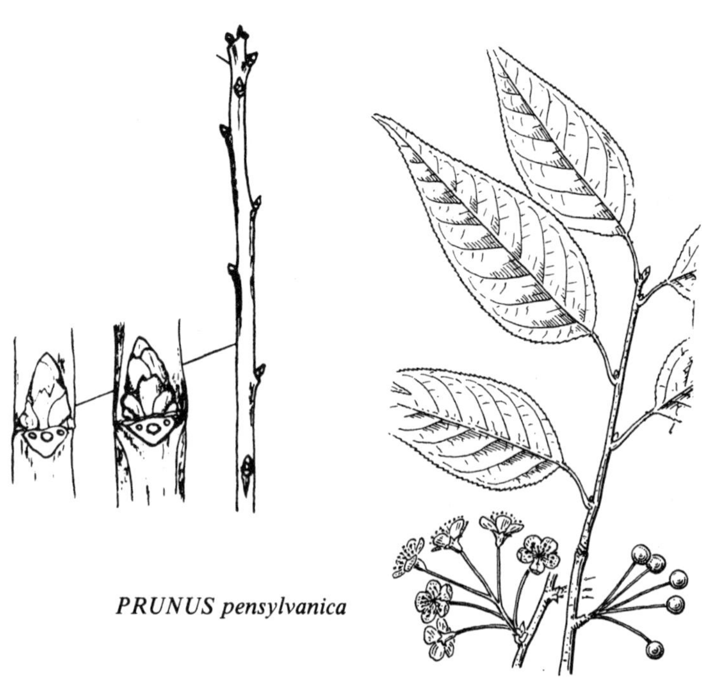

PRUNUS pensylvanica

P. serotina Ehrh. (late) **Wild Black Cherry**

A large tree to 35 m in height and 1.5 m in diameter; leaves oblong or elongate, sharp-pointed, **margin with fine incurved teeth;** flowers white, in elongated, spreading or drooping clusters; **fruit ripe in August-September, spherical, 8-10 mm in diameter, dark purple or black, slightly bitter.** Seeds and wilted leaves poisonous. Flowers in May. Woods.

WINTER

A large tree up to 35 m tall and 1.5 m in diameter; **buds about 4 mm long; scales chestnut-brown.** Old bark black, rough with small platelets turning outward at their edges. **Young bark smooth, black or slightly reddish-black with conspicuous horizontally elongated lenticels; inner bark with an unpleasant odor; the reddish brown twigs have a bitter almond taste.** A valuable timber tree in the original forest. Common in woods.

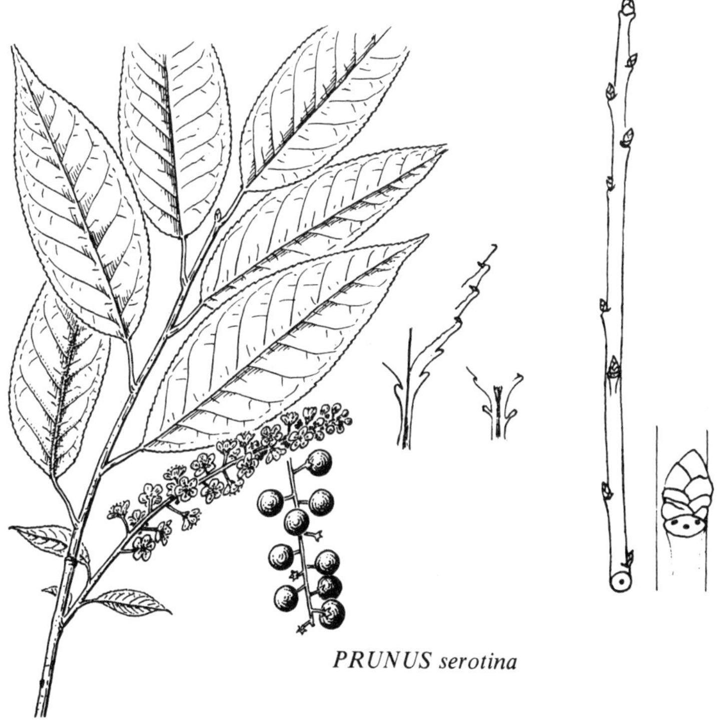

PRUNUS serotina

P. virginiana (Virginian) **Choke Cherry**

A tall shrub or small tree, 7.5 m or less high, with grayish bark, the inner layers with a disagreeable odor; **leaves oval, abruptly pointed, very sharply toothed with slender teeth;** flowers white, in terminal clusters; **fruit ripe August-October, red, turning to dark crimson, very bitter.** Seeds and wilted leaves poisonous. Flowers in May-June. Woods or on the borders of swamps.

WINTER

A small tree to 7.5 m high; **buds dull brown, oval with rough scales.** Bark grayish, the inner layers with a very unpleasant odor; twigs hairless, brown or gray. Woods, expecially on swamp borders.

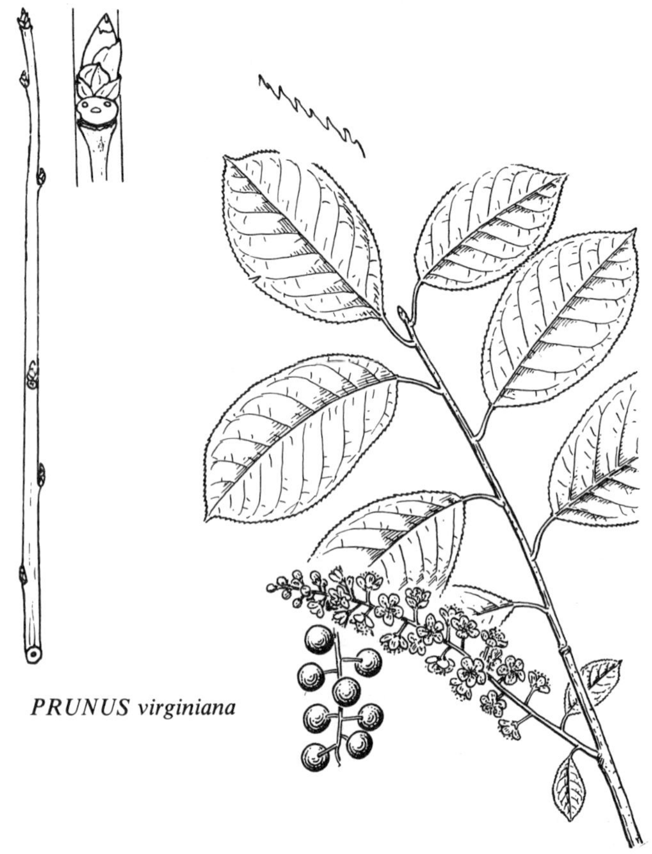

PRUNUS virginiana

GLEDITSIA L. **Honeylocust**

Large thorny trees with alternate pinnate and bipinnately compound leaves with stipules and small perfect or imperfect flowers in slender elongate clusters. Calyx 3-5 cleft. Petals 3-5, equal. Stamens 3-10, distinct. Ovary rudimentary or none in the staminate flowers, in the fertile ones oval or elongated. Legumes linear (our species) or oval.

G. triacanthos L. (three-thorned) **Honeylocust**

Tree with a maximum height of 50 m; bark on young trees grayish brown to black, smooth and marked by conspicuous lenticels, that of older trunks roughened by scaly ridges formed by strips of outer bark curling outward, inner bark in the fissures often pink; leaflets oblong-elongate, toothed, 1.6-3 cm long; flowers greenish, about 4 mm broad; fruit elongate-oblong, flat, 2-4.5 dm long, filled with a sweet edible pulp around the seeds, hence the name Honeylocust. **Trunk usually thickly covered with large branching thorns** (rarely thornless, in the *f. inermis* [Pursh] Schneid. [unarmed]). **Our only large tree having large branched thorns; our only tree having both pinnate and bipinnately compound leaves.** Flowers in May-July. In rich woods and bottomlands.

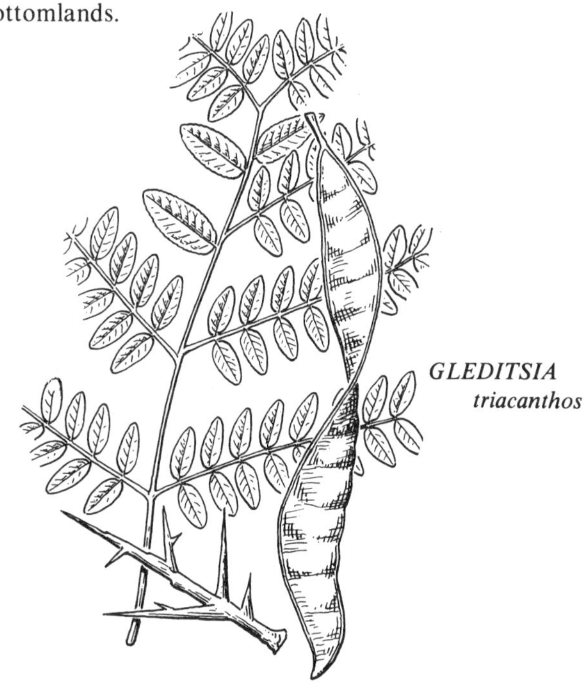

GLEDITSIA triacanthos

WINTER

Spreading deciduous trees usually armed with large multi-branched thorns arising above the leaf bases and persisting on the trunk. Thorns three-branched on young twigs and branches; bark on young trunks smooth and marked with large oblong conspicuous lenticels, on older trunks roughened by scattered shallow fissures and thick strips of upturned bark. Twigs zigzag, roundish, pith rounded, continuous pale or light pink. Buds hairless, sessile, occurring one above the other, more or less covered by the torn margin of the leaf scar (buds usually not evident); end bud lacking. Leaf scars alternate, relatively large, shield-shaped; bundle traces 3; stipule scars none. Fruit large, bean-like, reddish brown (when ripe) to 4 dm long. **Large, conspicuous, branched thorns are usually present on trunks and branches.**

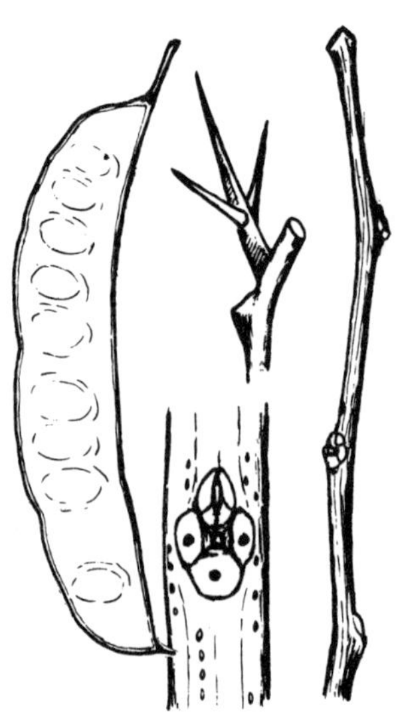

GLEDITSIA triacanthos

CERCIS L. **Redbud**

Deciduous shrubs or small trees with simple alternate, leaves and imperfectly butterfly-like flowers. Calyx 5-toothed. Corolla of 5 petals, the expanded upper petal smaller than the wings. Stamens 10, distinct. Ovary short-stalked, ovules numerous. Legume oblong, flat.

C. canadensis L. (Canadian) **Redbud.**

Shrub or small tree to 10 m high; **leaves simple, broad, entire margined, heart-shaped to round and palmately veined, hairy beneath,** 5-15 cm broad, the petiole swollen at both ends; **flowers several together in clusters, appearing before the leaves,** often borne on trunk and main branches; **corolla red-purple,** attractive, 8 mm long; legume 5-7.5 cm long. Flowers in April. In rich soil in open woods and old fields.

WINTER

Small tree up to 10 m high. Buds 2-3 mm long, smooth, the flower buds placed one above the other and stalked with several scales, the leaf buds sessile, oval with 2 scales; no terminal bud. Twigs reddish brown to black, slender, zigzag, rounded; pith roundish, continuous, white or pink. Leaf scars alternate, raised, with a fringe at the top, bluntly triangular, with 3 small ridges running along the stem, with 3 bundle traces; no stipule scars. Bark with dark brown to black scaly ridges. Fruit reddish brown, a legume 6-8 cm long, 10-12 mm wide, present on the tree in winter. **Blooms in early spring before the leaves appear. Rich woods and open fields.**

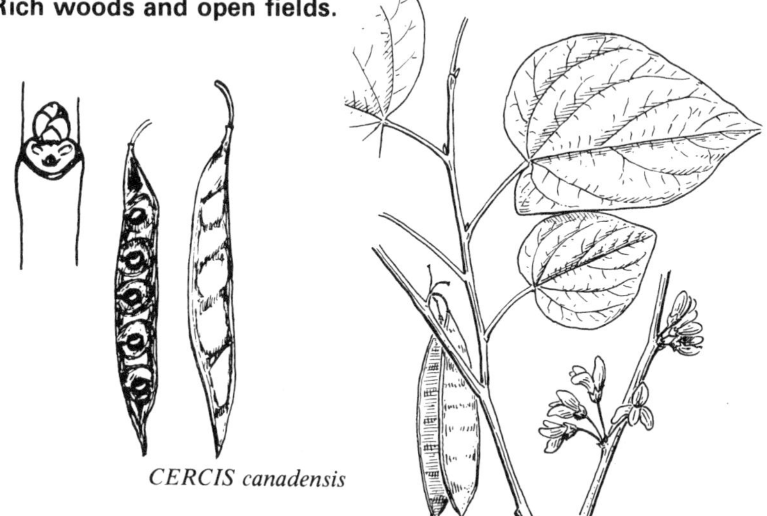

CERCIS canadensis

ROBINIA L. **Locust**

Trees or shrubs with alternate, pinnate leaves and axillary or terminal elongate clusters of showy flowers. Calyx teeth short, broad. Stamens united in 2 unequal sets. Ovary stalked, ovules numerous. Fruit flat, linear.

R. pseudoacacia L. (false acacia) **Black Locust**

Tree to 25 m high; branches hairless or nearly so; **stipules usually consist of two sharp spines at the nodes** (sometimes small and soft or absent); leaves odd-pinnate, flower cluster loose; flowers white, fragrant; legume gray-brown, smooth. Flowers in May-June. Limestone areas, strip mines and old fields.

WINTER

A tree up to 25 m high and 7 dm in diameter. Buds small, one placed above the other, partially covered by the leaf scar tissue (buds usually not evident); no terminal bud. Twigs often prickly, angled, zigzag, green to reddish brown; pith round, continuous. Leaf scars alternate, broadly 3-cornered, covered by a membrane that peels off, exposing the buds; bundle traces 3; stipules modified into two sharp spines which persist for several years. Bark deeply furrowed into rough dark brown ridges. Fruits gray-brown, up to 10 cm long, and 12 wide, usually present on trees in the winter. Common in thickets, strip mines and old fields.

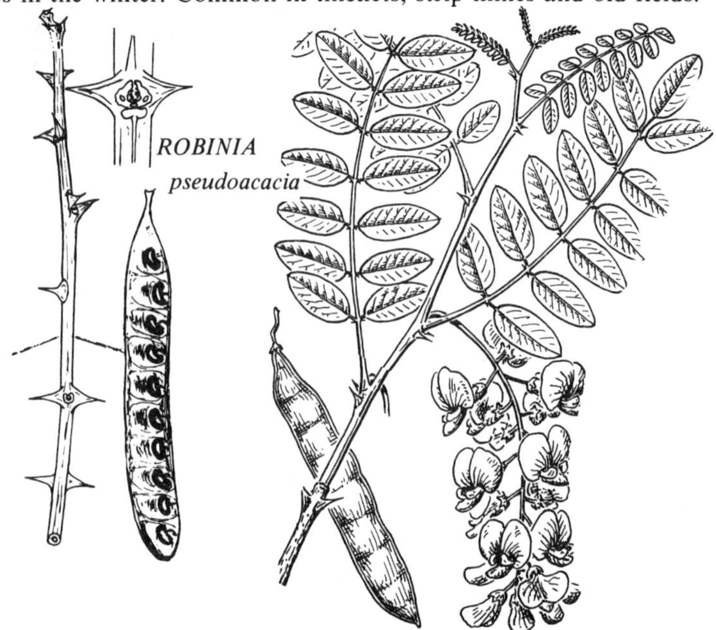

DESMODIUM Desv. **Sticktights, Tick-Treefoil**

Perennial erect ascending or trailing herbs with 3-parted leaves and small flowers in elongate clusters. Calyx tube short, the teeth somewhat united into 2 lips. Stamens united in one or two groups. Fruit with 2-many seeds. Fruit flat, several jointed, the joints readily separable.

D. nudiflorum (L.) DC. (with naked flowering stalk) **Sticktights**

Leaves all crowded at the summit of sterile stems; leaflets broadly oval, blunt, whitish beneath; inflorescence elongated on an ascending, mostly leafless stalk 6-10 dm high. Flowers in July-August. Dry woods. **Flat jointed fruits break apart and stick to clothing and animal fur, hence the name.**

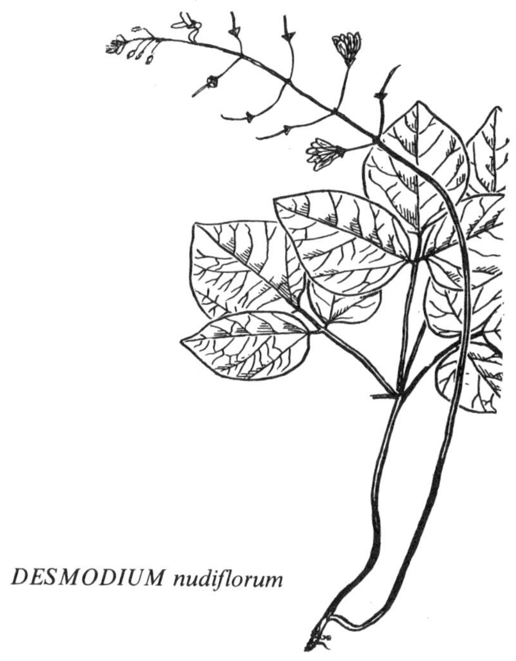

DESMODIUM nudiflorum

OXALIS L. **Oxalis, Wood Sorrel**

Sepals 5, persistent. Petals 5, soon withering. Stamens 10, usually united at base, alternately long and short. Styles 5, distinct. Capsule cylindric, or awl-shaped, thin walled; parts of fruit persistent, being fixed to the axis by the partitions.

O. montana Raf. (of the mountains), **White Wood Sorrel**

Perennial from a scaly rootstock; stems 5-15 cm high, hairy with scattered brownish hairs; leaves 3-6, long-petioled; leaflets heart-shaped with the point at the base, wider than long; flower stalks 1-flowered, 2-bracted above the middle; **petals white, with rose-colored veins;** capsule sub-round, 2-4 mm long, hairless. Flowers May-August. Damp woods, especially common in spruce-yellow birch forests, mostly at high elevations in the mountains. **This is the most common flowering plant in Red Spruce forests.**

OXALIS montana

GERANIUM L. **Geranium**

Herbs with stipulate, palmately lobed or divided leaves, and axillary 1-many flowered stalks. Stamens usually 10, generally 5 longer than the other 5, the longer ones with glands at the base. Ovary beaked with the compound style.

G. maculatum L. (mottled), **Wild Geranium, Wild Cranesbill**

Erect, hairy perennial, 3-6 dm high, simple or branching stem; basal leaves long-petioled, round in outline or broadly heart-shaped to kidney-shaped, 7.5-15 cm wide, deeply 3-5-parted, the divisions variosly toothed and cut; stem leaves 2, opposite, bearing a pair of leaves at the base of the inflorescence; flower stalks 2.5-5 cm long; flowers rose-purple, 2.5-4 cm broad; sepals awn-pointed; petals wooly at the base; fruits hairy; seed net-patterned. Flowers in April-July. In woods, thickets, and open fields.

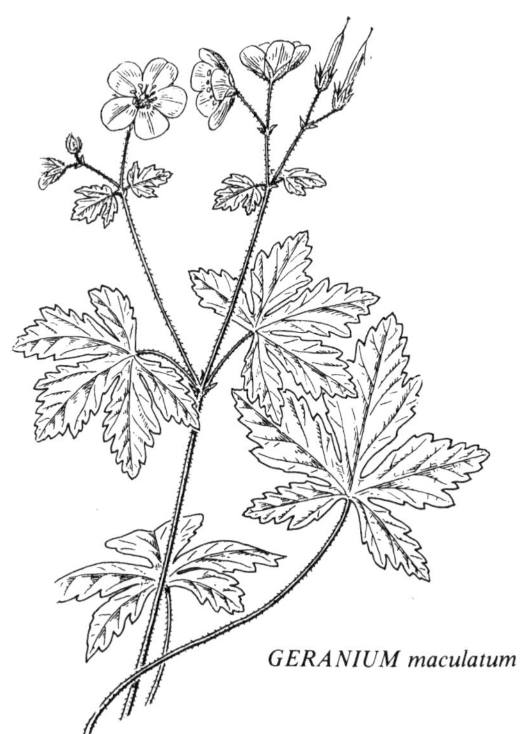

GERANIUM maculatum

RHUS L. **Sumac, Poison Ivy**

Leaves without stipules, alternate, mostly odd-pinnate, often bright orange or scarlet in autumn and very showy. Flowers greenish white or yellowish, with perfect flowers and separate staminate and pistillate flowers on the same plant, in terminal branched clusters. Calyx 5. Stamens 5, inserted under the edge or between the lobes of a flattened disk at the bottom of the calyx. Fruit dry, small, 1-seeded, subspherical, often hairy. Small trees, shrubs, or vines, some species poisonous.

SUMMER KEY

a. Leaflets normally more than 3. .... b
a. Leaflets normally 3. .... ***R. radicans***

b. Main axis of leaf winged, margin of leaflets not toothed, branchlets very minutely haired and round (not angled); leaf scars U-shaped. .... ***R. copallina***
b. Main axis of leaf not winged; branchlets smooth or hairy; leaflets regularly toothed to the base; fruit hairy with red hairs. c

c. Branchlets not hairy below the inflorescence, lower surface of the leaflets and main axis of the leaf smooth; branchlets more or less strongly angled. .... ***R. glabra***
c. Branchlets very hairy below the inflorescence, lower surface of the leaflets and main axis of leaf hairy; branchlets round or nearly so. .... ***R. typhina***

WINTER

Small trees, shrubs or vines, some species poisonous to the skin. Twigs round or somewhat 3-sided; pith large. Buds moderate or small, single, sessile, round to oval; terminal bud missing. Leaf scars alternate, almost round to horseshoe-shaped; bundle traces numerous and scattered in the round leaf scars, but 3 to 9 traces in the narrow leaf scars; stipule scars absent.

WINTER KEY

a. Leaf scars distinctly horseshoe- or U-shaped. .... b
a. Leaf scars broadly sickle-shaped, shield-shaped, or round. Climbing or bushy; twigs slender; buds stalked. .... ***R. radicans***

b. Leaf scars distinctly horseshoe-shaped. c
b. Leaf scars U-shaped; twigs round, hairless. .... ***R. copallina***

c. Twigs round, densely haired. .... ***R. typhina***
c. Twigs 3-angled, hairless. .... ***R. glabra***

R. typhina L. (like ***Typha,*** Cattail, i.e., velvety) **Staghorn Sumac**

Shrub or small tree to 10 m high, with orange-colored wood and densely hairy young twigs; **branchlets very hairy below the inflorescences;** leaves pinnate, 2-4 dm long; petioles and main axis of leaf densely velvet-hairy; the toothed leaflets 11-13, elongate-oblong, 7.5-12.5 cm long; inflorescences terminal, dense; **fruit spherical, 3-4 mm in diameter, very densely covered with long crimson spreading hairs** (sour to the taste). Flowers in June-July. Common on open hillsides and along roadsides.

WINTER

A small tree up to 10 m high and 1 dm in diameter; **twigs densely velvet-hairy; fruits round, in dense cone-shaped clusters; densely covered with long red hairs.** Present in early winter. Thickets, roadsides, and old fields.

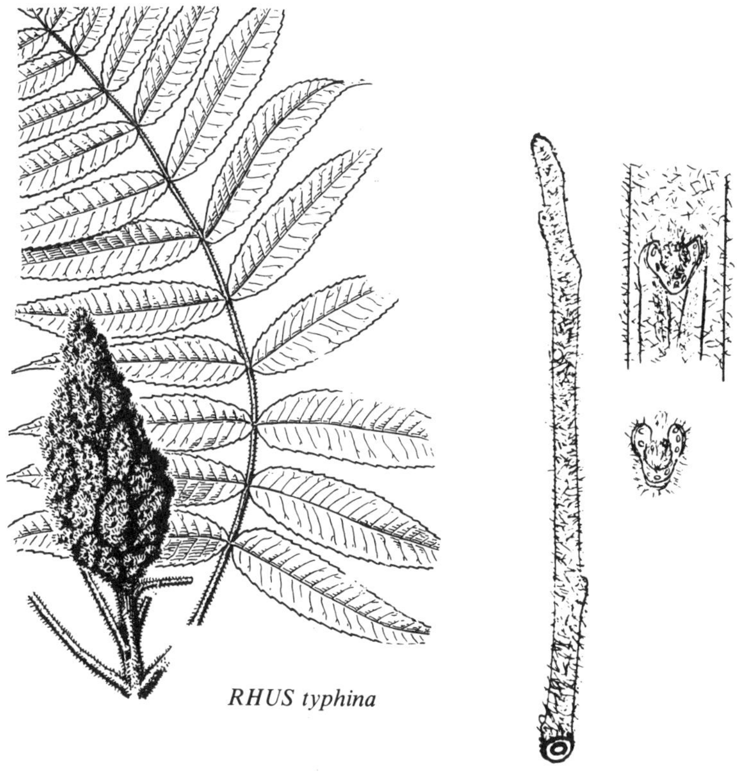

RHUS typhina

R. glabra L. (smooth) **Smooth Sumac**

Shrub or small tree to 5 m high, twigs hairless and somewhat whitened; leaves and fruit as in the preceding species except that the **petioles and twigs are hairless and the fruit is covered with short red hairs.** Flowers in June, July. Common in dry soil.

WINTER

A shrub up to 8 m high, **with angled hairless whitened twigs; fruits round in dense triangular clusters, covered with short red sticky hairs, present in early winter.** Thickets, waste places, roadsides.

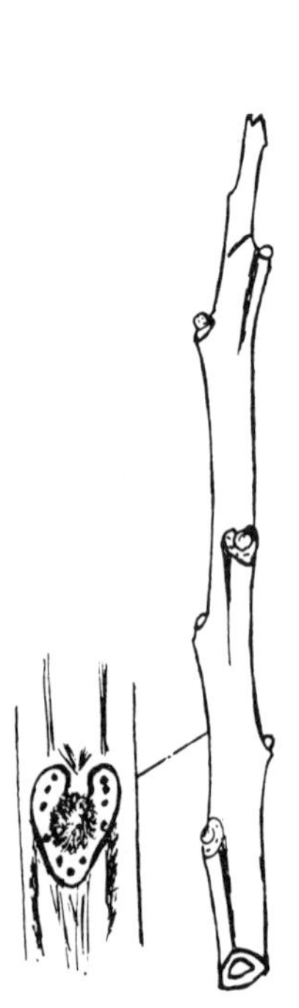

RHUS glabra

R. copallina L. (with copal-like droplets) **Shining Sumac**
Winged Sumac

Shrub or small tree to 10 m high and trunk diameter of 1.5 dm; leaves pinnate, 1.5-3 dm long, the **petiole and main axis more or less minutely hairy;** leaflets 11-23, elongate-oblong, 1-2 cm broad, not toothed on margin, **main axis wing-margined between the leaflets;** flower stalks and calyx finely haired; **fruit flattened, compressed, 4 mm in diameter, crimson, covered with short fine hairs.** Flowers in July-September. Abandoned fields and rocky hillsides.

WINTER

Small tree up to 10 m high; **the reddish brown twigs covered with minute downy hairs; fruits covered with short red hairs, present in winter.** In old fields and waste places.

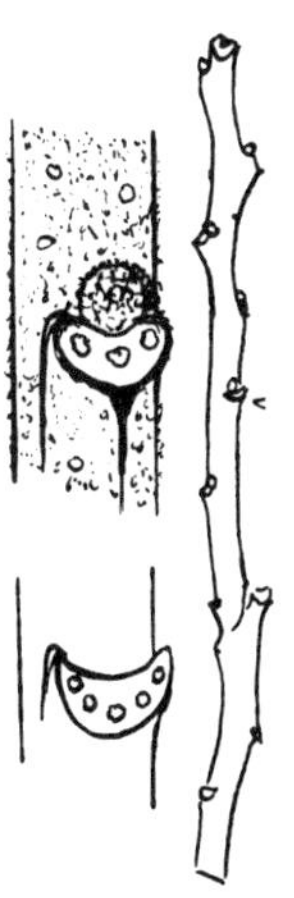

RHUS copallina

R. radicans L. (rooting) **Poison Ivy**

Vine or shrub, erect and bushy, scrambling over rocks, or high-climbing by aerial roots; **leaves 3-parted,** smooth; leaflets 2.5-10 cm long, entire or sparingly toothed or wavy-margined, **fruit similar to the preceding but smooth and yellowish green to white (not red).** Flowers in May-June. Thickets, along fences, roadbanks, etc.

WINTER

A variable vine becoming shrubby at times; **twigs slightly hairy or smooth; fruits green to yellowish white, persistent in winter.** Causes skin irritation to many persons in both summer and winter. Smoke from burning stems is especially bad. Abundant in thickets, fence-rows, and open woods.

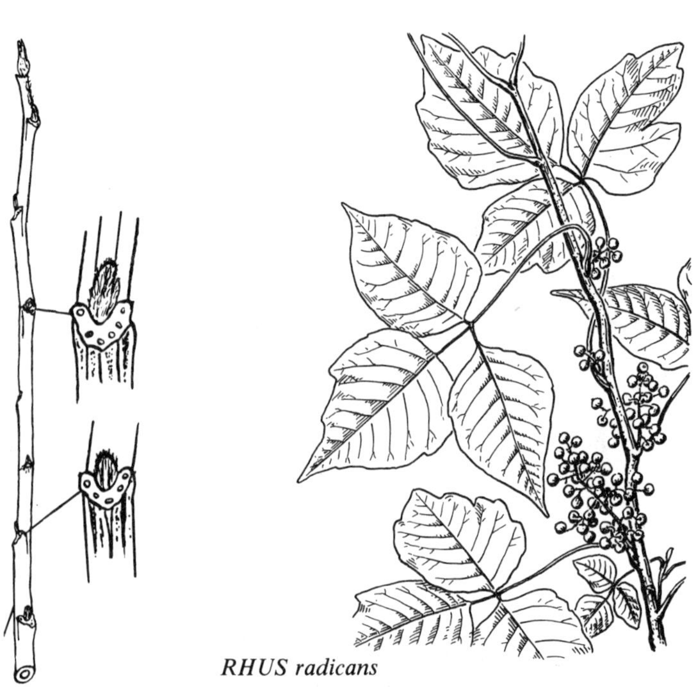

RHUS radicans

ILEX L. **Holly**

Shrubs or trees with alternate leaves, entire, toothed, or spiny-toothed, with tiny stipules. Calyx 4-9 toothed. Petals 4-9, separate or united only at the base, oval, blunt, spreading. Stamens 4-9. Fruit containing 4-9 nutlets.

SUMMER KEY

a. Leaves evergreen .... ***I. opaca***
a. Leaves deciduous. .... b

b. Fruits long-stalked .... ***I. collina***
b. Fruits short-stalked c

c. Nutlets ribbed on back, leaves thin, 6-12 cm long, usually hairless beneath .... ***I. montana***
c. Nutlets smooth on the back, leaves thick, 3-7 cm long, downy beneath .... ***I. verticillata***

WINTER

Shrubs or small trees, deciduous except for one species. Buds small, sessile, usually one above the other. Twigs slender, often spurlike with many crowded leaf scars; pith white, continuous. Leaf scars alternate, crescent-shaped with a single bundle trace; stipule scars tiny. Fruit fleshy, red (or rarely yellow), containing 4 to 6 hard nutlets.

WINTER KEY

a. Leaves evergreen .... ***I. opaca***
a. Leaves deciduous .... b

b. Buds more or less lying flat against the stem. c
b. Buds not lying flat against stem. .... ***I. verticillata***

c. Buds hairless except at apex; fruits on short stalks. ... ***I. montana***
c. Buds hairy; fruits on long stalks. .... ***I. collina***

I. opaca Ait. (opaque) **American Holly**

Tree to 20 m high, bearing **evergreen leaves with wide-spaced spiny teeth on the margins or rarely entire;** flowers small, greenish, in loose clusters; fruit red. A highly ornamental shrub or tree. Flowers in May-June. Trees are either male or female. Common in moist woods at lower elevations.

WINTER

Small tree up to 20 m high; buds short, blunt, downy; **leaves evergreen, oval, leathery, 5-10 cm long, usually with wavy margins and spiny teeth;** bark tight, rough, gray; twigs slender; **fruit bright red (rarely yellow),** 7-10 cm in diameter. Rich woods.

ILEX opaca

I. collina Alexander (growing on hills) **Long-stalked Holly**

A shrub to 4 m tall, with deciduous leaves, hairless on both sides, or sparingly hairy beneath; flowers small, on slender stalks 10-15 mm long; **fruits red, long-stalked.** Flowers in May-June. Moist woods. Restricted to the mid-Appalachians.

WINTER

Shrub up to 4 m tall; buds lying flat against the stem, hairy; twigs ashen, smooth; lenticels conspicuous; bark smooth, ashen; **fruits red, (rarely yellow) long-stalked,** 7-10 mm in diameter. Woods and thickets.

ILEX collina

I. montana T. & C. (of the mountains) **Mountain Holly**

Shrub or tree with a maximum height of about 12 m; **leaves deciduous, 6-12 cm long, thin, smooth on both sides;** fertile flowers on short stalks; **fruits red, short-stalked, the nutlets many-ribbed on the back.** Flowers in June. Moist woods in the mountains.

WINTER

Shrub up to 8 m high; **buds small, pointed, lying flattened against the stem, bud scales oval, keeled, acute, light brown, smooth, except fine hairs at the apex;** young twigs hairless, reddish brown, becoming gray with age, enlarged at the nodes, with ridges running down the stem from the leaf scars; bark thin, warty, brownish gray, with many lenticels; **fruits red, short-stalked,** about 1 cm in diameter. Moist woods and barrens in the mountains.

ILEX montana

I. verticillata (L.) Gray (whorled) **Black-alder, Winterberry**

Shrub to 6 m high; **leaves deciduous, 3-7 cm long, rather thick and leathery, turning black in autumn; flowers on short stalks; fruits bright red, clustered so as to appear whorled, very showy in late autumn and winter,** the prettiest of the deciduous hollies. Flowers in May-June. Low grounds, mostly in the mountains.

WINTER

Shrub up to 6 m high; **buds not lying close to the twig, blunt, the scales blunt;** twigs slender, hairless or slightly hairy; bark smooth. gray; **fruits red (rarely yellow),** 5-7 mm in diameter, **very crowded.** Moist woods and barrens.

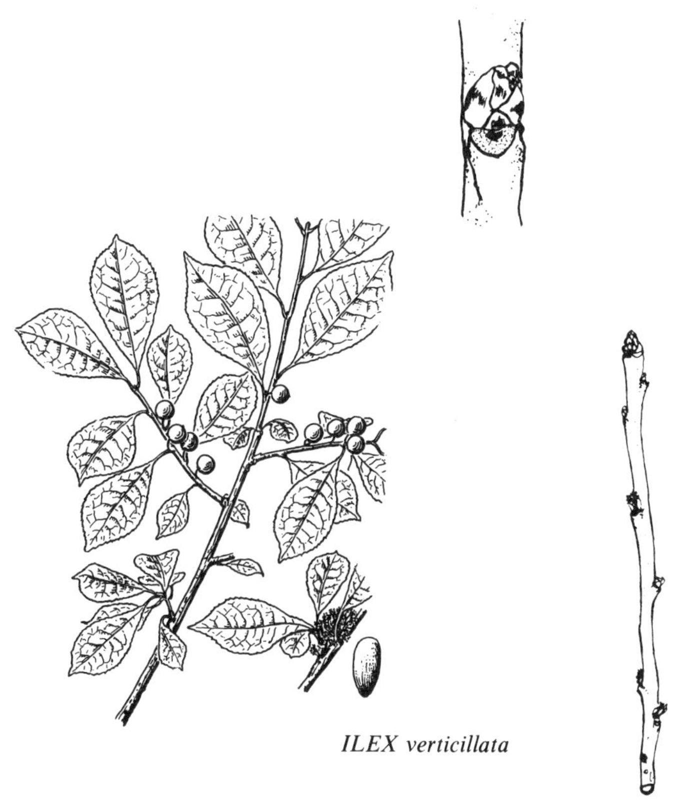

ILEX verticillata

NEMOPANTHUS Raf. **Mountain-holly**

Smooth shrub with slender-petioled, oblong, deciduous leaves and perfect or imperfect axillary small flowers. Calyx in the staminate flowers of 4-5 minute deciduous teeth; in the pistillate ones absent or almost so. Petals 4-5, oblong, linear, spreading, distinct. Stamens 4-5. Fruit with 4-5 bony nutlets, light red.

*N. **mucronata*** (L.) Trel. (abruptly short-tipped)
Mountain-holly, Catberry

Erect shrub to 3 m high, with ash-colored bark; **leaves elliptic or obovate, bristle-tipped,** 1-5 cm long; petioles 6-12 mm long; flowers of both kinds solitary or the staminate sometimes 2-4 together; **flower stalks very slender,** often 3-8 cm long; **fruit light red,** attractive, 6-8 mm in diameter. Flowers in May-June. Damp woods, margins of bogs at high elevations.

WINTER

Shrub with light gray bark; buds oval, single, tiny, sessile, pointed at the apex, with 2 hairy margined scales. Twigs slender, with a purplish to gray whitish coating; pith small, continuous. Leaf scars raised, 3-angled or crescent-shaped with 1 bundle trace; stipule scars absent. **Fruit red (rarely yellow), long-stalked, present in winter.** Damp wood, margins of bogs at high elevations.

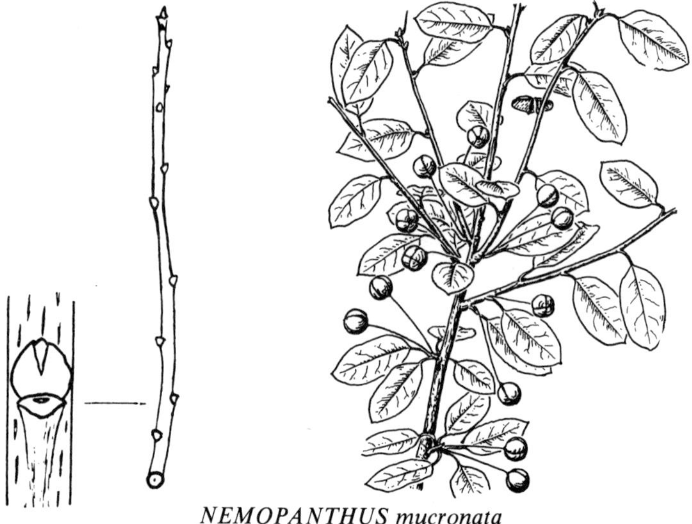

NEMOPANTHUS mucronata

STAPHYLEA L. **Bladdernut**

Shrubs with elongate or branched clusters of white flowers. Flower stalks jointed. Capsule 2-3-celled. Seeds spherical.

S. trifolia L. (three-leaved) **Bladdernut**

A branching shrub to 5 m high, with smooth white, striped, brownish bark; young leaves hairy, **mature foliage smooth opposite leaves with 3 leaflets;** stipules linear, 8-12 mm long, with an elongate tip; leaflets oval, 3-6 cm long, finely and sharply toothed; **flowers white, bell-shaped in branched inflorescences; capsule about 5 cm long, 2.5 cm wide, bladder-like, greenish, the 3 cells separated at the summit.** Flowers in mid-April to early June. In moist woods and thickets.

WINTER

A shrub to 5 m high; buds single, sessile, oval, smooth; terminal bud usualy absent leaving two opposite lateral buds in the terminal position. Bud scales 4, blunt. Twigs rounded, hairless; pith comparatively large, continuous, white. Leaf scars opposite, half-round with 3 bundle traces (or more); stipule scars rounded or elongated. bark on larger branches smooth, brownish with whitish stripes. **Fruit a papery inflated capsule turning brown and present in winter, the loose seeds rattling inside when the capsule is shaken.** Rich woods and thickets.

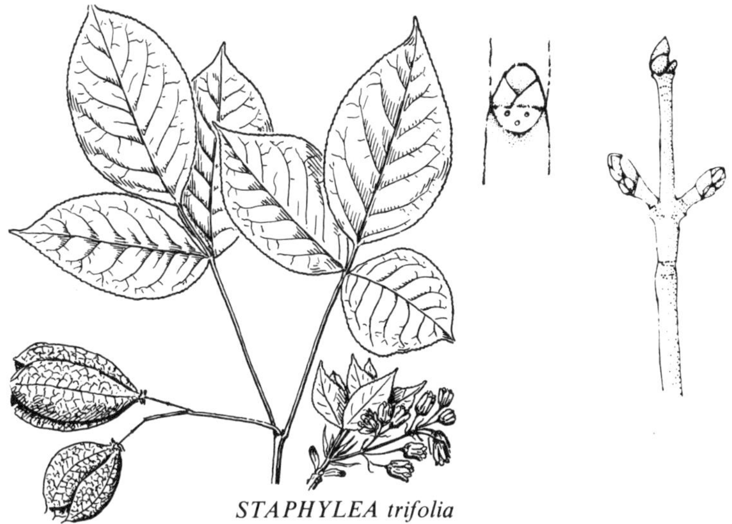

STAPHYLEA trifolia

ACER L. **Maple**

Deciduous trees or shrubs. Flowers perfect and imperfect on a single tree. Leaves opposite, simple, and palmately lobed or pinnately compound. Flowers green or red. Fruit double-winged, each cell usually 1-seeded.

SUMMER KEY

a. Flowers in terminal irregular or elongate clusters; leaves simple, palmately lobed. .... b
a. Flowers in short clusters. c

b. Irregular flower cluster erect; leaves coarsely single-toothed. .... ***A. spicatum***
b. Elongate flower cluster drooping; leaves finely double-toothed. .... ***A. pensylvanicum***

c. Flowers unfolding with the leaves; inflorescence sessile; leaves mostly 5-lobed, without hairs on both sides, pale beneath. ***A. saccharum***
c. Flowers unfolding before the leaves. .... d

d. Petals present; ovary not hairy; leaves not deeply lobed. ***A. rubrum***
d. Petals none; ovary wooly; leaves deeply lobed. ... ***A. saccharinum***

WINTER

Trees or shrubs. Leaf buds opposite, single or clustered, flower buds oval or cone-shaped, sessile or stalked, with 1 or more pairs of scales. Twigs rounded with continuous, pale pith. Leaf scars opposite, curved or U-shaped, the opposite leaf scars meeting in a "V"; bundle traces 3 or more; no stipule scars.

WINTER KEY

a. Bud scales 2, not overlapping. .... b
a. Bud scales more than 2, overlapping. c

b. Bud scales hairless, thick; buds blunt, 8-10 mm long. .... ***A. pensylvanicum***
b. Bud scales with tiny hairs; buds short, slender, 5 mm or less long. .... ***A. spicatum***

c. Buds dark gray to brown throughout the year, hairless, terminal buds usually 5 mm or less long; sap clear; twigs glossy, buff or reddish brown. .... ***A. saccharum***

c. Buds reddish or orange in winter (green in summer); scales about 4. d

d. Flowers red, beginning to bloom in March; twigs red; inner bark not unpleasantly scented. .... ***A. rubrum***

d. Flowers greenish yellow or reddish, beginning to open in February; twigs chestnut brown; inner bark unpleasantly scented. .... ***A. saccharinum***

A. spicatum Lam. (spiked) **Mountain Maple**

Shrub or small tree, with maximum height of 9 m and diameter of 2 dm; leaves 3-lobed, 7-13 cm long, hairy beneath at least when young, coarsely toothed; flowers in erect, irregular clusters 3 mm broad, greenish yellow, appearing after the leaves; winged fruits 1.8-2 cm long, the wings 6-8 mm wide. Flowers in May-June. Damp rocky woods. Mostly at elevations above 2,500 feet. **Inflorescence upright. Leaves coarsely single-toothed.**

WINTER

Small tree up to 9 m high; buds on short stalks, with 2 nonoverlapping scales; hairy; about 5 mm long; terminal buds larger; young twigs grayish, hairy; with thin, smooth, brown or grayish bark, spotted with gray patches. Cool woods, mostly at elevations above 2,500 feet. **Our only maple with small, hairy, red buds with nonoverlapping scales in winter.**

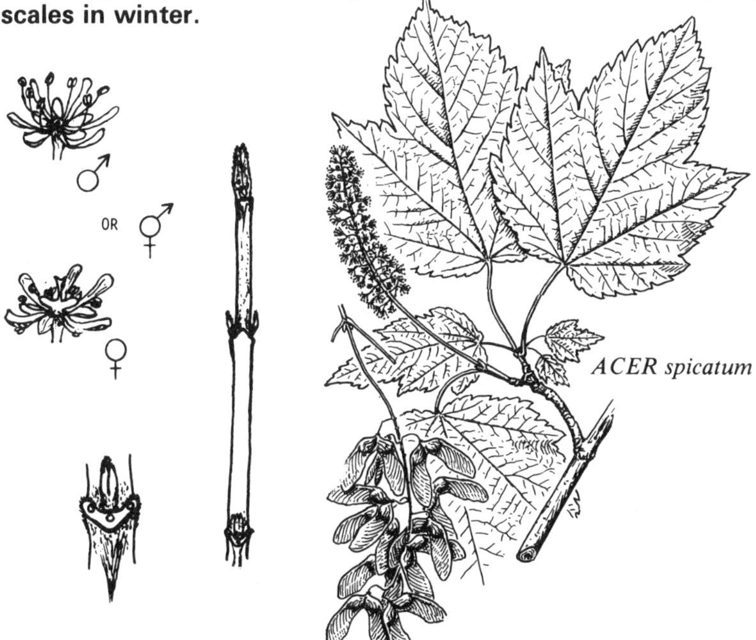

ACER spicatum

A. pensylvanicum L. (of Pennsylvania) **Striped Maple Goosefoot Maple, Moosewood**

Small tree, 10 m high or less, 2.5 dm in diameter; leaves 1.5-2.5 dm in diameter or less, heart-shaped or straight at base, finely toothed, 3-lobed with long, sharp tips; elongate flower cluster terminal, drooping, 7-10 cm long; flowers greenish yellow, 6-8 mm broad, appearing after the leaves; winged fruits 2.5 cm long, the wings 8-10 mm wide. Flowers in May-June. In rocky woods especially at elevations above 2,500 feet. **The whitish inner bark is revealed in long stripes in the green outer bark. Inflorescence drooping, leaves finely double-toothed.**

WINTER

A tree up to 10 m high; buds stalked with 2 nonoverlapping scales, red in winter, about 1 cm long, blunt-pointed, glossy, smooth except for the long-haired margins of the scales; **bark smooth, green, becoming striped with white lines;** twigs thick, smooth, green, changing to red (young growth) in winter; lenticels few; leaf scars U-shaped; almost meeting around the twig. Cool woods, mostly at elevations above 2,500 feet. Our only maple with large, hairless, red buds with nonoverlapping scales in winter.

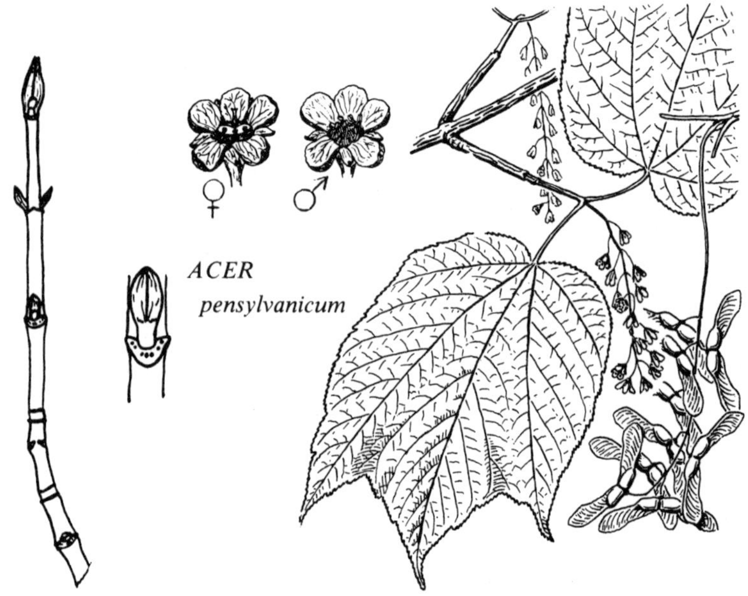

A. saccharum Marsh. (sugar) **Sugar Maple, Hard Maple**

A large and valuable tree with maximum height of 30-36 m and trunk diameter to 10 dm; leaves 7.5-15 cm long, dark green above, pale and hairless or slightly downy beneath, 3-7-lobed (usually 5), **unlike all other maples listed here, the margin of the leaf is not toothed (scattered sharp tips of lobes not considered),** the angles rounded, brilliant yellow or scarlet in autumn; flowers greenish yellow, in lateral or terminal compact clusters, drooping on thin stalks, appearing with the leaves; petals none; winged fruits hairless, 2.5-4 cm long, the wings 6-10 mm wide. Flowers in April-May. Rich woods and coves, usually on nonacid soil.

WINTER

Large timber tree up to 36 m high, with a diameter to 10 dm. Bark gray, furrowed (on very large trees resembling white oak bark), but easily distinguished by the small opposite twigs; twigs slender, hairless, not shiny, reddish brown. **Except for black maple, this is our only maple having overlapping, scaled, brownish, sharp-pointed buds in winter;** opposite leaf scars meeting in a "V" (as in all of our maples). Rich woods, one of our most valuable trees.

ACER saccharum

A. rubrum L. (red) **Red Maple, Soft Maple**

Large trees with maximum height of 40 m and diameter to 13 dm; bark on young trunks smooth and gray, on older trunks grayish, rough and often platy and black at base; twigs slender, green, becoming glossy red in winter; buds blunt, almost globe-shaped, green in summer, turning reddish in winter; leaves 8-15 cm long, heart-shaped at base, sharply 3-5-lobed, the lobes irregularly toothed, whitish or silvery green beneath; **flowers in sessile lateral clusters, preceding the leaves; petals narrow; ovary hairless; winged fruits hairless,** 1.8-2.4 cm long, the wings 6-8 mm wide. Flowers in March-April. Swamps and moist woods, usually on acid, upland soils. **Only red and silver maples have green summer buds with overlapping scales.**

WINTER

Tree up to 40 m high and 13 dm in diameter; buds green, turning reddish, blunt and nearly globe-shaped, flower buds developing towards spring; twigs slender, green in summer, becoming glossy red during winter; young trees with smooth, light gray bark, older trunks have rough dark grayish bark becoming scaley on large trees, platey and black at base of trunk; **flowers red, beginning to bloom in March.** Rich soil in a variety of situations. **Only red and silver maples have red, overlapping bud scales in winter.**

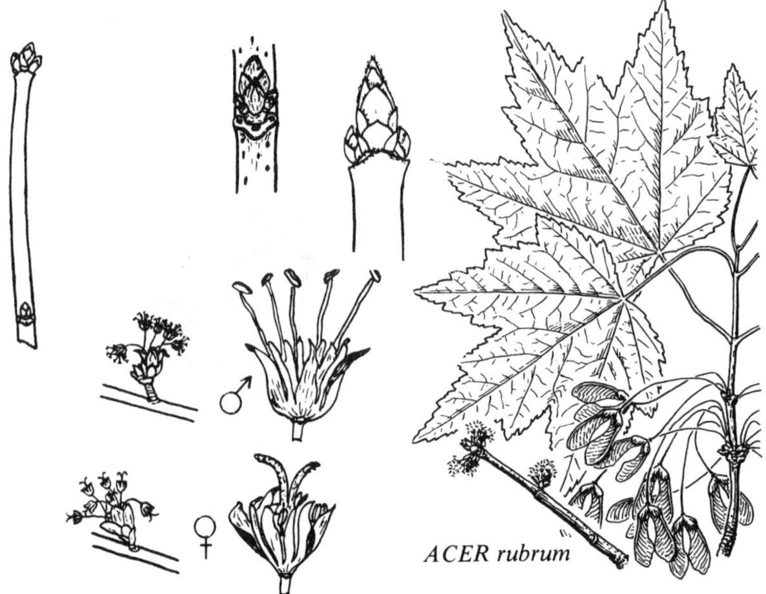

ACER rubrum

A. saccharinum L. (sugary) **Silver Maple, Water Maple**

Tree with flaky bark, maximum height to 40 m; trunk diameter to 15 dm; crushed twigs with a rank odor; leaves 10-15 cm long, deeply 5-lobed, the lobes coarsely toothed, silvery white below; flowers greenish to red in nearly sessile, lateral compact clusters preceding the leaves; **petals none; ovaries and winged fruits hairy when young,** becoming 5 cm long, the wings often 12 mm wide. Flowers in February-April. Margins of rivers and creeks and on bottomlands.

WINTER

A large tree reaching a height of 40 m and a diameter of 15 dm; buds reddish, blunt, almost globe-shaped, sessile or short-stalked; flower buds round, margin of scales hairy, and light-colored; crushed twigs have an unpleasant odor; young trees have smooth and light gray bark, on older trees this becomes brown and very shallowly furrowed; **flowers greenish yellow or reddish, blooms as early as February.** Riverbanks and moist bottomlands.

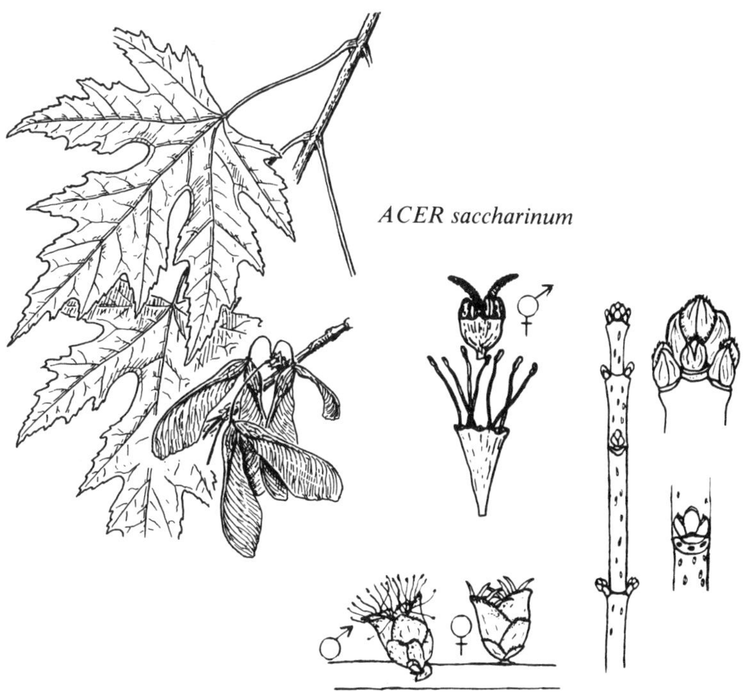

ACER saccharinum

AESCULUS L. **Buckeye**

Our only native trees having opposite, palmately compound leaves. Our native species have tan to light reddish brown nonresinous buds. Seeds large, dark brown or black, shining, starchy, containing a bitter, somewhat poisonous material.

A. octandra Marsh. (with eight stamens) **Yellow Buckeye, Sweet Buckeye**

Tree with a maximum height of 30 m and trunk diameter to 9 dm; bark dark brown, scaly on older trees; bark smooth, gray with whitish vertical marking on younger trees; **leaves opposite, palmately compound, leaflets 5,** 10-17.5 cm long, hairless or hairy, finely toothed; inflorescences loose, with tiny hairs; flowers pale yellow; petals 4; fruit 5-7.5 cm long, smooth. Flowers in May-June. Scattered but common on rich, moist soil.

WINTER

A tree reaching a height of 30 m and a diameter of 9 dm. Buds, especially the terminal, quite large, somewhat pointed, sessile, with 6 or more pairs of tan overlapping scales; covered with a thin wax-like layer. Twigs thick, light to reddish brown; pith large, continuous. **Leaf scars opposite, large, shield-shaped; bundle traces 3 or more; no stipule scars.** Bark light brown to grayish brown splitting into thin scales. A terminal fruit scar is sometimes present. Rich woods and lowlands.

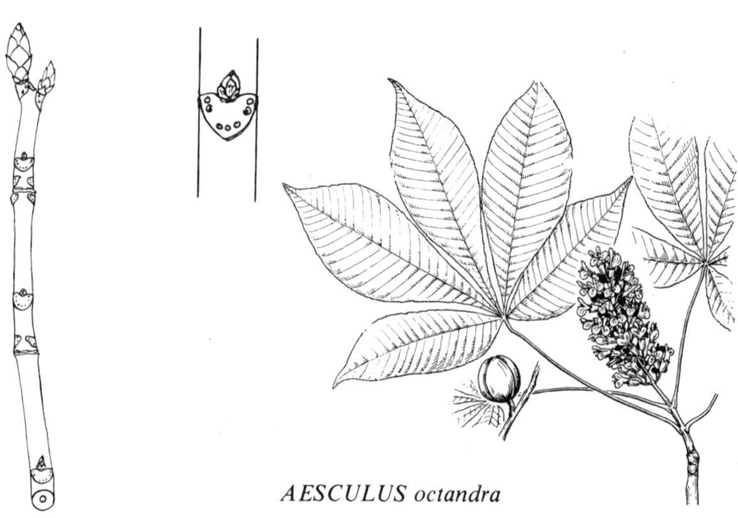

AESCULUS octandra

CEANOTHUS L. **New Jersey Tea**

Shrubs with alternate, petioled leaves and terminal or axillary clusters of perfect, white flowers. Calyx 5-lobed, incurved. Petals 5, hooded, spreading, on slender bases, longer than the calyx. Stamens 5, filaments filliform, elongated. Fruit a capsule, 3-lobed, dry and splitting into 3 cavities when ripe.

C. americanus L. (American) **New Jersey Tea, Red Root**

Low shrub with erect or ascending, branching stems from a deep reddish root; leaves ovate or ovate-oblong, mostly 5-10 cm long, 2.5-6 cm wide, sharp at the apex, blunt or heart-shaped at the base, finely hairy, especially beneath, toothed all around, strongly 3-nerved; flowers small, white; stalks 6-12 mm long; fruit depressed, about 4 mm high, nearly black. Flowers from May to September. Dry hillsides, open woods, thickets and roadsides.

WINTER

Low, upright, shrub less than 1 m high; buds small, single, sessile, oval; with slender branches; twigs slender, with fine hairs, greenish or brown; pith large, white, continuous. Leaf scars alternate, half-oval, small with 1 bundle trace forming a tranverse line or sometimes compound; stipule scars small and narrow or stipules present. Roots dark red. Fruits may be present in winter. Dry roadsides and banks and open woods.

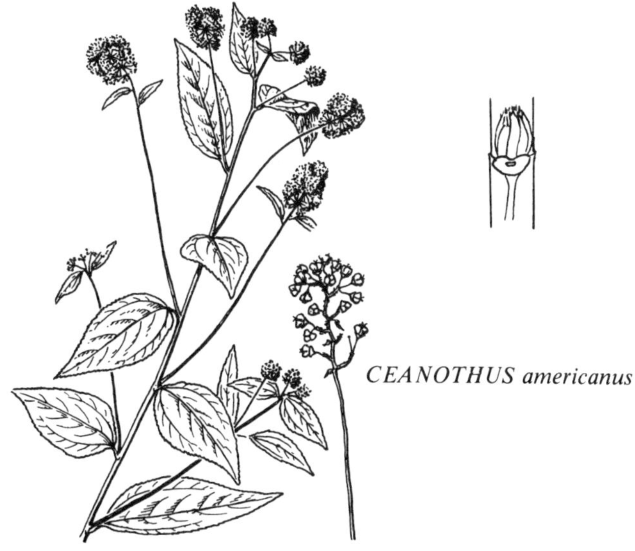

CEANOTHUS americanus

PARTHENOCISSUS Planch. **Virginia Creeper**

Climbing or trailing deciduous woody vines, the tendrils often tipped with adhering pads or disks, or sometimes merely coiling; leaves alternate, palmately compound. Flowers in compound flat or spreading inflorescences. Petals 5, spreading. Stamens 5. Ovary 2-celled, seeds 2 in each cavity; style short and thick. Berry 1-4 seeded, the flesh thin.

P. quinquefolia (L.) Planch. (five-leaved) **Virginia Creeper**

High climbing or trailing woody vine; tendrils usually numerous and often tipped with terminal adhering pads; **leaves 5-foliate;** leaflets stalked, oval, elliptic, or narrowly oval, 5-15 cm long, sharp-pointed, coarsely toothed, **brilliant red in autumn;** inflorescences erect or spreading in fruit; fruits only in the sun, **berries blue,** about 12 mm in diameter, usually 2-3-seeded, inedible for humans but important as a fall and winter food for birds; stalks of the inflorescences and flowers red. Flowers in July. In woods, thickets, fencerows, and hillsides. **Our only woody vine with palmately compound leaves with 5 leaflets.**

WINTER

Slender woody vines. Buds frequently multiple, sessile, conical; no terminal bud. Stems round, slender with swollen nodes and relatively large, continuous pith; twigs usually hairy. Leaf scars oval; **tendrils opposite the leaf scars, except every third node; tendrils branching with terminal adhesive disks;** stipule scars elongate. Open woods and thickets.

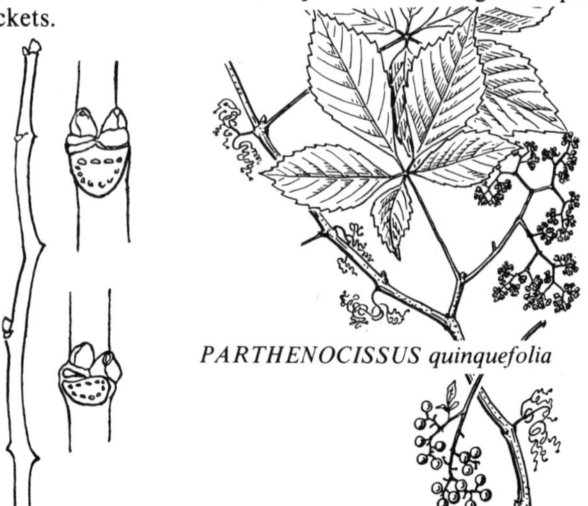

PARTHENOCISSUS quinquefolia

VITIS L. **Grape**

Woody vines trailing or climbing by the coiling of tendrils. Leaves simple, usually palmately lobed or toothed. Flowers mostly of one sex on a plant or sometimes mixed or perfect, 5-parted. Calyx very short, or none. Petals separating only at base and falling off without expanding. Disk of 5 nectar-bearing glands alternate with the stamens. Berry spherical or oval, few-seeded, pulpy, usually edible.

V. aestivalis Michx. (of summer) **Summer Grape, Pigeon Grape**

High-climbing; **leaves large,** 3-5-lobed, **dull green above; tendrils on young shoots red and conspicuous;** berries 0.6-1 cm in diameter, acid, dark purple to black and slightly covered with a blue-gray waxy coating. Flowers in May-June. Fruit ripe September-October. In the var. ***argentifolia*** (Munson) Fernald (silvery-leaved) **Silverleaf Grape, the lower leaf surface, and the joints of the young stems are strongly whitened.** Extreme specimens are distinct, but many specimens show much intergradation. The variety seems nearly as common as the typical form. In woods and thickets.

WINTER

A woody, vine climbing high into the treetops; buds subspherical, covered with 2 scales; no terminal bud. Medium or short internodes and pubescent twigs. Stems striped, rounded, bark very stringy. Leaf scars alternate, hemispherical or crescent-shaped; bundle traces several forming a curved line; stipule scars elongate. Withered fruits or at least remains of the inflorescence present in winter. **Tendrils opposite most of the leaf scars.** Open woods, often forming dense canopies.

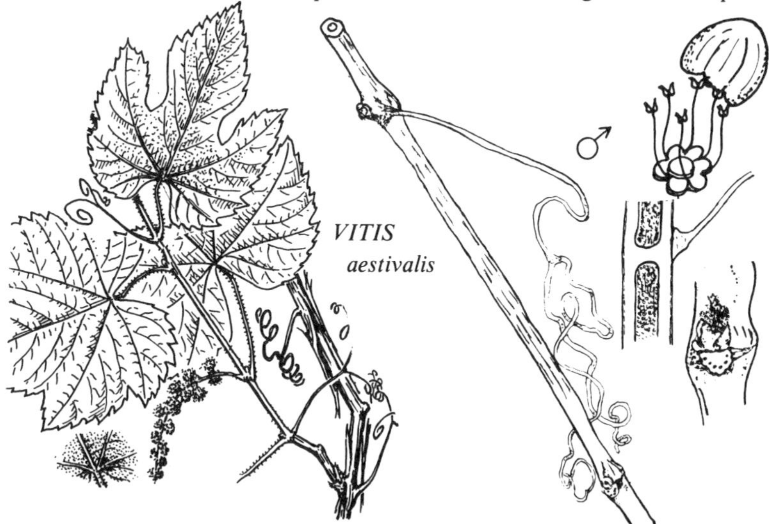

TILIA L. **Basswood, Linden**

Deciduous trees with smooth, zigzag twigs, soft white wood, and very tough inner bark, useful in making fabrics or baskets and suggesting the name bastwood (basswood). Leaves alternate, simple, toothed, usually having a lopsided heart-shaped base and the petiole swollen at both ends. Flowers yellowish white, nectar-bearing, fragrant, an important honey source, borne in small flat clusters hanging on an axillary stalk which is united to a tongue-like bract. Pistil with a 5-celled ovary, a single style, and a 5-toothed stigma. Fruit dry and woody, does not break open, spherical.

SUMMER KEY

a. Twigs relatively stout, 4 mm thick, leaves sometimes slightly whitened beneath. .... ***T. americana***
a. Twigs moderate, 2-3 mm thick; leaves strongly whitened beneath. .... ***T. heterophylla***

WINTER

Large trees up to 40 m high and 11 dm in diameter. Buds single, sessile, rather large, unequally oval, with 2 red scales in winter; no terminal bud. Twigs reddish, smooth, zigzag; pith pale, continuous. Leaf scars alternate, somewhat elevated, half-oval; bundle traces 3, scattered; stipule scars uneven. Separation of the two native species is difficult in winter unless the withered leaves are present.

WINTER KEY

Use the above key for winter identification.

T. americana L. (American) **American Linden, Basswood, Linn**

A large tree up to 40 m high, **leaves 5-12.5 cm wide, leathery, hairless on both sides or with some hairs on the veins or the undersurface,** sharply toothed with glandular teeth abruptly sharp-pointed; **unequally heart-shaped at base,** petiole swollen at both ends; floral bracts 5-10 cm long, often narrowed at the base, strongly veined; inflorescences drooping, 6-20-flowered; flowers 10-14 mm broad; fruit spherical-oval, 8-10 mm in diameter. Flowers in May-June. In rich woods and along river bottoms.

WINTER

A tree growing up to 40 m high, with gray, shallowly furrowed bark and hairless twigs and buds, the green buds and twigs turning pink to red in winter; no terminal bud. **Withered leaves the same color on both sides.** Rich coves and hillsides.

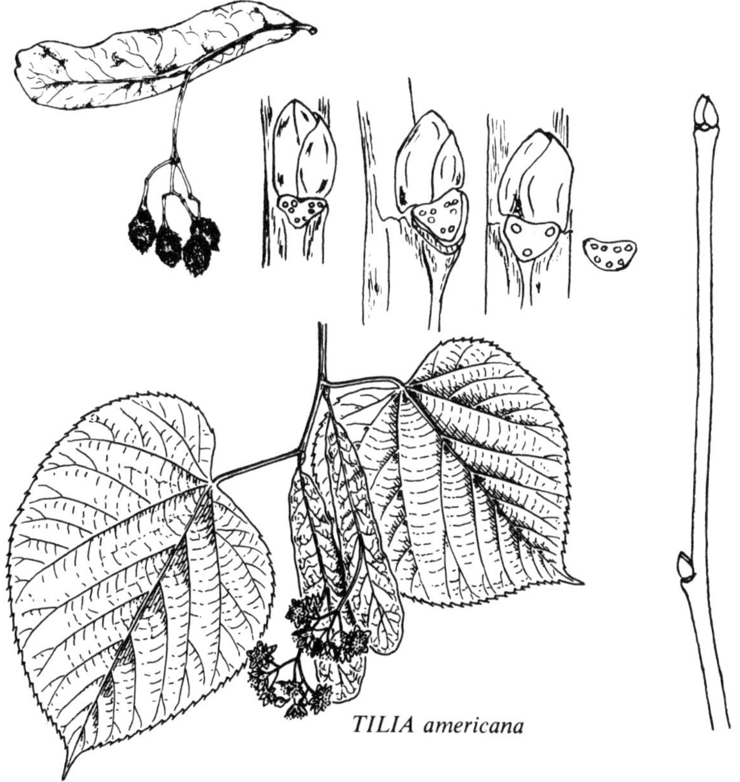

TILIA americana

T. heterophylla Vent. (diverse-leaved) **White Basswood, Linn**

A large tree to 30 m high, with a diameter of 1.5 m; bark at first gray and smooth, becoming shallowly furrowed into flat ridges; twigs smooth, reddish, or yellowish brown; **leaves large, 15-20 cm long, asymetrical at the base, smooth and dark green above, white beneath with fine downy hairs,** apex sharp-pointed; floral bracts 7.5-12.5 cm long, narrowed at the base; flowers slightly larger than in the preceding species; fruit oval, about 10 mm in diameter. Flowers in June-July. In woods.

WINTER

A tree up to 30 m high and a diameter of 1.5 m, twigs smooth, reddish or yellowish brown; bark smooth, on older trees becoming roughened into flat ridges. **Withered leaves whitened beneath.** Rich woods, especially east of the mountains.

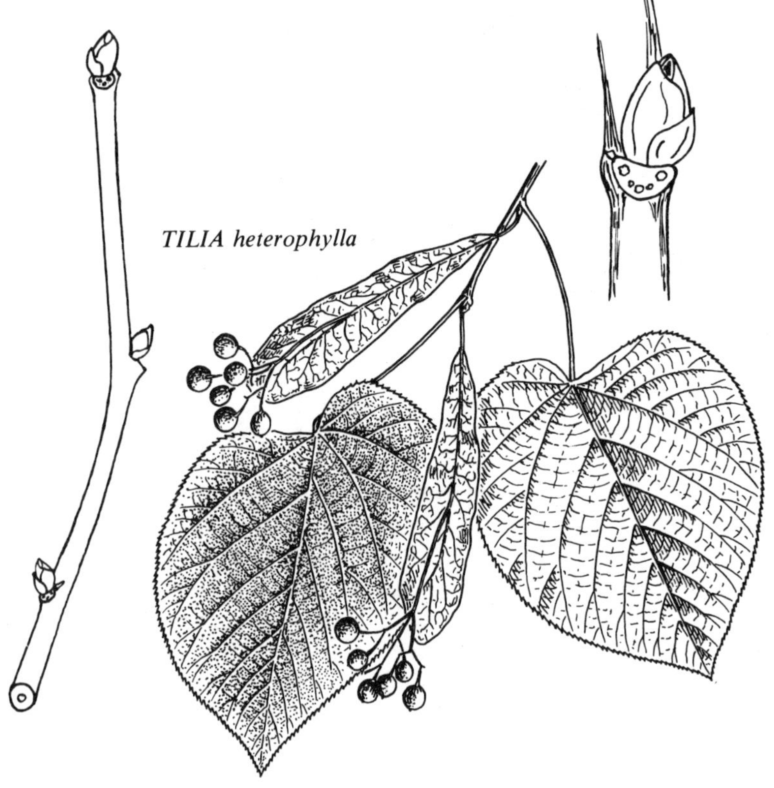

HYPERICUM L. **St. John's Wort**

Herbs or shrubs with opposite leaves and flowers in flat-topped clusters. Sepals 5, equal. Petals 5. Stamens numerous; more or less grouped in 3-5 clusters. Ovary 1-6-celled. Fruit a capsule.

H. prolificum L. (prolific; producing offsets) **Shrubby St. John's Wort**

SUMMER

Shrubby, diffusely branched, to 2.5 m high, the **branchlets 2-edged;** leaves narrowly oblong, 3-7 cm long, mostly obtuse, narrowed ovoid. Flowers in July-September. Dry or damp sandy soil.

WINTER

Shrub to 2.5 m high, very bushy; buds single, sessile, tiny; **twigs 2-edged,** slender, with large pith, porous, or missing in older stems. Leaf scars opposite, small, 3-cornered with 1 bundle trace; stipule scars missing. **Fruit consisting of a small brown capsule, is present in winter.** Dry or damp thickets.

HYPERICUM prolificum

VIOLA L. **Violet**

Leafy stemmed or stemless herbs, bearing showy flowers with petals mostly in early spring, usually followed by closed flowers, often underground, which normally are without petals and never open but bear abundant seed. Sepals prolonged into a lobe at the base. Petals unequal, the lower one spurred at the base. Stamens distinct but closely surrounding the ovary and sometimes slightly coherent to each other. Closely allied species often hybridize and produce very confusing forms.

a. Plant stemless; leaves kidney- or heart-shaped, petioles and flower stalks mostly smooth; flowers violet-blue to purple, overtopping the leaves; beard of the lateral petals knobbed; sepals with long lobes. .... ***V. cucullata***
a. Plants with leafy stems. .... b

b. Flowers yellow; stipule entire. c
b. Flowers white with yellow center, pale lavender on back; stipules lance-shaped, entire. .... ***V. canadensis***

c. Leaves arrowhead shaped, 2-4 at the summit of the stem, not lobed or divided; stipules less than 3 mm long. .... ***V. hastata***
c. Leaves heart-shaped, not lobed or divided; stipules more than 5 mm long; stems several, ascending, leafy; basal leaves present; plants sparingly hairy to smooth. .... ***V. pensylvanica***

V. cucullata Ait. (hooded, from the inrolled young leaves)

Marsh Blue Violet

Rootstock branching, becoming matted in old clumps; stemless; plant smooth, or with a very few hairs scattered along petioles and flower stalks; leaves heart-shaped, toothed, wavy, margined, normally sharp-pointed at apex; **flowers with petals large, typically violet-blue, decidedly darker toward the center, with a large white center,** smooth spurred petal shorter than the lateral ones; dense tufts of knobby beard on the lateral petals; long, spreading lobes of the elongate sepals usually distinctive. Flowers in April-June. In open or semi-shady marshy places and along streams.

VIOLA cucullata

V. hastata Michx. (hastate) **Halberd-Leaf Yellow Violet**

Rootstock long, horizontal, underground creeping, white, brittle; stems slender, smooth, arising singly or in pairs at intervals along the rootstock; **stem leaves mostly 2-4, clustered near the summit, lance-shaped or heart-shaped,** singly serrate, sharp at apex. Stipules ovate, sharp-pointed, entire or sparingly toothed, 2-10 mm long; **flowers yellow,** 1.5-2 cm long, lateral petals slightly bearded; spur very short; capsule smooth. Flowers in April-May. Dry woods, mostly in the mountains.

VIOLA hastata

VIOLA pensylvanica

V. pensylvanica Michx. (Pennsylvanian) **Smooth Yellow Violet**

Plant smooth or often somewhat hairy; stems mostly in clusters of 2-several, inclined, **leafy from near the base,** with a few or several spreading basal leaves; hairs, when present, mostly confined to the petioles and veins on the undersurface of the younger leaves; **leaves broadly oval, mostly with an abrupt acute point,** heart-shaped or cut off at the decurrent base, wavy or toothed margins, normally about 4 cm long; stipules ovate, sharp-pointed, mostly more than 1 cm long; **flowers yellow, purple-veined.** Flowers in April-May. Moist open woods.

V. canadensis L. (Canadian) **Canada Violet**

Plant smooth or nearly so throughout; **stem often 4 dm high (our tallest violet):** stipules elongate, sharp-pointed, about 1.5 cm long; leaves normally about 8 cm long by 6 cm wide; toothed, heart-shaped at base, sharp-pointed at apex; flowers with petals at intervals throughout the summer, the earliest ones often 2.5 cm wide, **petals white on the face with a yellow center, the spurred petal striped with fine, dark lines; spur very short; backs of the upper petals flushed with purple;** lateral petals bearded; sepals long and narrow, sharp-pointed; capsules subspherical, 6-10 mm long, often hairy; seeds brown. Flowers in May-July. Rich woods, especially at elevations above 2,500 feet.

VIOLA canadensis

DIRCA L. **Leatherwood**

Leaves alternate, thin, short-petioled, deciduous. Flowers yellowish, in stalked clusters of 2-4; calyx corolla-like, tubular, funnel-shaped, appearing cut off at the base. Stamens 8, inserted on the calyx, the alternate ones longer. Ovary nearly sessile, 1-celled. The tough twigs were used by the Indians for cords and are the source of the name "Leatherbark" applied to several geographic locations.

D. palustris L. (of the swamps) **Leatherwood**

Shrub to 3 m high with **flexible branches and very tough bark;** wood white, soft and very brittle; leaves oval, blunt at the apex, rounded or narrowed at base, 5-7 cm long; flowers expanding before the leaves; calyx 4-6 mm long; drupe ovoid, about 1.2 cm long, yellowish, rarely seen. Flowers in April-May. In moist rich woods, thickets, and along streams.

WINTER

Low shrub up to 3 m high; buds with long dark hairs, small, single, sessile, conical, no terminal bud. Twigs rounded, glossy, slender, forking, light brown, or greenish, enlarged upwards in each annual growth forming swollen nodes; pith small, rounded, continuous. Leaf scars alternate, nearly meeting around the bud; with 5 or more bundle traces; no stipule scars, **branches flexible with very tough bark.** Rich woods, thickets and along streams.

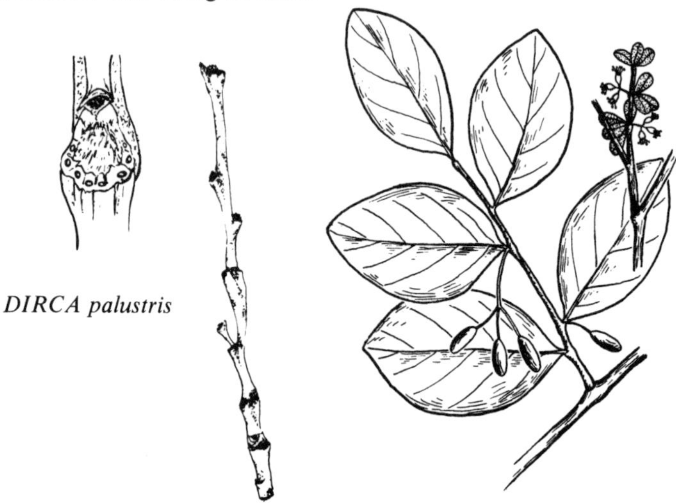

DIRCA palustris

NYSSA L. **Gum, Tupelo**

Perfect and/or imperfect flowers on the same tree; flowers 5-parted; petals small or none; style recurved or coiled at the summit; fruit with thin outercovering and ridged or winged inner layer; trees with entire or few-toothed leaves, the staminate flowers in a stalked, inflorescence, the pistillate (which sonmetimes have stamens on very short filaments) solitary or few, sessile.

N. sylvatica Marsh. (of the woods) **Black Gum, Sour Gum**

Large tree to 40 m; leaves oval, not toothed, lateral veins run nearly parallel to the leaf margin as in dogwood, sharp-pointed, 1-3 dm long, bright crimson in autumn; pistillate flower solitary, at the end of a slender stalk; fruit oval, 1 cm long, acid, blue-black, important as wildlife food. Flowers in April-May. Rich soil, either moist or dry.

WINTER

A large tree growing up to 40 m with a diameter of 1.5 m; twigs smooth, young growth olive brown, rounded; pith white, usually with firmer plates at intervals. Buds minutely soft-haired, olive-brown, sessile or slightly stalked, single or placed one above the other, oval with 4 scales; terminal bud somewhat larger than the lateral buds. Leaf scars alternate, crescent-shaped or triangular with 3 bundle traces; no stipule scars. Young bark smooth and grayish, older bark scaly, ridged, reddish brown or grayish black, and **bark on very old trees forming a blocky pattern.** Dry or moist woods.

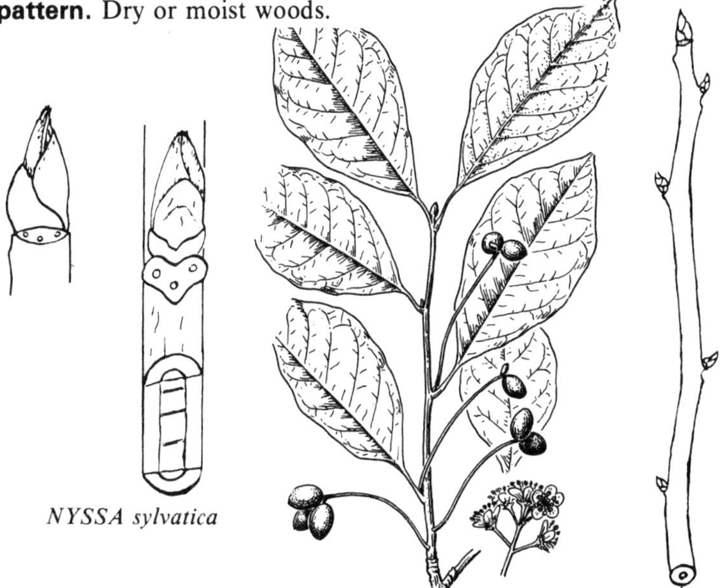

NYSSA sylvatica

ARALIA L. **Aralia**

Flowers white or greenish, perfect or imperfect on the same plant; petals 5, sheathing at the base; flower stalks jointed below the flowers. Stamens 5. Ovary 5-celled. Fruit a small berry enclosing about 5 seeds.

SUMMER KEY

a. Inflorescences numerous in a large compound cluster. .... b
a. Inflorescences mostly 2-7, flattened; stem short, somewhat woody, plant bristly, stem leafy, erect. .... ***A. hispida***

b. Spiny shrub or small tree. .... ***A. spinosa***
b. Branching unarmed herb. .... ***A. racemosa***

WINTER

Deciduous shrubs, small trees, or herbs, sometimes with surface prickles on the stems and branches. Twigs stout, rounded with large, continuous pith. Leaf scars alternate, crescent-shaped, reaching halfway around the twigs with about 15 bundle traces forming a line; stipule scars absent.

WINTER KEY

a. Tree or shrub with a thick stem having stout prickles. ***A. spinosa***
a. Small shrub with a moderately thick stem having hair-like bristles. .... ***A. hispida***

(***A. racemosa*** is not present in winter)

A. spinosa L. (spiny) **Hercules' Club, Devil's Walking Stick**

Shrub or small tree attaining a maximum height of 12 m; stem, branches, and petioles spiny; **spines on stem in circles at the nodes, irregularly scattered spines on the internodes; leaves long-petioled, two or more times compound;** leaflets sharp-pointed, stalked, toothed; flowers white, 4 mm broad; fruit ovoid, black, 5-lobed, about 5 mm long. **Our only small, spiny tree having alternate, bipinnately compound leaves.** Flowers in June-August. Rich woods, bluffs and roadsides.

WINTER

A shrub or small tree, reaching 12 m high, branches gray or tan, smooth; inflorescence large, in compound clusters, dark blue berries, present into early winter; **with extremely prickly, stout stems.** Woods, road banks.

ARALIA spinosa

A. racemosa L. (racemose) **American Spikenard**

Herbaceous, from large spicy-aromatic roots, divergently branched, unarmed, to 18 dm high, smooth or slightly hairy; **leaves three or five times compound;** leaflets broadly oval, thin; flowers greenish, about 2 mm broad; fruit nearly spherical, dark purple or reddish brown, about 6 mm in diameter. Flowers in July-August. In rich woods. **Not present in winter.**

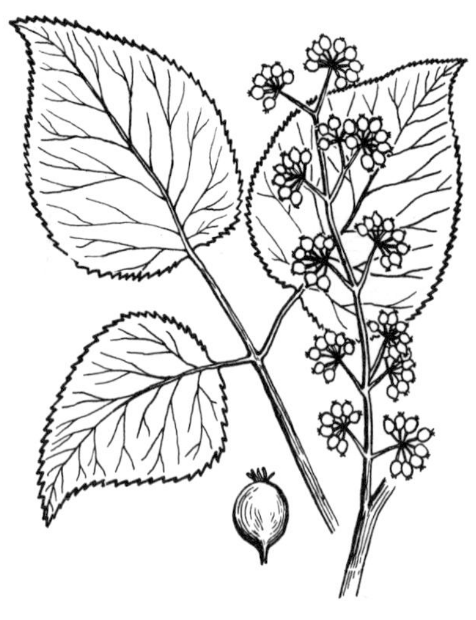

ARALIA racemosa

A. hispida Vent. (with straight hairs) **Bristly Sarsaparilla**

Erect to 9 dm high, the stem and petioles covered with slender bristles; **leaves twice pinnate;** leaflets oblong-oval, sharp-pointed, sharply toothed; flowers white, 2 mm broad; fruit purplish-black, 6-8 mm in diameter. Flowers in June-July. Exposed rocky and sandy places especially in barren places at high elevations.

WINTER

Short stem up to 9 dm high, bristly at the base, not very woody. Rocky woods and clearings especially in barren places at high elevations.

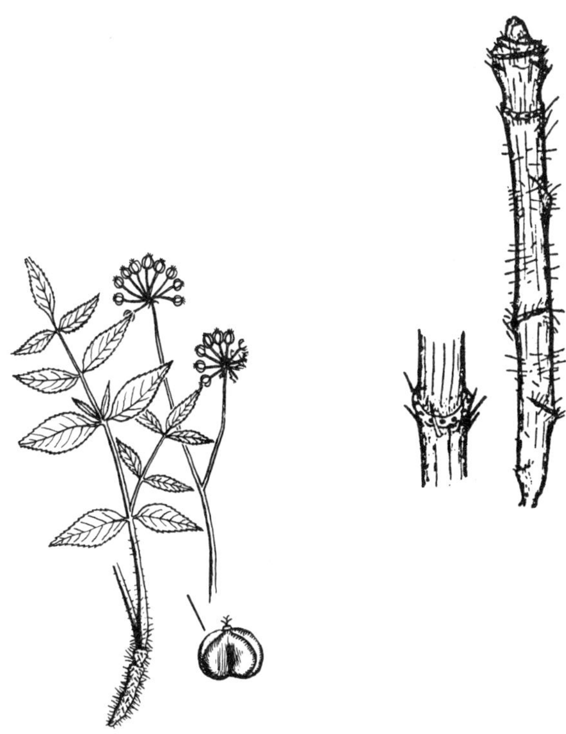

ARALIA hispida

PANAX L. **Ginseng, Sang**

Erect perennial herbs from aromatic roots, with a whorl of palmate leaves at the summit of the stem. Inflorescences solitary, terminal. Flowers greenish or white, perfect and/or imperfect. Petals 5. Carpels 2-3. Fruit a berry.

P. quinquefolius L. (five-leaved) **Ginseng, Sang**

Root large and spindle-shaped; often forked, 1-2 dm high; **leaves palmately compound,** leaflets large and thin, oval-oblong, pointed, 5-12.5 cm wide; stalk of inflorescence slender, 2.2-5 cm long; inflorescence 6-20-flowered; flowers about 2 mm broad; styles usually 2; **fruit bright crimson,** 10 mm broad. Flowers in July-August. Rich cool woods. Extensively collected for its valuable roots. **The collection of ginseng roots is regulated by law.**

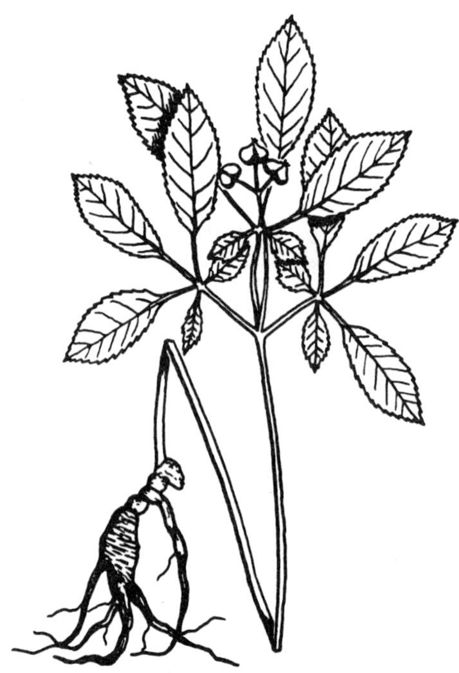

PANAX quinquefolius

CORNUS L. Dogwood

Shrubs or trees with simple, entire leaves (all but one species with opposite leaves), the terminal pair of lateral veins curving forward and meeting in the apex (all lateral veins run nearly parallel to the smooth leaf margin as in black gum). Flowers small, greenish, or purple, in flat clusters. Calyx minutely 4-toothed, petals 4, oblong, spreading.Stamens 4, filaments slender, style slender; stigma terminal, flat or capped. Drupe small, with a 2-celled and 2-seeded stone.

SUMMER KEY

a. Leaves opposite. .... b
a. Leaves alternate. .... ***C. alternifolia***

b. Flowers greenish, in a dense cluster surrounded by usually 4 showy white or pinkish bracts; fruit bright red; shrub or tree to 12 m high. .... ***C. florida***
b. Flowers white in open, flat inflorescences; bracts none; fruit white or blue. c

c. Leaves downy-haired beneath, at least when young, oval or oval-elongate, rounded at the base, green beneath, hairs brown, reddish, or grayish. .... ***C. amomum***
c. Leaves smooth or minutely hairy beneath; twigs olive-gray; fruit white. .... ***C. racemosa***

WINTER

Small trees or shrubs with slender, round twigs; pith round, continuous or becoming porous. Buds single, stalked or sessile, oval. Leaf scars opposite (alternate in 1 species), crescent-shaped, raised; with 3 bundle traces; stipule scars absent; leaf scars may meet or may be joined by a line.

WINTER KEY

a. Leaf scars distinctly opposite. .... b
a. Leaf scars indistinctly alternate (very crowded at the ends of the twigs). .... ***C. alternifolia***

b. Leaf scars of previous summer raised; petiole bases cover the leaf buds; flower buds onion-shaped, conspicuous, found in the winter; pith white. .... *C. florida*
b. Leaf buds visible; pith of young twigs brown or gray; branchlets reddish or purplish; leaves rounded at the base. c

c. Remains of inflorescence flat-topped; twigs reddish. *C. amomum*
c. Remains of inflorescence branched, not flat-topped; twigs gray. ... . *C. racemosa*

C. florida L. (flowering) **Flowering Dogwood**

Shrub or small tree to 12 m with **brownish "alligator" bark on older trees and green or purplish, smooth branchlets; leaves ovate, pointed, acute at base;** bracts of inflorescence somewhat heart-shaped, 3-6 cm long, white, or rarely pink; fruit oval, bright red. Flowers in April-June. Dry, acid woods.

WINTER

A small tree sometimes reaching a height of 12 m; twigs green of purplish, smooth; pith white; bark on older trees becoming blocky; fruit football-shaped, 1 cm long, red (rarely yellow), persistent into winter. Common in woodlands. **Flower buds of next year present in winter.**

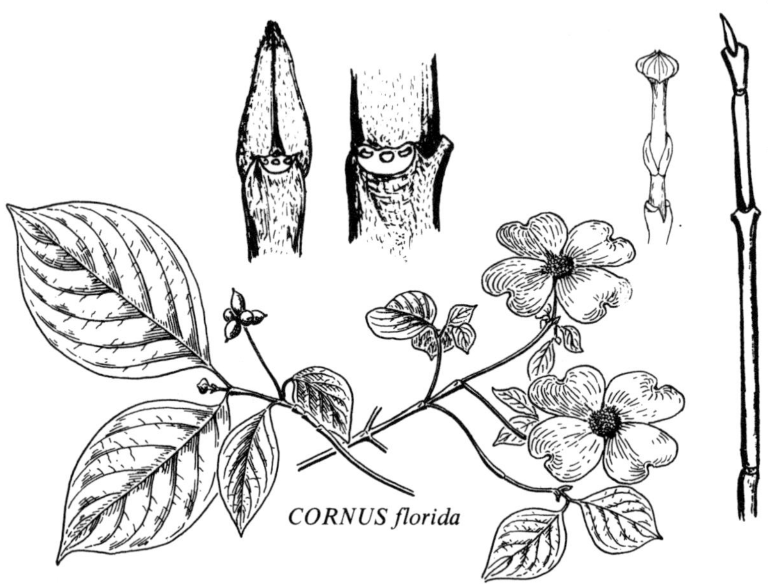
CORNUS florida

C. amomum Mill. (Latin name of some shrub) **Silky Cornel, Kinnikinnik**

A many-stemmed shrub to 3 m high, with **loose, branching, green twigs, becoming purplish red and bearing silky, downy rusty hairs; pith brown;** leaves ovate or ovate-lanceolate, abruptly sharp-pointed at the apex, narrowed or rounded at the base, **usually finely haired with white or brownish red hairs beneath,** 2.5-12.5 cm long, averaging more than half as long as broad; flowers white in rather compact flat clusters; fruit light blue, globe-shaped. Flowers in May-June. Swamps and damp thickets.

WINTER

A shrub up to 3 m high, buds sessile; twigs green in summer, becoming purplish red in winter, bearing fine, downy, rusty hairs; pith brown, the lower branches may root in wet soil. Damp thickets and woodland borders.

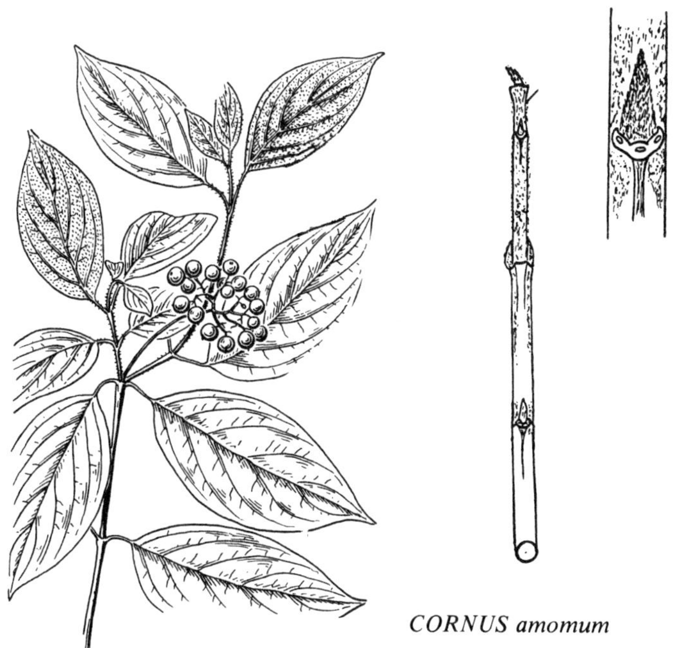

CORNUS amomum

C. racemosa Lam. (a type of inflorescence) **Panicled Dogwood**

Shrub to 5 m high with **smooth olive-gray bark and smooth gray branchlets; pith sometimes white but generally brown, especially in 2-year-old branchlets;** leaves ovate-lance-shaped, taper-pointed, sharp at base, **whitish beneath but not downy;** inflorescences convex, loose, often branched; **fruit white,** depressed, spherical, on bright red stalks. Flowers in June, July. Moist or dry soil. Note: Inflorescence is a panicle as indicated by the common name.

WINTER

A shrub up to 5 m high, with **smooth gray bark and twigs; pith usually brownish, sometimes white in young twigs.** Dry open woods and borders.

CORNUS racemosa

C. alternifolia L.f. (alternate-leaved) **Alternate-leaved Dogwood**

Tree-shaped shrub or small tree to 8 m high, the branches spreading in irregular whorls to form horizontal tiers (for this reason it may be called Pagoda Dogwood); **branchlets smooth, greenish, the alternate leaves clustered at the ends;** whitish and minutely hairy; **fruit globe-shaped, deep blue on reddish stalks.** Flowers in May-June. Thickets and open woods.

WINTER

Tree-shaped shrub or small tree up to 8 m high, the branches characteristically form horizontal layers; **branchlets smooth, greenish; leaf-scars actually alternate, but are so crowded as to appear whorled.** Dry open woods.

CORNUS alternifolia

RHODODENDRON L. **Rhododendron, Azalea, "Honeysuckle"**

Shrubs with alternate, petioled, entire leaves and showy flowers usually borne in terminal clusters; calyx usually 5-parted, frequently quite small, corolla showy, round,to bell-shaped or funnel form, sometimes tubular, mostly slightly irregular, usually 5-lobed; stamens 5-10, anthers opening by apical pores; ovary 5-10 celled, many ovuled, with a slender style and a capitate stigma; capsule ovoid to oblong with numerous minute seeds.

In West Virginia the evergreen members of this genus usually receive the common name "Big Laurel" or "Rhododendron." The deciduous members are often called "Honeysuckle" but this name is better applied to the Honeysuckle Family; a more distinctive name is "Azalea."

SUMMER KEY

a. Leaves thick, leathery and evergreen (**Rhododendrons**). .... b
a. Leaves thin, deciduous (**Azaleas**). c

b. Leaves usually acute at both ends; calyx lobes oblong, obtuse. .... ***R. maximum***
b. Leaves usually obtuse at both ends; calyx lobes short, acute. .... ***R. catawbiense***

c. Flowers appearing before or with the leaves. .... d
c. Flowers appearing after the leaves. .... ***R. arborescens***

d. Flowers orange, yellow or red; leaves white-haired beneath. .... ***R. calendulaceum***
d. Flowers pink or white. .... e

e. Leaves with stiff hairs beneath along midrib; corolla tube hairy. .. .. ***R. nudiflorum***
e. Leaves grayish, hairy beneath. .... ***R. roseum***

WINTER

Evergreen or deciduous shrubs. Buds single, sessile, the upper oval with 6 or more scales with hairy margins, flower buds present in winter much larger than leaf buds; twigs round having small roundish, continuous pith. Leaf scars alternate, shield-shaped, with 1 or more bundle traces; stipule scars absent. Fruit a dry capsule splitting into 5 sections. Persistent into winter.

WINTER

a. Leaves leathery, evergreen. .... b
a. Leaves thin, deciduous. c

b. Leaves usually acute at both ends. .... ***R. maximum***
b. Leaves rounded at both ends. .... ***R. catawbiense***

c. Buds mostly hairless. .... d
c. Buds hairy. .... e

d. Twigs hairless. .... ***R. arborescens***
d. Twigs with a few long hairs. .... f

e. Twigs reddish. .... ***R. calendulaceum***
e. Twigs tan or gray. .... g

f. Buds brown. .... ***R. calendulaceum***
f. Buds reddish. .... ***R. nudiflorum***

g. Twigs with small hairs at least near the tip. .... ***R. roseum***
g. Twigs with a few straight stiff hairs. .... ***R. nudiflorum***

R. maximum L. (greatest) **Great Rhododendron, Great Laurel**

Shrub or small tree; **leaves very thick and leathery, elliptical-oblong or lance-oblong, acute at both ends,** very smooth, 0.8-2 dm long; flower stems sticky, **corolla bell-shaped,** 3.5-5 cm broad, **rose-colored varying to white, greenish in the throat on upper side, and marked with yellowish or orange spots,** capsule oblong, finely haired, 1-1.4 cm long. Flowers in June, July. Often forming nearly impenetrable thickets in the mountains. This is the state flower of West Virginia.

WINTER

Evergreen shrub up to 12 m high, but usually much shorter, the young twigs hairy; **leaves up to 20 cm long, thick, leathery, acute at both ends.** Moist woods, most common in the mountains.

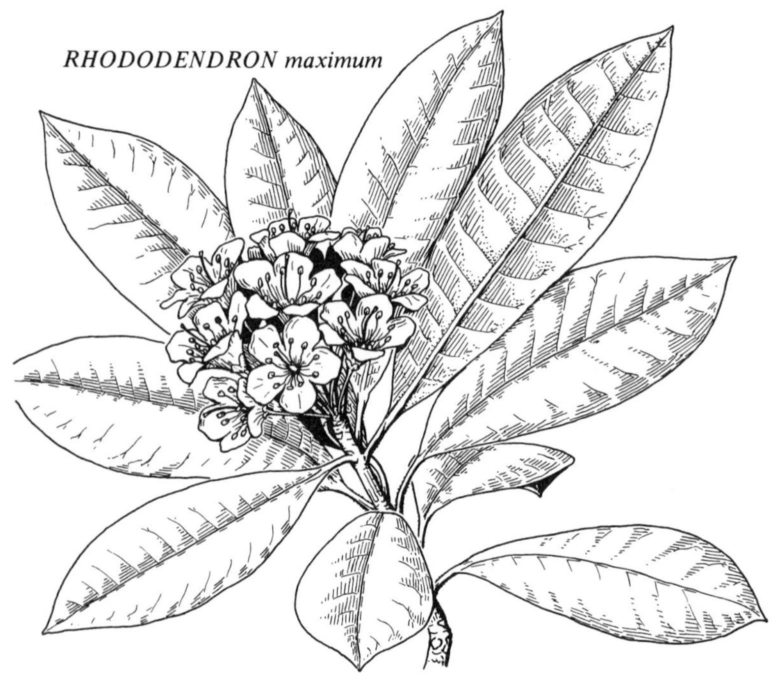

RHODODENDRON maximum

R. catawbiense Michx. (from Catawba River, N.C.)
Mountain Rose Bay, Purple Laurel

Leaves oval or oblong, usually rounded or obtuse at both ends, 7.5-12.5 cm long, 3.5-5 cm wide, dark green above, paler beneath; flower stems hairy, becoming hairless; **corolla broadly bell-shaped, lilac-purple,** 3.5-5 cm long, 5-6.5 cm broad; capsule linear-oblong, with small hairs, 1.6-2 cm long. Flowers in May, June. High mountain woods in the southeastern counties reaching its northernmost known limit in Pocahontas County.

WINTER

Evergreen shrub up to 6 m high; **leaves rounded at both ends,** 5-15 cm long. Moist woods. Rare in our area.

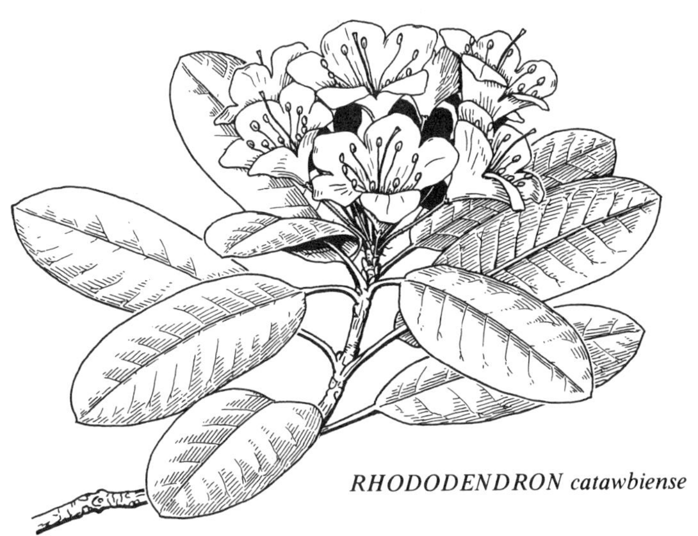

RHODODENDRON catawbiense

R. calendulaceum (Michx.) Torr. (colored like ***Calendula***)
Flame Azalea, Yellow "Honeysuckle"

Young twigs hairy with fine, stiff hairs, leaves oval, 4-8 cm long, acute and gland-tipped, finely-haired above and more or less densely so beneath (when young); **flowers yellow or orange, nearly odorless,** corolla about 5 cm across, glandular, and hairy, tube 1.5-2 cm long, flower stems usually with small bristles and usually glandular; capsule oval-oblong, 1.5-2 cm long, bristly and hairy. Flowers in May-June. Dry woods, most common on the western slopes of the mountains, occasionally found in the hilly counties west of the mountains.

WINTER

Deciduous shrub up to 3 m high; leaf buds light brown, smooth except for marginal hairs on the scales, the flower buds greenish; the young twigs with small hairs near the tips; capsule present in winter, long, oval, hairy. About 2 cm long. Rocky barrens and pastures, espcially in the mountains.

RHODODENDRON calendulaceum

R. nudiflorum (L.) Torr. (naked-flowered) **Pinxter Flower, Pink "Honeysuckle", Pink Azalea**

Twigs hairless or with stiff hairs; leave oval, acute at both ends, with small hairs or hairless except for stiff hairs on the margins and the midrib (beneath), 5-10 cm long; flower stem stiff-haired; **flowers flesh-colored, pink or purple, sometimes nearly white, expanding while the branches are still bare,** corolla somewhat 2-lipped, 3.5-5 cm broad, shorter than the narrow tube; capsule with stiff hairs; 1.5-3 cm long. Flowers in May-June. Open woods, probably in every county of the state, often quite abundant and showy, especially in the mountains.

WINTER

Deciduous shrub up to 2 m high; buds smooth, or bearing glands or small hairs; twigs tan or gray, with a few long hairs or becoming smooth; capsules about 2 cm long with upright long hairs, not glandular or sticky. Open woods, pasture fields and old burns.

RHODODENDRON nudiflorum

R. roseum (Loisel.) Rehd. (rosy) **Rose Azalea**

Twigs finely hairy and usually with fine stiff hairs; leaves oval, 3-7 cm long, acute or with a sharp point, sparingly haired above; flowers fragrant; corolla bright pink (rarely white), about 4 cm across, tube rather gradually dilated, 1.5-2 cm long, **flower stems long-haired and glandular;** capsule 1.5-2 cm long, slightly hairy and glandular. Flowers in May-June. Open woods, mostly at high elevations in the mountains.

WINTER

A deciduous shrub up to 5 m high; buds with small hairs; tan or gray twigs with fine hairs; capsules glandular, up to 1.8 cm long. Thickets, open woods and along streams.

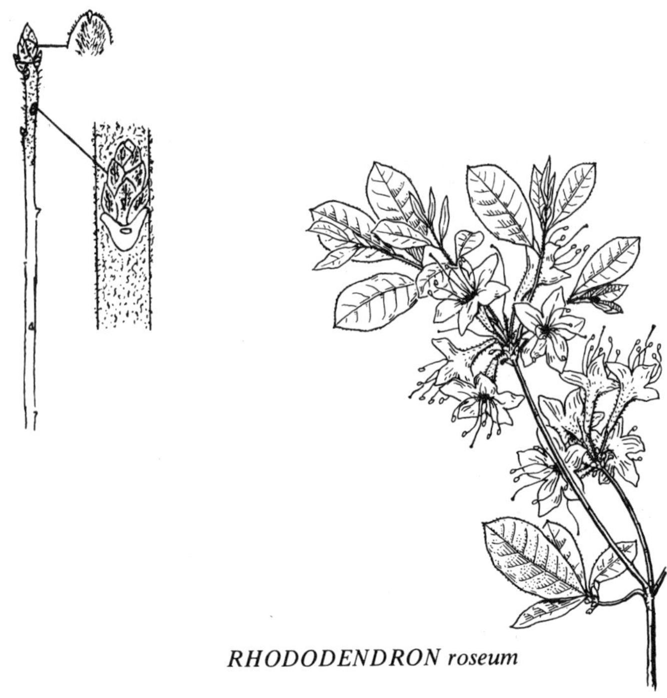

RHODODENDRON roseum

R. arborescens (Pursh) Torr. (tree-like) **White "Honeysuckle," Smooth Azalea**

Loosely branched shrub to 6 m high, hairless or nearly so throughout; leaves obovate, 5-10 cm long, bristly on the margins; **flowers appearing after the leaves, white or rose-colored,** fragrant, corolla 3-5 cm broad, about as long as the slender glandular tube; flower stem short, glandular (sometimes glandless); stamens and style red, long extended; capsule oblong-ovoid, 1-1.7 cm long. Flowers in June-July. rocky woods, stream banks and swamps, mostly on the western slopes of the mountains.

WINTER

Deciduous shrub up to 6 m high; twigs usually hairless; buds and flower stems contain a few stalked glands, otherwise glandless; capsules oblong, with dense glands, up to 1.6 cm long. Moist areas and stream banks.

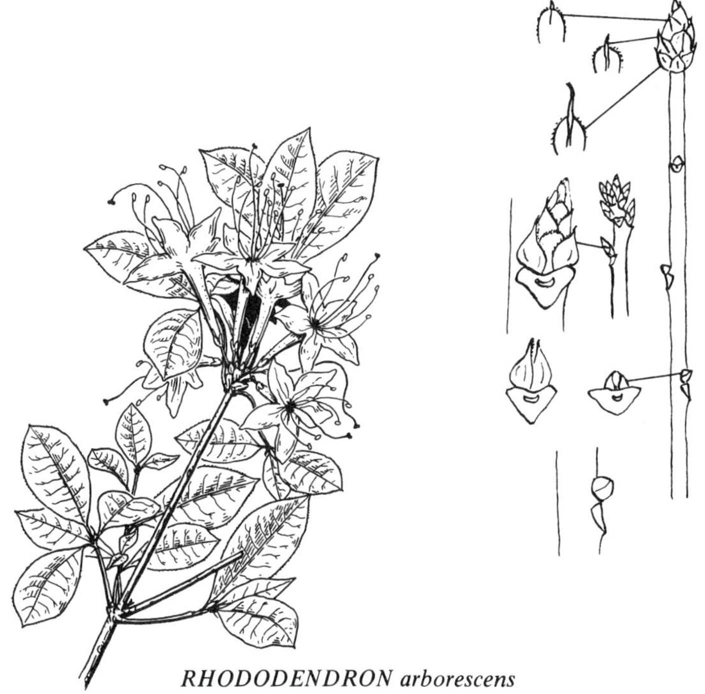

RHODODENDRON arborescens

KALMIA L. **Laurel**

Shrubs with alternate, entire, evergreen, leathery leaves and clusters of showy flowers; calyx 5-parted; corolla 5-lobed, saucer-shaped, stamens 10, shorter than the corolla, filaments curved outward with the anthers inserted in the pouches of the corolla, but straightening elastically when the flower becomes fully opened; capsule round, 5-celled; many seeded.

K. latifolia L. (broad-leaved) **Mountain Laurel, Sheepkill**

Leaves hairless, not toothed, bright green on both sides, oval, generally acute at each end, 2.5-12.5 cm long; flowers pink to white, 1.8-2.4 cm broad; **stamens tucked in pockets of the corolla and held with tension on the filaments,** calyx and corolla glandular capsule round, 5-lobed, glandular, 4-6 mm in diameter. Flowers May-July. Rocky or gravelly soil in acid woods, but most abundant in the mountains.

WINTER

Shrub usually less than 3 m high with hairless round twigs; leaves leathery, oval, evergreen, 5-10 cm long, not toothed, acute at both ends. Fruit a glandular capsule, 5-7 mm in diameter, present in winter. Rocky woods, barrens and old pastures.

KALMIA latifolia

EPIGAEA L. **Trailing Arbutus**

Plants prostrate or trailing, slightly shrubby, with oval, alternate leaves and rose-colored flowers in small axillary clusters. Sepals 5, persistent; corolla with a short tube splitting into 5 lobes at the top; stamens 10. Capsule round, fleshy, hairy, 5-celled.

E. repens L. (creeping on the ground) **Trailing Arbutus**

Twigs hairy, branches 1.5-3.8 dm long, **prostrate or trailing; leaves evergreen,** oval to round, thick, 2.5-7.5 cm long; flowers 10-16 mm long; capsule splitting into 5 valves, exposing the white fleshy interior. Flowers March-May. Sandy or rocky woods, especially under evergreens, often forming large patches which persist in open fields after the trees have been removed; especially common in the mountains.

WINTER

Small trailing evergreen shrub. Buds single or clustered, very hairy. Slender twigs with red-bristly hairs; pith round, continuous. **Leaves alternate, evergreen, oval to round, entire, with marginal hairs, veins net-like;** peeling bark.

EPIGAEA repens

MENZIESIA Sm. **Menziesia**

Erect shrubs with alternate, entire leaves and small nodding greenish purple flowers in terminal clusters; calyx small, flattish, 4-toothed or 4-lobed, persistent; corolla urn-shaped, becoming bell-shaped or globe-shaped, 4-toothed or 4-lobed; stamens 8; ovary mostly 4-celled, 4-valved, many seeded.

M. pilosa (Michx.) Juss. (hairy) **Allegheny Menziesia, Minnie-bush**

Shrub to 1.8 m high, more or less **chaffy and with stiff hairs; leaves oblong, thin, glandular, glandular-pointed at the tip,** rough-haired above, 2.5-5 cm long, **margins hairy;** petioles 4-10 mm long, hairy; flowers few on slender glandular stems 1.2-5 cm long. May-July. Rocky woods and thickets in the mountain counties, common on heath barrens at high elevations. Often confused with azaleas when not in flower.

WINTER

Shrubs up to 2 m high; buds single, sessile, oval, small, the terminal and flower buds larger; twigs slender with small, continuous pith. Leaf scars alternate but crowded toward the ends of the twigs, small, triangular or elongate; with one bundle trace; no stipule scars. Bark shredding. Fruit a bristly-glandular capsule, about 4 mm long, present in winter. Open woods and barrens at higher elevations.

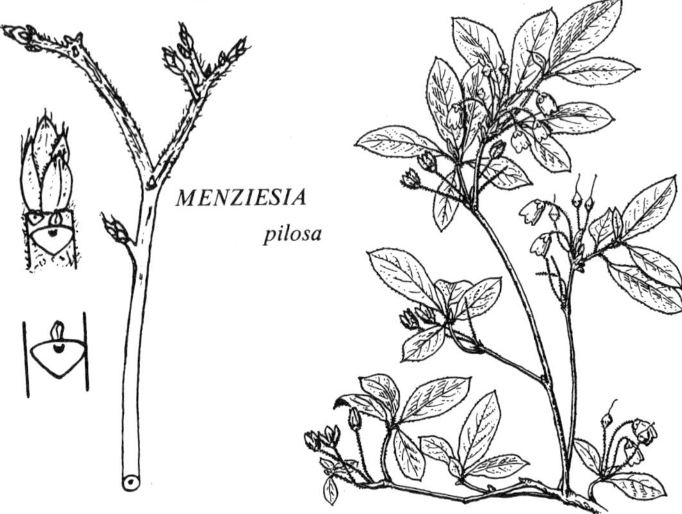

LYONIA Nutt. **Lyonia**

Shrub with hairy leaves and small white flowers in terminal or axillary clusters. Calyx 4-5 lobed. Corolla globe-shaped, 4-5 toothed, hairy. Stamens 8-10. Ovary 4-5 celled. Capsule round ovoid, 4-5 angled; seeds numerous.

L. ligustrina (L.) DC. (resembling ***Ligustrum,*** privet), **Maleberry, Seedy Buckberry, "He-Huckleberry"**

Shrub to 3 m high; leaves oval, 2.5-8.5 cm long, toothed or entire, hairy on the veins beneath or hairless; corolla globe-shaped, 3 mm in diameter; capsule depressed-round, 3 mm in diameter. The common names refer to the fact that the plants somewhat resemble blueberries or huckleberries, **produce only dry fruits.** May-July. Swamps and wet soil throughtout but more common in the mountains.

WINTER

Deciduous shrubs; buds single, sessile, oblong, lying close to the stem, covered by 2 scales; twigs slender 3-sided, pith round, continuous. Leaf scars alternate, small semicircular, with 1 bundle trace; no stipule scars. **Fruit a round capsule about 3 mm in diameter, present in winter.** Wet swampy woods in higher elevations.

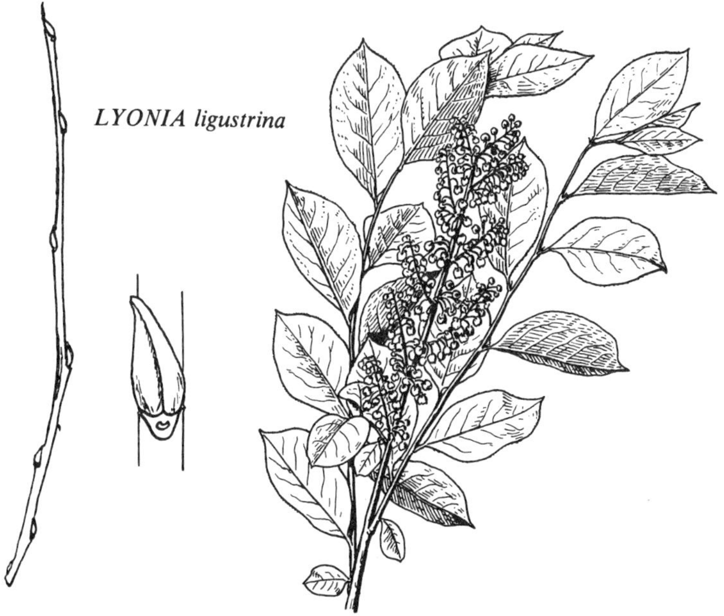

LYONIA ligustrina

GAULTHERIA L. **Teaberry**

Low shrubs with alternate, evergreen leaves and small, axillary flowers. Calyx 5-parted, persistent. Corolla urn-shaped, 5-toothed. Stamens 10. Capsule flattened-spherical, fleshy.

G. procumbens L. (lying flat), **Teaberry, Wintergreen, Mountain Tea**

Stems slender, creeping at or below the surface, the flowering branches erect to 10 cm high; leaves oval, obscurely toothed; flowers few, usually solitary in the axils, nodding; corolla white, 4-6 mm long; **fruit berry-like, bright red, 8-12 mm in diameter, mealy, very spicy.** Flowers in June-September. In woods, especially under coniferous trees.

WINTER

Small trailing shrub with upright branches less than 10 cm high. Buds single, sessile, oval, tiny. Leaves up to 5 cm long. Twigs slender, rounded with small pith. **Leaves evergreen, alternate, simple, oval and entire. Fruit a red, mealy, spicy, spherical capsule resembling a berry, present in winter.** Dry woods and roadbanks.

GAULTHERIA procumbens

PIERIS D. Don. **Mountain Fetterbush**

Shrubs with evergreen, leathery, broad, mostly toothed leaves. Flowers white, in terminal and axillary clusters. Calyx deeply 5-parted. Corolla oval-urn-shaped, 5-toothed. Stamens 10. Capsule round.

P. floribunda (Pursh) B. & H. (full of flowers) **Mountain Fetterbush**

Shrub to 15 dm high **with very leafy, stiff-haired branches; leaves oblong, acute, toothed with hairy margins,** glandular-dotted beneath, 4-6 cm long, 1-2.5 cm wide; flowers white, in terminal, slender, dense clusters; corolla slightly 5-angled; capsule round-oval, 4 mm high. May. Moist slopes, in the Alleghenies, with a very restricted range.

WINTER

Evergreen shrubs up to 15 dm high. Lateral buds small, round, no terminal bud. Twigs slender; pith 3-sided, continuous. Leaves alternate, oblong. Leaf scars small, semicircular with 1 bundle trace; stipule scars small, semicircular with 1 bundle trace; stipule scars absent. **Fruit a round capsule 5-6 mm long, present in winter. Clusters of next season's flower buds also present.**

PIERIS floribunda

OXYDENDRUM (L.) DC. **Sourwood**

Trees with deciduous sour-tasting foliage and twigs with white flowers in one-sided racemes clustered in terminal panicles. Calyx of 5 nearly distinct sepals. Corolla ovate, 5-toothed. Stamens 10. Capsule 5-celled, ovoid-pyramidal; seeds numerous.

O. arboreum (L.) DC. (becoming a tree) **Sourwood**

Trees with ridged bark, growing to 20 m and over in height and 4 dm in diameter; leaves oblong, hairless on the upper surface, usually with scattered long whitish hairs on the midrib, minutely toothed, 1-1.5 dm long, 2.5-7.5 cm wide, **bright scarlet in autumn;** flowers 6-8 mm long; capsule 4-6 mm long. **The flower buds and flowers (June-July) are drooping but the capsules (fall) bend upright when mature.** Light, well-drained acid soils, common in all sections west of the Alleghenies. An important source of honey. **The leaves somewhat resemble those of Black Gum, however the margin is minutely toothed, and the lateral veins do not run parallel to the leaf margin.**

WINTER

Medium sized to 20 m high; buds small, red, mound-like, single, sessile, covered with about 6 scales; no terminal bud. Twigs slender, zigzag, pink to red with whitish, continuous pith. Leaf scars alternate, small, semicircular with 1 U-shaped bundle trace, no stipule scars. Young bark smooth becoming deeply fissured with age. **Capsules present in winter, about 5 mm long, in one-sided clusters. Bark on older trees often confused with that of Sassafras or younger Black Gum.**

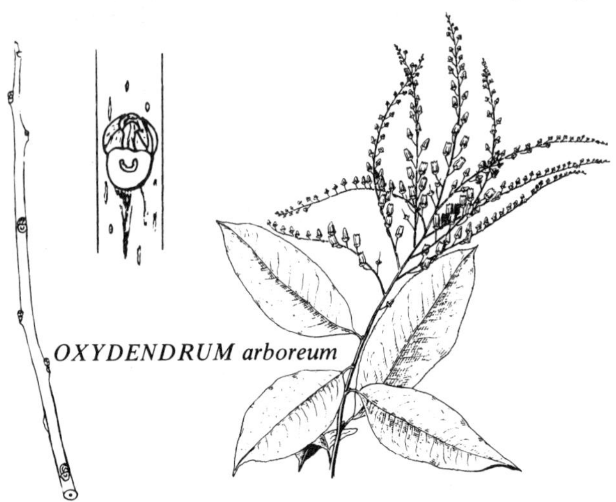

OXYDENDRUM arboreum

GAYLUSSACIA HBK. **Huckleberry**

Branching shrubs with alternate leaves dotted with resin, with or without teeth, small flowers in lateral clusters. Calyx tube short, 5-toothed, persistent. Corolla flask-shaped or bell-shaped, the flared portion 5-lobed. Stamens 10. Fruit berry-like, with 10 seed-like nutlets each containing a single seed. **May be separated from the blueberries by the resin dots on the leaves and the 10 relatively large seeds. Blueberries lack the resin dots and have many tiny seeds.**

G. baccata (Wang.) K. Koch (berry-bearing) **Black Huckleberry**

Much-branched rigid shrub to 1 m high; leaves oval or oblong, entire, resin-dotted, 2.5-5 cm long; flowers pink or red, in one-sided clusters; corolla oval to cone-shaped, 4-5 mm long; **fruit black, about 6 mm in diameter, sweet but "seedy."** Flowers in May-June. Dry sandy or rocky acid soil in thickets and woods.

WINTER

Small shrub up to 1 m high. Buds single, sessile, oval, small, with no terminal bud. Young twigs slender, very resinous with some hairs present, pith small, continuous. Leaf scars alternate, triangular with 1 bundle trace; stipule scars absent. Thickets, woods and barrens, especially in burned over areas at high elevations.

GAYLUSSACIA baccata

VACCINIUM L. **Blueberry**

Shrubs with alternate deciduous or persistent leaves and clustered flowers produced in spring or early summer. Calyx tube attached to the ovary. Expanded portion of corolla 4-5-cleft. Stamens 8 or 10. Berry 4-5-celled (or 8-10-celled by false partitions), with many tiny seeds. Called "huckleberry" by natives of the mountains. **May be separated from the true huckleberries by the lack of resin dots on the leaves and the many, tiny seeds.**

SUMMER KEY

a. Corolla open-bell-shaped, 5-lobed or 5-toothed; bracts of inflor-florescence much smaller than foliage leaves, 2-10 mm broad, mature leaves 5-9 cm long. .... ***V. stamineum***
a. Corolla cylindric to spherical, 5-lobed or 5-toothed. .... b

b. Leaves entire. c
b. Leaves toothed, small, 1-3 cm long. .... ***V. angustifolium.***

c. Leaves very hairy with stiff hairs. .... ***V. myrtilloides.***
c. Leaves toothed, small, 1-3 cm long. .... ***V. vacillans.***

WINTER

Small shrubs, usually less than 1 m tall. Buds small, single, sessile, with 2 or more scales; no terminal bud. Twigs slender, angled; with small, continuous pith. Leaf scars alternate, small, semicircular with 1 bundle trace; stipule scars absent.

WINTER KEY

a. Buds oval, erect or lying close to stem. .... b
a. Buds subspherical or oval, divergent from the stem. ***V. stamineum.***

b. Twigs not angled or grooved, densely hairy. .... ***V. myrtilloides.***
b. Twigs angular or grooved above the bud; not hairy. c

c. Twigs smooth, reddish. .... ***V. angustifolium.***
c. Twigs warty with low glands; greenish. .... ***V. vacillans.***

V. stamineum L. (with prominent stamens) **Squaw Huckleberry Buckberry, Deerberry**

Much-branch shrub to 9 dm high, young branches hairy; leaves hairy on lower side, oval, pale beneath, 2.5-20 cm long; calyx smooth; **corolla greenish white or purplish,** 4-6 mm long; **stamens much extended beyond the corolla;** bracts persistent; **berry spherical, green or yellow,** 8-10 mm in diameter, sour. Flowers in April-June. In dry woods and thickets.

WINTER

A greatly branched shrub up to 9 dm high; buds reddish brown; twigs slender, glossy red, zigzag, pith greenish, subspherical. Dry open woods and thickets.

VACCINIUM stamineum

V. myrtilloides Michx. (like *V. myrtillus,* of Europe) **Sourtop, Velvetleaf Blueberry**

Shrub to 6 dm high, the **crowded branches densely hairy; leaves with fine hairs on both sides; 2-4 cm long, elliptic to oblong lance-shaped, entire; corolla 4-6 mm long, white or pinkish; berry blue,** 4-7 mm in diameter, sour, but of good flavor. Flowers in May, June. Usually in swamps or moist woods.

WINTER

A low shrub up to 6 dm high; buds lying close to the stems, with 2 elongate outer scales. **Twigs roundish, slender, very hairy;** leaf scars small, half-round. Moist open woods and barrens.

VACCINIUM myrtilloides

V. vacillans Torr. (vacillating, i.e., variable) **Late Low Blueberry**

Shrub to 9 dm high, hairless, with **yellowish green warty branchlets; leaves whitened beneath,** 2.5-4.5 cm long, entire, corolla 5-8 mm long, white or greenish white or tinged with red; fruit blue, 5-8 mm in diameter, sweet. Flowers in May. Common in acid soil in higher elevations.

WINTER

Low shrub up to 9 dm high with very warty, yellowish green, or reddish twigs, grooved above the buds; buds red to reddish green; leaf scars alternate, slightly raised. Acid soil in open woods and barrens.

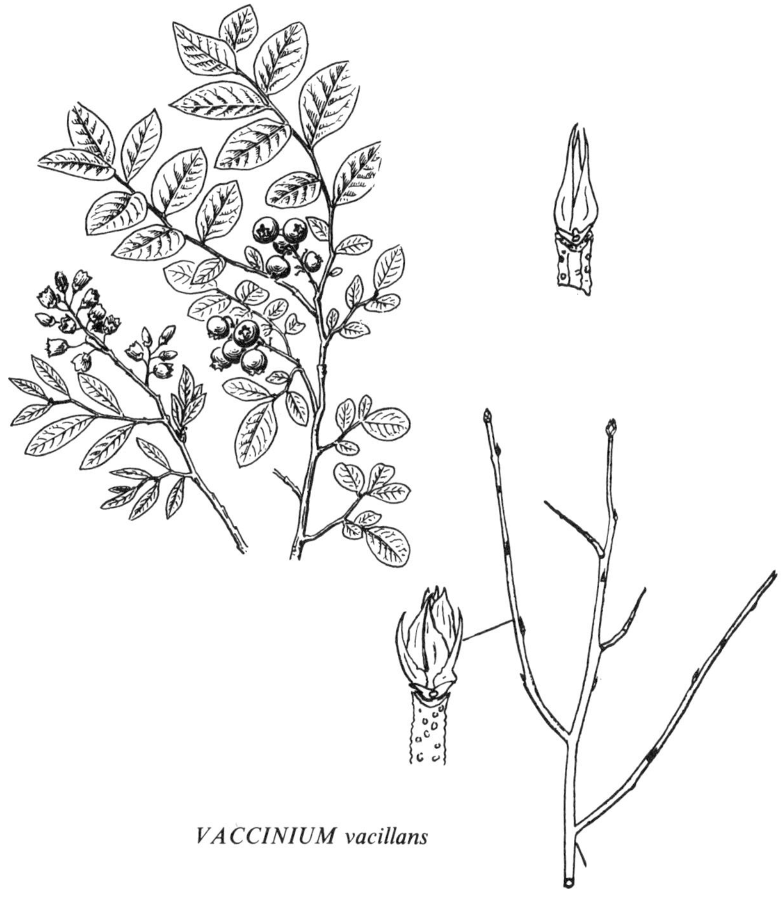

VACCINIUM vacillans

V. angustifolium Ait. (narrow leaved) **Early Low Blueberry Lowbush Blueberry**

Plants to 2 dm high, in dense, often extensive colonies; **leaves green,** hairless, narrowly elliptic, **sharply toothed,** 1-2.5 cm long; corolla white or pink, 3-6 mm long; **berry bright blue,** 5-7 mm in diameter, of excellent flavor. Flowers in May, June. Dry open rocky or sandy soil.

WINTER

A low shrub up to 2 dm high. Leaf buds smooth, brown to pink, with 2 long exposed scales; flower buds plump with several smooth scales. Twigs very slender, hairless when mature, olive green to reddish with numerous pale, warty dots. Leaf scars semicircular. Open barrens, especially at high elevations.

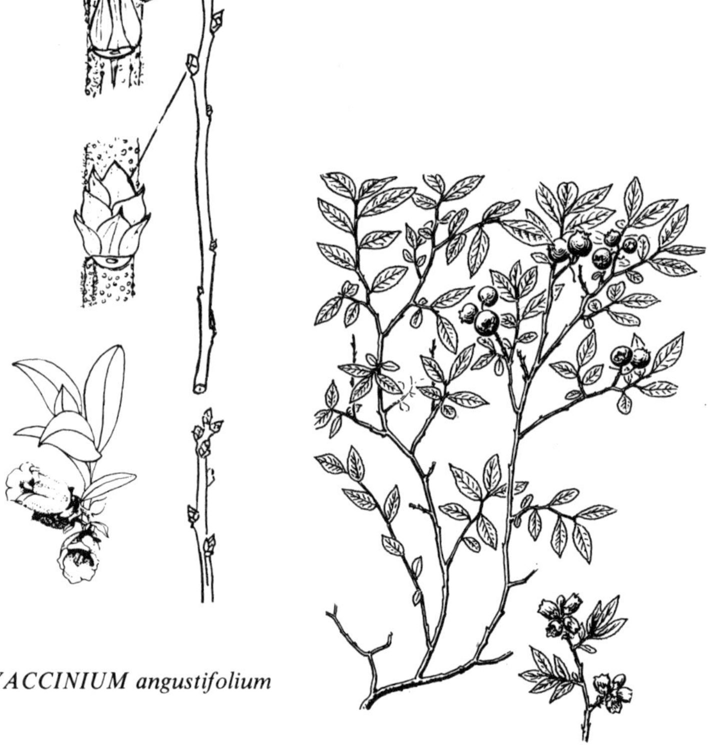

VACCINIUM angustifolium

DIOSPYROS L. Persimmon

Broad-leaved trees or shrubs having perfect or imperfect flowers on same tree, clustered or solitary flowers, usually the pistillate solitary and the staminate clustered; stamens 8-20 in the sterile flowers, few or several and mostly imperfect or none in the pistillate flowers; ovary spherical or oval, its cavities twice as many as the styles. Ovary rudimentary in the sterile flowers. Berry large, pulpy.

D. virginiana L. (Virginian) Persimmon

Tree attaining a hight of 30 m and trunk diameter of 6 dm, usually smaller **with black, blocky, "alligator" bark on older trees;** leaves alternate, simple, not toothed, thickish, hairless or nearly so, having a metallic green sheen above, 5-12 cm long; calyx 4-parted; corolla pale yellow, fertile flowers 1-1.5 cm long, about twice as large as the sterile flowers; stamens of staminate flowers about 16, of perfect flowers 8 or fewer; styles 4, 2-lobed at the apex; ovary 8-celled; **fruit spherical, about 2.5 cm long, reddish yellow, astringent when green, sweet when ripe.** Flowers in June. Dry woods and old fields.

WINTER

A small tree up to 30 m high; buds single, sessile, triangular to oval, with 2 overlapping scales; no terminal bud. Twigs round, zigzag, gray-brown; pith continuous, sometimes becoming porous with age; leaf scars alternate, half-oval with 1 curved bundle trace; no stipule scars; mature bark dark, deeply divided and blocky. **Fruit a large, juicy berry, edible when fully ripe, 2-3.5 cm across, yellowish or orangish, withered fruit present into early winter; the short, usually 3-branched flower stalks persistent on the twig through winter.** Dry, open woods and old fields.

DIOSPYROS virginiana

FRAXINUS L. **Ash**

Trees with opposite, pinnately compound leaves and small, perfect or imperfect, clustered flowers. Calyx small, 4-cleft, entire or none. Petals 2-4 or none. Stamens 2 (rarely 3 or 4). Fruit with one thin straight wing and an elongated seed cavity.

F. americana L. (American) **White Ash**

Large trees to 40 m high, branchlets and petioles usually hairless; **opposite, pinnately compound leaves, leaflets usually 7,** stalked, oval to oval lance-shaped, 6-15 cm long, hairless beneath or slightly hairy, entire or sparingly toothed; fruit 2.5-5 cm long, the seed area round, the wing straw-colored. Flowers in April, May. Rich moist woods.

WINTER

A tree growing up to 40 m high, and 1 m or more in diameter. The opposite buds sessile, one above the other, with 4-6 scales, dark brown, the terminal bud oval, blunt, larger than the lateral buds. Twigs thick, stiff, spreading; pith obscurely angled. **Leaf scars opposite,** deeply notched at the top; bundle traces form a curved line; no stipule scars. **The branching pattern consisting of large opposite branches is a good winter character in large trees. Older bark almost black, interlacing ridges produce a diamond-shaped pattern (sometimes the bark is blocky and resembles persimmon).** Rich woods and moist bottomlands.

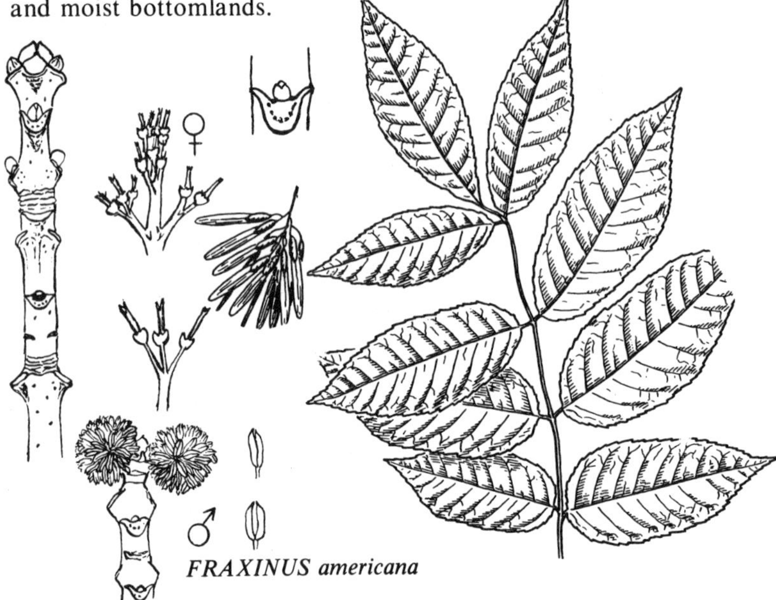

FRAXINUS americana

MITCHELLA L. **Partridge Berry**

Evergreen creeping herbs, with opposite, entire leaves, and axillary or terminal stalked "twin" flowers (i.e., with ovaries united); calyx tube oval, the expanded portion 3-6-lobed (usually 4-lobed); corolla funnelform, usually 4-lobed, bearded on the inner side; stamens as many as the lobes of the corolla and inserted on its throat; ovary 4-celled with 1 ovule in each cell; fruit a berrylike double drupe crowned with the calyx teeth of the two flowers.

M. repens L. (creeping). **Partridge Berry.**

Stems trailing, rooting at the nodes, 1-3 dm long, branching, smooth or slightly hairy; **leaves oval or circular, petioled, blunt, 6-20 mm long, dark green, often variegated with white, shining;** stalks of the inflorescences shorter than the leaves; flowers white; often purple-tinged, fragrent; corolla 10-12 mm long; drupes red (rarely white), 4-8 mm in diamter, persistent through the winter, edible. Flowers in June, July. In woods.

WINTER

Stems prostrate, 1-3 dm long, forming mats. Leaves round to ovate, 1-2 cm long, dark green and glossy above, somewhat paler beneath, hairless or nearly so; tips rounded; bases rounded to heart-shaped, margins entire. **Fruits bright red, 6-8 mm in diameter, each formed from two fused ovaries and crowned by the persistent calyx teeth of the two flowers.** Fruits ripe in fall, persisting through winter and spring. In moist or dry woods. An important food plant for upland game birds, especially ruffed grouse.

MITCHELLA repens

CEPHALANTHUS L. **Buttonbush**

Shrubs or small trees with opposite or whorled entire leaves, and terminal or axillary flowers in dense, globe-shaped heads; calyx tube pyramidal, its limb with 4 obtuse lobes; corolla tubular-funnelform with 4 short erect or spreading lobes; stamens 4, inserted on the throat of the corolla; ovary 2-celled, with 1 ovule in each cell; fruit dry, wedge-shaped.

C. occidentalis L. (western, i.e., of the Western Hemisphere) **Buttonbush**

A shrub or small tree to 5 m high, hairless or somewhat hairy; **leaves opposite or in whorls of three, petioled,** oval, 7-15 cm long, 2-7 cm wide; flower clusters and fruiting heads spherical, about 2.5 cm in diameter; flowers sessile, white, 8-12 mm long; style very slender, about twice the length of the corolla. Flowers in June-September. In swamps and stream margins.

WINTER

Shrubs up to 5 m tall; buds single, conical; no terminal bud. Twigs slender, round, hairless, reddish and glossy; pith small, angled, brown, continuous. **Leaf scars in whorls of 3, or opposite,** round with 1 U-shaped bundle trace; stipule scars meeting around the stem; stipules sometimes persist through the winter. Along streams and in wet soil.

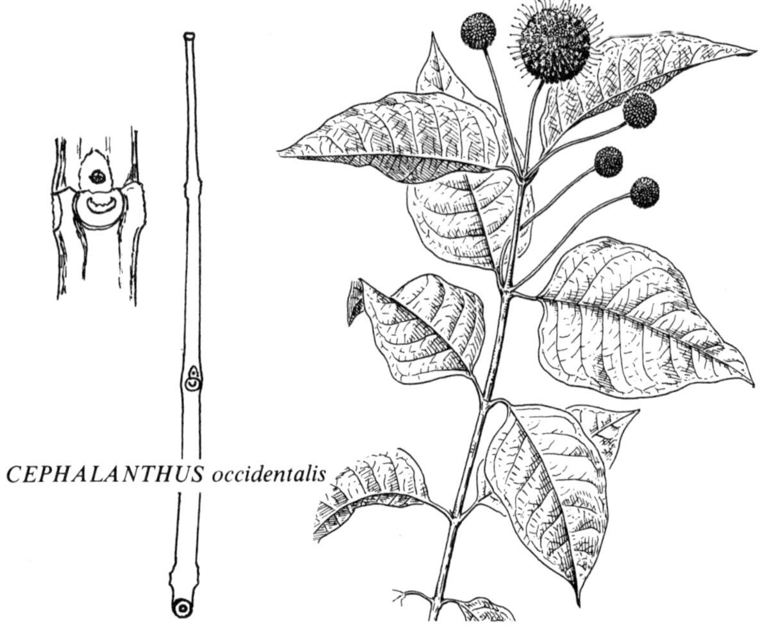

CEPHALANTHUS occidentalis

LONICERA L. **Honeysuckle**

Erect or climbing shrubs with entire opposite leaves and flowers in spikes, heads or twined. Calyx slightly 5-toothed. Corolla tubular, 5-lobed, oblique or 2-lipped. Stamens 5. Fruit a several-seeded berry.

L. canadensis Marsh (Canadian) **Fly Honeysuckle**

Straggling shrub 1.5 m high; **leaves thin, oval, opposite, entire,** petioled, hairy on the margin, downy beneath when young, 2.5-10 cm long; **flowers in pairs from the axils of the leaves, greenish yellow,** 2 cm long; **berries separate, red,** 6 mm thick. Flowers in May. Moist, mountain woods.

WINTER

A small shrub to 1.5 m high. Buds opposite, solitary or one above the other, sessile, oval or nearly spherical, smooth, scales sharp-pointed; twigs smooth, rounded, slender; pith white, continuous, or lacking between the nodes. **Leaf scars opposite, crescent-shaped, small, connected by lines around the stem.** Bundle traces 3; stipule scars missing. Cool woods and thickets.

LONICERA canadensis

VIBURNUM L. **Viburnum**

Shrubs or small trees with with simple, opposite, entire or toothed, lobed or unlobed leaves and perfect, white (rarely pink) flowers in flat compound clusters. Calyx 5-toothed. Corolla round, regular, 5-lobed. Stamens 5. Ovary 1-3-celled. Fruit oval or spherical.

SUMMER KEY

a. Outer flowers of the inflorescences large, showy; fruit red (ultimately maturing to black); leaves doubly toothed, pinnately veined. .... ***V. alnifolium***
a. Flowers not as above; fruit blue or black. .... b

b. Leaves palmately veined, mostly 3-lobed. .... ***V. acerifolium***
b. Leaves pinnatley veined. c

c. Leaves coarsely toothed; petioles 6-40 mm long. .... d
c. Leaves entire, wavy or toothed. .... e

d. Leaves hairless or nearly so. .... ***V. recognitum***
d. Leaves hairy beneath. .... ***V. dentatum***

e. Inflorescences on a stalk. .... ***V. cassinoides***
e. Inflorescence sessile or nearly so; leaves blunt or sharp, hairless or nearly so beneath, not red-dotted. .... ***V. prunifolium***

WINTER

Deciduous shrubs with slender, angled twigs; pith continuous. Buds single or one above the other, mostly stalked, oval. Leaf scars opposite, crescent-shaped, triangular, connected with lines around the stem; bundle traces 3; stipule scars missing. Fruits persistent in winter.

WINTER KEY

a. Leaf scars broadly triangular; twigs purplish, with star-shaped scales; fruits red (ripening to black). .... ***V. alnifolium***
a. Leaf scars thin; twigs brownish or gray; fruits not red. .... b

b. Buds with 2 visible scales, not overlapping, oblong, brown-scurfy or gray. c
b. Buds with more than 2 visible scales. .... d

c. Branches many, often short and spreading. .... ***V. prunifolium***
c. Branches fewer, elongate, flexous. .... ***V. cassinoides***

d. Twigs do not have star-shaped hairs, usually smooth. .... e
d. Young twigs with dense, star-shaped hairs, becoming smooth with age. .... *V. dentatum*

e. Lower bud scales very short; twigs hairy. .... *V. acerifolium*
e. Lower bud scales longer, may be as long as the bud; twigs smooth. .... *V. recognitum*

V. alnifolium March (alder-leaved) **Hobblebush, Moosewood**

A shrub to 3 m high, irregularly branched, the **branches often trailing and rooting, likely to trip pedestrians (hence one common name); leaves circular or oval, 7-20 cm broad, heart-shaped at the base, with star-shaped hairs; inflorescence sessile,** the exterior flowers showy and sterile, about 2.5 cm broad; fruit ovoid-oblong, 10-12 mm long. Flowers in May-June. In moist woods.

WINTER

Shrub to 3 m high, **lower branches often trailing and rooting.** Buds densely covered with brown star-shaped hairs. Buds without true scales but covered with a pair of modified leaves. Twigs with branched hairs near the tips. Older stems purplish and hairless. Leaf scars broad with 3 bundle traces. Cool woods at higher elevations in northern hardwood and spruce forests.

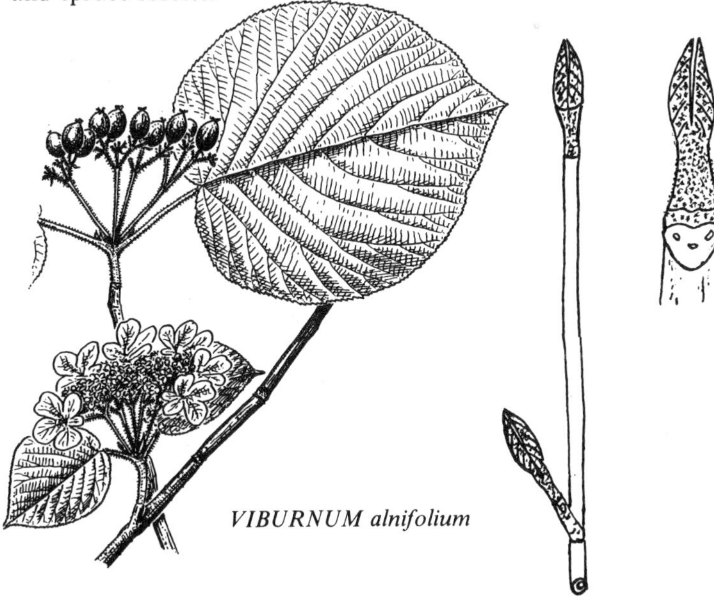

VIBURNUM alnifolium

V. cassinoides L. (like Ilex cassine) **Wild Raisin**

Shrub or tree to 4 m high; leaves oval, thick, 2.5-7.5 cm long, with rounded teeth or entire; inflorescence 5-rayed; **fruit oval to spherical, 6-9 mm long, pink and showy while maturing, blue-black when fully ripe.** Flowers in June-July. Swamps and wet soil.

WINTER

Erect shrub up to 4 m high with dull, scaly, elongated, flexible twigs; buds covered by 2 yellowish brown scales; leaf scars opposite, narrowly V-shaped with 3 bundle traces. Pith cream-colored. **Fruit blue-black,** up to 9 mm long. Thickets and open woods.

VIBURNUM cassinoides

V. prunifolium L. (plum-leaved) **Black Haw**

Shrub or tree to 8 m high; leaves oval, finely and sharply toothed, 2-7 cm long, hairless or nearly so; inflorescence sessile, or short-stalked, several-rayed, 5-10 cm broad; flowers numerous, all perfect; **drupes oval, bluish black, 8-12 mm long, with sweet pulp.** Flowers in April-June. In dry soil.

WINTER

Large shrub or small tree to 8 m high, much branched with stiff, usually crooked branches; buds acute, reddish, hairy, with 1 pair of brown scales; twigs hairless. Leaf scars opposite, crescent to U-shaped; dark on older stems. **Fruit blue-black, about 1 cm long.** Thickets and open woods.

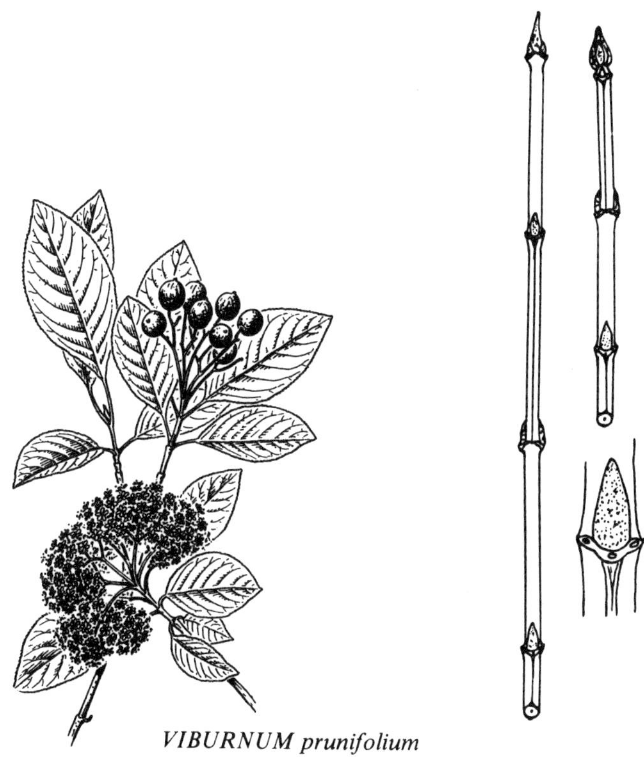

VIBURNUM prunifolium

V. dentatum L. (toothed) **Rough Arrowwood**

Shrub to 3 m high; **leaves usually with dense star-shaped hairs beneath,** oblong to oval, 4-10 cm long, fine-toothed; inflorescences 5-8 cm broad; fruit spherical-ovoid, blue, 5-8 mm in diameter. Flowers in May-June. Woods and banks of streams.

WINTER

Shrub growing to 3 m high. Twigs often densely haired, sometimes becoming smooth. Leaf scars crescent to U-shaped with 3 bundle traces. bark tight, gray; **fruit blue-black,** oval, up to 10 mm long. Open woods and thickets.

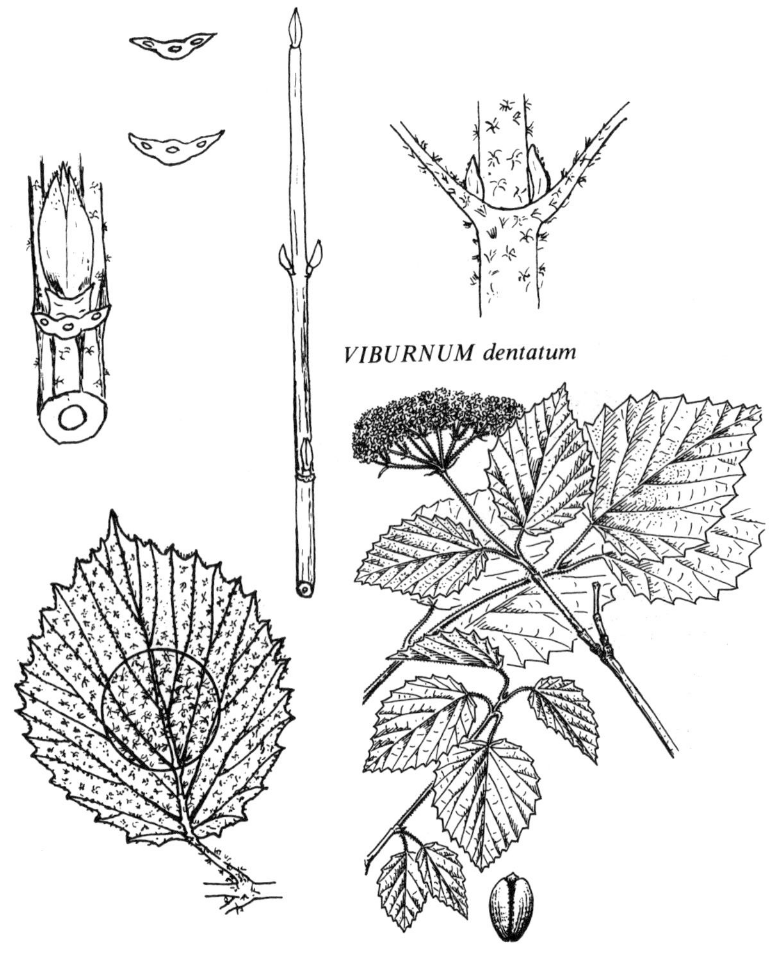

V. recognitum Fernald (restudied) **Smooth Arrowwood**

Shrub to 3 m high, with slender straight branches; **leaves oval to circular, coarsely toothed all around,** 4-7 cm broad, **hairless on both sides except for the axils of the veins beneath; inflorescence long-stalked,** 5-8 cm broad; flowers all perfect; fruit spherical-oval, about 6 mm in diameter, blue-black. Flowers in May-June. Moist or wet ground.

WINTER

Shrub up to 3 m high; buds reddish to reddish brown, hairless except for hairs along the margins of the scales; twigs hairless, slightly 4-angled, pale grayish brown; leaf scars crescent or V-shaped; pith white. Damp thickets and open woods.

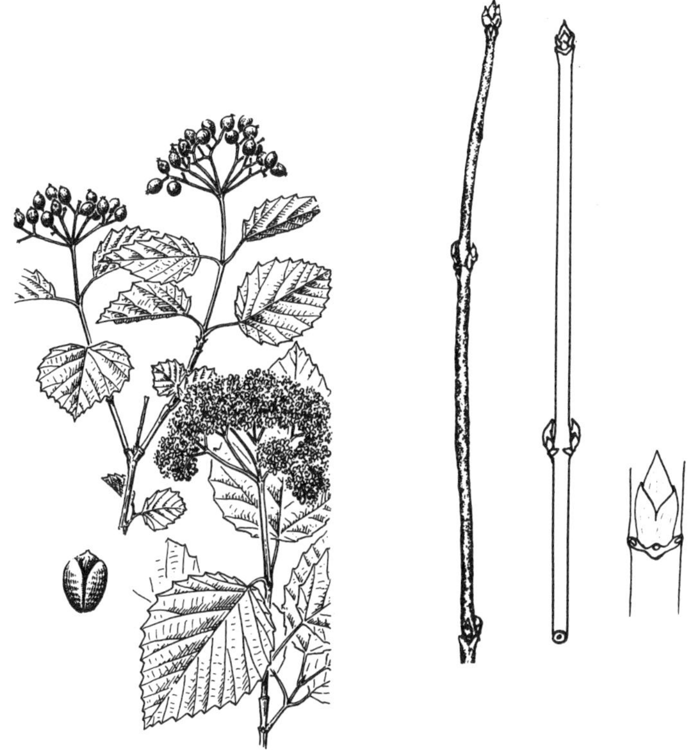

VIBURNUM recognitum

V. acerifolium L. (maple-leaved) **Dockmackie, Maple-Leaf Arrowwood**

Shrub to 2 m high with hairy twigs; **leaves oval or circular, mostly deeply 3-lobed, coarsely toothed, black-dotted beneath,** 5-12 cm broad; **inflorescence long-stalked,** 4-7 cm broad; all flowers perfect, 4-6 mm broad; fruit nearly black, 6-8 mm long. Flowers in May-June. Dry rocky woods. Leaves soft and velvety to the touch.

WINTER

Shrub up to 2 m high. Buds stalked, lying close to stem, 4 scales. Twigs round, grayish brown, with tiny star-shaped hairs or smooth; pith large, white. Leaf scars opposite, crescent to U-shaped with 3 bundle traces. Fruits ellipsoid, purple-black. Rocky woods.

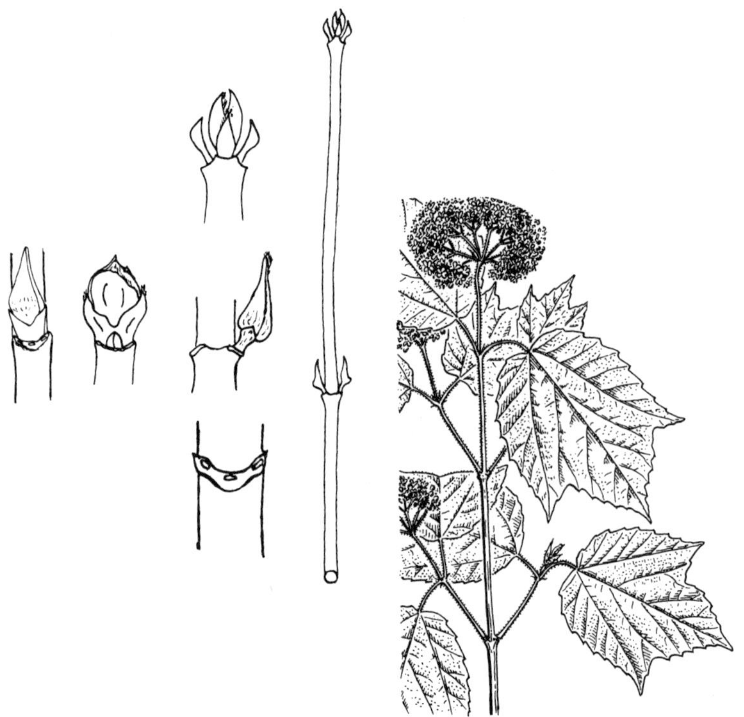

VIBURNUM acerifolium

SAMBUCUS L. **Elderberry**

Shrubs with opposite pinnate leaves and small flowers in compound clusters. Calyx 3-5-toothed or lobed. Corolla round, regular, 3-5-lobed, stamens 5. Ovary 3-5-celled. Fruit a berry-like drupe.

SUMMER KEY

a. Inflorescence flat; fruit black. .... ***S. canadensis***
a. Inflorescence pyramidal; fruit red. .... ***S. pubens***

WINTER

Shrubs with thick, angled twigs with conspicuous wart-like lenticels. Buds single or clustered; terminal bud often absent. Pith large, soft, continuous. Leaf scars opposite, large, crescent-shaped or triangular, connected by lines around the stem.

WINTER KEY

a. Pith white, most common at lower elevations. .... ***S. canadensis***
a. Pith brown, found only at high elevations. .... ***S. pubens***

S. canadensis L. (Canadian) **Common Elder, Black Elderberry**

Shrub to 4 m high, not very woody, the younger twigs with white pith; leaflets 5-11, oblong, smooth, sharply toothed, 5-12 cm long; inflorescence flat; flowers white, about 3 mm long; **fruit purple or black,** nearly 6 mm in diameter, edible. Flowers in June-July. Rich moist soil.

WINTER

A stoloniferous shrub up to 4 m tall; pith white. Leaf scars opposite, large, V-shaped with 3-7 bundle traces; stipule scars absent, but leaf scars often connected by lines; bark thin, light brown, warty. Damp rich bottomlands.

SAMBUCUS canadensis

S. pubens Michx. (pubescent) **Red Elderberry**

Shrub to 3.5 cm high, not very woody, the **pith orange-brown;** bark warty; leaflets 5-7 oval-lance-shaped, 5-12 cm long, downy underneath; inflorescences cone-shaped; **flowers yellowish white; fruit scarlet or red,** 4-6 mm in diameter, very showy when mature. Flowers in April-May. Fruit June-August. Rocky woods at 3,500 feet or higher.

WINTER

Shrub up to 3 m tall, with pale brown twigs with large wart-like lenticels; **pith orange-brown;** leaf scars opposite, half-round with 5 bundle traces. Found only at higher elevations; in rocky woods and along roadsides.

SAMBUCUS pubens

SENECIO L. **Ragwort**

Annual or perennial herbs with alternate and basal leaves and many-flowered heads of both tubular and ray flowers. Receptacle flat. Rays yellow, pistillate, fertile. Disk flowers yellow, perfect, fertile. Achenes round. Fruit with numerous thin white bristles.

S. aureus L. (golden) **Golden Ragwort**

Perennial; smooth or nearly so throughout; stems slender, 3-8 dm high; basal leaves heart-shaped-oval or heart-shaped-circular or kidney-shaped, small-toothed, clasping; heads several, 1.6-2 cm broad, showy; rays 8-12, fruits smooth. Flowers in May-July. In swamps and wet meadows.

SENECIO aureus

SOLIDAGO L. **Goldenrod**

Perennial herbs with wandlike stems and sessile (or nearly sessile) stem leaves. Heads several-flowered, with ray flowers only, the rays 1-16, pistillate.

a. Inflorescences not in 1-sided branches, mostly of small axillary clusters or forming a terminal cluster; stem leaves nearly uniform in size, only gradually reduced upwards. .... b
a. Inflorescences 1-sided, the heads borne on the upper side of the branches. c

b. Stems smooth, whitened, round; fruits hairy. .... ***S. caesia***
b. Stems hairy; leaves narrow, lance-shaped; involucre 3-5 mm high; fruits smooth. .... ***S. puberula***

c. Basal leaves much larger than the upper ones; stem leaves mostly fewer than 40; stems with small ash-colored hairs. ***S. nemoralis***
c. Basal leaves not much larger than the upper ones; stem leaves 20-100 or more. .... d

d. Leaves pinnately veined, gradually narrow to the base, coarsely toothed, hairy beneath. .... ***S. ulmifolia***
d. Leaves three-nerved; upper portion of the stem (below the inflorescence) with dense long hairs; involucres 2-3 mm high; disk corollas about the same length. .... ***S. altissima***

S. caesia L. (bluish gray) **Wreath Goldenrod**

Stem erect, round, slender, smooth, whitened, green to purplish, 0.3-1 m high; lower stem leaves lance-shaped, sessile, sharply toothed, smooth except for rough margins, 5-12 cm long, 0.6-3 cm wide; **median and upper stem leaves similar except gradually reduced upward;** inflorescence smooth except on ultimate branches and flower stalks, inflorescence in axils of leaves, involucre 3-5 mm high; phyllaries oblong, obtuse with swollen green tips; rays 2-6; disk flowers 3-7; fruits 1-1.5 mm long, hairy. Flowers in August-October. Rich deciduous woods.

SOLIDAGO caesia

S. puberula Nutt. (minutely pubescent) **Downy Goldenrod**

Stem erect, round, with tiny hairs, 0.2-1 m high; basal leaves lance-shaped, toothed, narrowed to long, winged petioles, lower stem leaves lance-shaped, sharp narrowed to winged petioles; toothed with tiny hairs, 2.5-15 cm long; **median and upper stem leaves similar, becoming elliptic and reduced in size upward;** inflorescence with tiny hairs; involucre 3-4 mm high; phyllaries linear-awl-shaped, very sharp, hairy or smooth; rays 7-12; disk flowers 4-12; fruits 1-1.5 mm long, smooth. Flowers in August, September. Dry rocky or sandy soil, open banks, margins of woodlands, or in sparse woodland.

SOLIDAGO puberula

S. nemoralis Ait. (of woodland) **Oldfield Goldenrod**

Stem erect, round, with tiny gray hairs, 0.15-1 m high; basal leaves lance-shaped, with rounded teeth, long-petioled; sharp, gradually narrowed to petiolate base, densely and minutely hairy on both surfaces, 7.5-15 cm long; **middle and upper stem leaves similar except smaller, the upper abruptly much reduced,** elongate, lance-shaped, entire; **inflorescence densely haired, wand-shaped with recurved tip** to broadly pyramidal; heads strongly one-sided; involucre 3-4.5 mm high; phyllaries linear-oblong, light yellowish, blunt; rays 1-9; disk flowers 4-10; fruits 1-1.5 mm long, hairy. Flowers in August-November. Dry open fields, clearings, sparse woods.

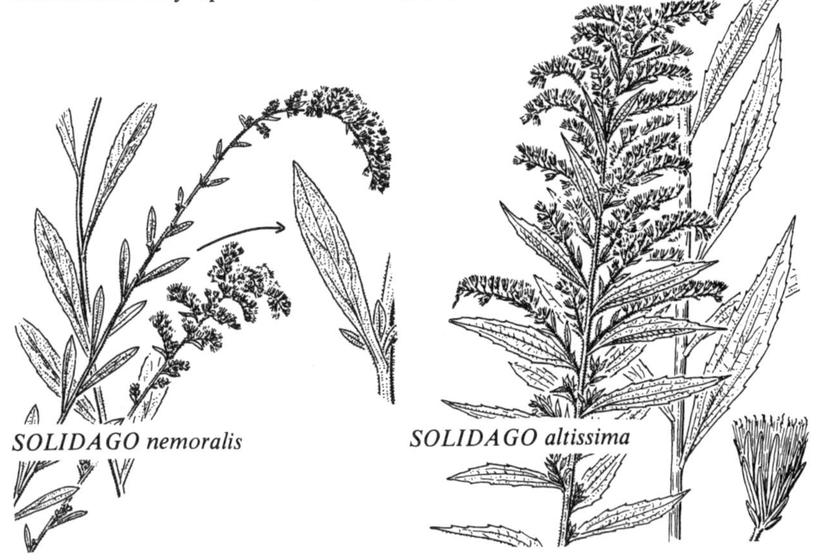

SOLIDAGO nemoralis　　*SOLIDAGO altissima*

S. altissima L. (very tall) **Tall Goldenrod**

Stem erect, round, short hairy with stiff hairs, 0.7-2 m high; basal leaves lance-shaped to elliptic; wedge-shaped at base, sharp-pointed, sharply toothed to almost entire, rough above, hairy beneath, narrowed to sessile, or very short-petioled base, 7-15 cm long; median and upper stem leaves similar to lower except gradually reduced and more nearly entire; inflorescence hairy, from a narrow to broad pyramidal branched inflorescence; lower inflorescence sometimes branched, elongated, leafy below and recurved at tip; heads strongly one-sided; involucre 3-4.5 mm high; nearly cylindrical; phyllaries elongate, sharp or sometimes blunt; rays 9-15; disk flowers 2-5; fruits 1-1.5 mm long, hairy. August-November. Fields and waste places.

S. ulmifolia Muhl. (elm-leaved) **Elm-Leaf Goldenrod**

Stem erect, round, smooth below, hairy in upper part, green, 0.6-1.2 m high; **lower stem leaves** oval, lance-shaped, sharp-pointed, narrowed into short, margined petioles, **coarsely toothed, smooth or hairy with appressed hairs,** 7-13 cm long; middle and upper stem leaves similar to lower except smaller, upper lance-shaped, sessile, inflorescence hairy, variable; involucre 3-4 mm high; phyllaries oblong-lance-shaped, sharp or blunt, ribbed; rays 1-6; disk flowers 2-6; fruits 1.5-2 mm long, hairy. July-September. Dry borders of woods, open woods, thickets.

SOLIDAGO ulmifolia

INDEX